A Destiny Denied...

A Dignity Restored

"... FOR THE HEALING OF THE NATIONS."

REV. 22:2

Harry Smith

7710-T Cherry Park Dr, Ste 224
Houston, TX 77095
713-766-4271

Cover design by Nigel Smith (www.wolfandbear.co).

ISBN: 9780578430614

Contents

Bridging the Gap

Part 2: A Dignity Restored

Appendix I

Appendix II

Appendix III

Introduction

My overall stimulus for writing this book is one of obedience, closely followed by something akin to a compulsion. When the Apostle Paul writes to the Corinthians about reconciliation, he says, *"For Christ's love compels us..."* (2 Corinthians 5:14) It is as if God puts something in your heart that becomes a driving force in what you do. This has certainly been my experience, and it is in part a telling of my story, a journey that God has brought me on.

As a follower of Creator God, who has been involved in UK and Irish reconciliation issues, since the early 1990s, I became acutely aware that much had also been done detrimentally to other people groups around the world in His name, that had not been sanctioned by Him. The history of Ireland, my homeland, through its relationship with England and Scotland, is a sad testimony of that! Finding that our ancestors, "with the sword in one hand and the Bible in the other," had suppressed people groups all over the world during the centuries of Empire expansion, has motivated a growing body of people in the United Kingdom and the Republic of Ireland to reach out and seek the healing of those ancient wounds—reconciliation! There was also an awareness that such negative actions of my forefathers had become a barrier, a "stumbling block" to people finding God. (2 Corinthians 6:3) Even in more recent times, missionaries have sadly heard, "Why should I follow your God when Catholics and Protestants are fighting in Ireland?"—unaware of the finer nuances of life here and that the words Catholic and Protestant also carry with them other political and cultural connotations.

My ancestry on my mother's side is English and is culturally Ulster Scots on my father's. I'm from a Protestant background! I did not grow up overtly sectarian, though Catholics were different, somehow inferior, and we didn't play with "them." I believe that there is sufficient in my DNA, physical and spiritual, to identify with the wounding, which both streams of my ancestry committed on Irish and American soil.

In writing this book, I do not want in any way to put myself forward as an expert, there are too many historical and sociological complexities for that! So, this is not a definitive history but rather a record of my journey, one in which I have sought to embrace God's heart and what I sense He has been saying to me regarding my own tribal identity or that of the Irish, Native and Euro-Americans. Nor do I want to appear to stand on the eastern seaboard of the Atlantic and point the finger of condemnation at the later. That is not my place! I write having deeply searched my heart.

Our histories are profoundly connected. My people went to America bringing with them much that was good, but they also brought some spiritual, political and social belief systems that were and continue to be wrong and extremely detrimental to the First Nation Peoples. They brought their cultural hurts, wounds, etc., (often because of persecution at home) with them. These were not only detrimental to themselves but also consequently to us, their descendants today, as we continued to live out of them in Ireland and America.

Many left the shores of what is now the United Kingdom and the Irish Republic, with their own destinies being denied, through persecution. Yes, they brought their Christian faith with them and led many Indians to a living faith in Christ, but it was the wrong packaging of that faith that also led to conflict, land removal, genocide, meaning that many Native Americas had their destinies also denied. One only needs to examine the effects of broken treaties; go unto the Sioux Reservations in South Dakota or speak to people who continue to suffer the pain of the Residential Schools.

God has been taking me to America for more than 12 years now, to listen and learn. I can identify with Nehemiah when he writes, *"When I heard these things, I sat down and wept ... and prayed before the God of heaven, 'I confess the sins we... including myself and our father's house have committed against you...'"* (Nehemiah 1:4, 6-7). I can truly say, "I am sorry for the wrongs that my tribe brought with them to America, and I have at times experienced a profound sorrow in my heart for what we did to the Native tribes."

Whatever else God has for me in the future, regarding this, I do not know, but I sense this is but the beginning of a journey for me. If what I have written in this book becomes a catalyst to drawing others, White and Native Americans into a healing process, I rejoice and give thanks to our Creator. One thing is sure: ownership and repentance are needed by individuals as well as our spiritual and political leadership on both sides of the Atlantic. If the spiritual and political foundations are wrong, then what we have built on them is wrong!

Over these years, I have not only sat with people who have a heart for reconciliation—both White and Native, but I have also been reading widely: many "histories" of the Scots; the Scots-Irish; the Puritans; the colonies; Native American tribes and the growth of the United States of America. That has included the European roots of those histories and the effects these have had (positively and negatively) on the Native American tribes. I have found that over the centuries a variety of interpretations of the details have been recorded, new documentation becomes available and at times the revisionists have moved in, all of which makes accuracy in writing impossible. I can only hope through my reading and research that I have gained a broad sense of the history of the peoples I am writing about.

Also, in any of the issues mentioned, I have tried to keep in mind that I am writing to the average person on the street and to those who are engaged in intercession and reconciliation in the UK, Ireland, and the United States. This is purposely not an in-depth academic study, but if you have been stimulated to dig deeper, scholarly works are out there in plenty. Regarding the historical content of this book I also hope that all the quotes and references are correct. I have also submitted sections of this book to others in the UK and America for their critical input. Grace is needed if my interpretations of events are in any way different from yours!

One key slant, that I seek to bring in this book, is to take our thinking a step further on from the historical and sociological into the realm of the spiritual, to ask: what has taken place in the spirit realms as a result of the interactions—positive and negative—between the various people groups? This is based on the premise that God made man, in all the multiplicity of people groups, ethnicities and tribes, in His image. Each is unique in His eyes; each has something special to bring to the whole, and each has its boundaries set. *"From one man he made every nation of men, that they should inhabit the whole earth; and he determined the times set for them and the exact place where they should live."* (Acts 17:26) Unfortunately, what God wanted us to reflect of Himself through this diversity was marred in our rebellion—with help from God's archenemy, Satan! We were created to live in perfect harmony with Him, with our fellow man, and remarkably, with ourselves—the rebellion recorded in Genesis 3 changed all that! We are now players in a spiritual battle between God and Satan!

We need to bear in mind that none of our leaders, both White and Native, have been able to lead us perfectly into our personal and national destinies, as they have at times also made wrong choices. Added to that we also need to be aware that we have so often tended to operate solely on the horizontal plane, forgetting that God has instructed us that our earthly battles and struggles are primarily not *"against flesh and blood, but against the rulers, against the authorities, against the powers of this dark world and against the spiritual forces of evil in the heavenly realms."* (Ephesians 6:12) Through our imperfections, we have inadvertently given Satan legal footholds into our lives and communities. (Ephesians 4:26) If these are not appropriately dealt with, they affect not only our yesterdays but also our tomorrows and generationally the tomorrows of others.

In the light of that, when I read authors stating in their writings, that the Puritans and Scotch-Irish were only doing in warfare against the Native Americans what other European nations were doing in the Americas; that we should no longer drag up the past but need to move on, "get over it," this does not sit easy with me. If they acted in ways that were not God's ways, then that has to be acknowledged and not rationalized away! As an associate of mine once said, "We can only truly move forward after we have truly looked back!" Or to put it another way, my Navajo friend Mark Charles recently wrote: "Until we deal with our past, we will remain incapable of walking into a better future."

Through my travels, research and reconciliation work, I have become acutely aware that so much of what I have observed comes down to a clash between culture and God's Kingdom. Sadly, for too many, both are synonymous! I have needed to ask myself: "Can I, as a Christian look at my culture, my upbringing, my denomination, the experiences in life that make up 'me' and with the help of the Holy Spirit, Scripture and my interaction with other people, determine what is truly of God and what is not, and respond to it were necessary, with repentance and subsequent change of action?" Along with a growing number of people here in Ireland, I have grappled long and hard regarding the negative intertwining of history, culture and so much of what makes up Catholic/Protestant nationalist and religious identities.

As I grew up, a lot of my Protestant identity was defined by what we weren't, leading to the production of a list full of do's and don'ts. At the same time, it was deemed by many Christians as an honorable thing to be a member of the Orange Order or a Masonic Lodge. If a Catholic became Protestant, they were rigorously submitted to this framework, and all too often paraded around as "trophies of grace." Except for reconciliation purposes, I don't particularly like being identified any longer as "Protestant." We are in a desperate need of a new identity, a new Reformation!

One of the challenges in this current part of my journey has been to try and discover what is redeemable, signs that God was already at work in a culture: issues related to how we do mission, of contextualization and syncretism (e.g., Paul at the Areopagus, Acts 17). Part of this is, I am sure, connected to having lived for 18 years in a residential community of reconciliation, with Christians from other traditions and cultures—that was, to put it mildly, extremely transformative! I now know, love and respect so many wonderful Catholic Christians, and there is so much of what was identified culturally as "Catholic" and Irish, their music, dance, etc., which I now like and feel I was deprived of as I grew up. Can I not be Irish and Christian—period? Can Native Americans not also be Native and Christian? I sense this is also the experience of many white American Christians labeled as "Evangelical," regarding what God is doing in their hearts, as they get to know their Native brothers and sisters in Christ. Mutual enrichment and growth are available to all who embrace this journey together.

The overriding message of the Jewish and Christian scriptures is one of God's desire for our restoration. Through the title of this book, "*A Destiny Denied, A Dignity Restored.*" I want to reflect on that. Aspects of our destinies can probably never be fully restored; some things will have been lost forever, but I do believe that our dignity can be restored IN HIM! I also believe that out of all the pain of our individual and corporate histories, God can also give us a new sense of our identity, again IN HIM! He can redeem and restore us as we bring our pain, woundedness, anger, disappointments, and bitterness to Him!

For some people that journey starts when a person goes in a spirit of humility to somebody from the other tribe and confesses, "I am sorry for what my people did to yours... that action of mine and my people were wrong." I have seen that happen time and time again in Ireland and in the United States as I have gone in that spirit to people from Catholic Nationalist or Native American backgrounds. They have needed to hear it! Other aspects of the healing process may follow, including reconciliation, restoration, restitution, etc. Repentance is crucial to the opening of a door for a new journey to begin!

An overview

I have been very conscious in my research and writing, that I am not just dealing with facts and figures. We are dealing here with people, families, nations, cultures. Many years ago, when I was a Clinical Nurse Tutor, I pointed out to the students that the patient in the bed was not just a Hospital Number with something wrong with their body. I also encouraged them to ask questions. What was going on in the patient, physically, mentally, spiritually? They also had brothers, sisters, children, friends—what were they experiencing during this time of hospitalization? Some patients would either die there or at home because of their illness. If they died from injuries sustained in the ethnic violence, we were experiencing daily—what were the repercussions for their family and society? Many today, decades later, still live out of the anger, fear, hatred that has been stirred up. Wounded places that Satan can use, that God wants to heal!

My desire, living in Ireland and traveling in and out of the States, is to see the healing of our nations. It is multi-directional: the ongoing need for healing here in Ireland (North and South); between each of the nations in the United Kingdom; those nations towards the United States; the internal healing of the USA regarding its own historical development, especially between the Native and Euro-Americans.

Part 1 A Destiny Denied

In the first section of this book, there are some 'thumbnail' sketches of relevant history. These are grouped as three main threads:

1. The unpacking, in Chapters 3-5, of a key issue—the Doctrine of Discovery—as it developed in the Catholic Church in Europe and then traversed the Reformation to undergird the expansion of the British Empire. The Holy Wars of Europe were, by extension, being played out in North America!

2. In Chapters 6-10, the beginnings of British colonization: the Company's established; the development of Puritanism in England and Ireland; the key role this played in forming the early colonists and their early contact with the local Native American tribes.

3. The Ulster-Scots, Chapters 11-14. Looking at their roots in Scotland and Ulster; what made them into the ideal frontiers people in the American colonies; how their negative relationship with England in Scotland and Ulster was central to England's defeat in the War of Independence.

For many white Americans, these are your roots, the history of your ancestors, your political, cultural and spiritual foundations—what makes you tick!

I have also included specific chapters on Manifest Destiny, the Residential Boarding Schools and some teaching on prayer. These have been significant milestones on my journey in understanding God's heart and the need for reconciliation.

In all of these, what was key, is how my ancestors perceived the Native American tribes, the primary inhabitants in the land and how they dealt with them on it. Principles of engagement were being established. Every negative encounter on both sides was giving Satan footholds regarding future encounters. The fruit lives on!

Part 2 A Dignity Restored

Here are some of the issues explored:

- Repentance, Reconciliation, Restitution–God's idea!
- What if you don't get all the land back? Justice—what if there is no justice, but dignity is restored. A higher way: You-in charge; 2nd-mile people; Brother offends-go!
- God and covenant. The real thing!
- Dignity. It's there for all.
- A new destiny! Being part of the 'body of Christ' is two ways! We are one—all expressions!
- Knowing our identity; Building your part of the wall is ok!
- Issues related to syncretism and contextualization—worshipping Creator in culturally relevant ways!

Appendices

- The Doctrine of Discovery—overview
- The Fort Wayne Acknowledgement.
- A repudiation document regarding the Doctrine of Discovery, by the Episcopal Church.

—oooOooo—

Lastly, as you read this book, I ask you to read it with your hearts and minds open to God. In Chapter 19, "Reconciled to reconcile," I quote the Apostle Paul, who wrote to us, as followers of God's way, that we...

"... should no longer live for themselves but for him

who died for them and was raised again. So, from now on we regard no one from a worldly point of view... if anyone is in Christ, the new creation has come; the old has gone the new is here! All this is from God, who reconciled us to himself through **Christ** *and* **gave us the ministry of reconciliation.***"** (2 Corinthians 5:15-18)

The words in bold tell us who we are, this is our calling. If you find yourself negatively reacting to something I have written, be open to asking yourself, why? I am still on this journey—so it may be that you are reacting to something I have misunderstood, some errors in my thinking. On the other hand, you may be coming across new information to be processed. You could also be "face to face" with a particular cultural or theological belief that is a "stronghold" in your life, *"a worldly point of view"* that needs to be submitted to Christ? I know this happened as people read my first book "Heal not Lightly." Some were set free, reconciled with God, others and themselves, to become reconcilers; others, at times have strongly dismissed it!

So, here goes!

"Through the Chosen One, Creator has removed the hostility between human beings and himself... [He] has chosen us to represent him in the sacred task of helping others find and walk this path of peacemaking." 2 Corinthians 5:18. First Nations Version.

(Courtesy of Terry Wildman, *RainSong*)

Part 1

A Destiny Denied

Chapter 1

My Journey This Far

Have you ever felt that you have been "set-up"—that someone has been working behind the scenes to get you to a specific place for a specific purpose? I was party to one of those occasions some years ago when my brother-in-law was treated to a surprise birthday celebration. As I look back over my life, I have a strong sense that God also does this, as He works behind the scenes in the circumstances and experiences of life, to bring us to a place, where He begins to reveal something integral to the next stage of the journey. It is often only as we look back that we can see the threads coming together; a theme that has been developing.

For about fourteen years now, I have been carrying something deep in my heart for a people group, far removed geographically from our shores here in Ireland, and yet, as I am increasingly being made aware, so strongly connected through history. I speak of the First Nations or indigenous peoples of North America, and in particular, for the purposes of this book, the United States of America.

I have asked myself and God, many times, "Why me?" I will probably never get a complete answer to that, but part of it lies in the forty-years-long journey I have been on since the early days of what became known euphemistically as "the troubles" here in Northern Ireland. It has been a journey of prayer, reconciliation, research and seeking understanding regarding the conflict here between the two major "tribes"—Protestant/Unionist and Catholic/Nationalist. God was using it in preparation for something around the corner. Something I could never have imagined myself being connected to.

I invite you to come with me as I give you an overview of the journey so far, and how the experiences, the threads of yesterday, are showing themselves to be so connected to the place I now find myself standing at the threshold of the next part of my journey with God! At times, it will be autobiographical and at others historical and theological. It is my journey, yet nevertheless one traveled with many others, not least by my wife, Dorothy. I believe it has, for the most part, been ordained of God (or as I have heard my Native American friends address Him—Creator or Grand Father).

Irish apartheid

To give what I share later some context, I will bring you back to 1969 when I started training in September of that year as a male nurse in one of Belfast's major Accident and Emergency Hospitals—The Royal Victoria—just as "the Troubles" broke out all around us. Before that, while it was peaceful, I nevertheless grew up in an 'apartheid' system. We, as Protestants, were in the ascendancy—better jobs, career prospects, etc. We also grew up going to separate schools; played different games; listened to different music and back then, what we considered as the added bonus, not having to learn Irish!

Along with many other students from Northern Ireland, third-level education gave me my first meaningful contact with people from "the other side," as we learned together how to treat the physical and emotional wounds of patients coming through the hospital doors. That sadly included people suffering from the effects of riots, petrol bombs, shootings, car bombs, etc., that we were inflicting on each other's communities in the name of "God and Ulster" and "God and Ireland" Many stereotypes had to be faced! Their blood was nevertheless the same color as ours—RED!

God broke the rules

In the early 1970s I had a radical encounter with God, as the Holy Spirit moved throughout Ireland in what became known as the Charismatic Renewal Movement. It was all the more significant, considering I had grown up in a Church which taught that any such move attributed to the Holy Spirit was, to put it mildly, suspect! Almost overnight, I found myself being able to worship and pray together with Catholics who had also encountered God at this same deep personal level. God was "breaking the rules," He should not have been doing that to them—never mind, me! But the reality was, He did, and to validate my experience meant that I also had to do so with theirs. If we were embracing the same God, by the same Spirit, then we were brothers and sisters in Christ—bottom line! Theologically and culturally we were poles apart regarding many issues, but now undeniably members of the one family, the body of Christ. That was made all the more powerful, giving the backdrop of civil unrest all around.

For many years to come, God would use this outpouring of His Spirit to bring healing and reconciliation to many people within our divided communities. Cross-community Prayer Groups and residential Communities of Reconciliation sprung up across Ireland. My wife Dorothy and I had the privilege of living in one, The Christian Renewal Centre, for eighteen years (until in June 2010 we passed the baton to Youth With A Mission, Ireland). The Centre, established in 1974 by an Anglican clergyman, the Rev. Cecil Kerr and his wife Myrtle, was strategically situated on the border between Northern Ireland and the Republic of Ireland.

We went there in 1992 when I took up the position of Prayer Coordinator, subsequently taking the reins of leadership for ten years. One of my roles during that time, along with other colleagues in the Irish Prayer Movement, was to research and gain further insight into the roots of the centuries-old problems here. We realized that this was an essential part of the intercessory process, as together we faced some of the historical "skeletons in the cupboard," from both sides. Out of this place of corporate ownership often came forth deep levels of confession, repentance, and reconciliation.

Connections
This would also connect me over many years to others in the United Kingdom who were doing similar research within their regions of these islands: The Prayer Forum of the British Isles and Ireland (formerly the British and Irish Prayer Leaders Conference) and Interweave (formerly the English Reconciliation Coalition, which expanded to embrace the other nations in the UK and Ireland). Both groups being acutely aware of many of the negative aspects of

4

Britain's Empire expansion, especially throughout the sixteenth to eighteenth centuries.

At an international level, I have also experienced invaluable input from ministries like the International Reconciliation Coalition led by John Dawson, (author of two significant books: "Taking Your Cities for God." and "Healing Americas Wounds"); Reignbridge, overseen by Joey and Fawn Parish; Intercessors International founded by Johannes Facius; InterPrayer led by Brian Mills (who along with Roger Mitchell, co-authored "Sins of the Fathers"); and Alistair Petrie of Partnership Ministries.

Root issues

Ireland, positioned as it is on the edge of Europe and close to England, inevitably became its oldest colony, with the political and spiritual battles of Europe—before and particularly after the Reformation— often being played out here. In many ways "the troubles" of the last forty plus years have been the outworking of those painful roots.

It is within this context, of reconciliation and research in Ireland, that God spoke to me 20 years ago through a vivid dream. Without going into all the details, I was made aware of a covenant made in Ireland in 1912 by the main Protestant Churches here (Presbyterian, Church of Ireland and Methodist)—The Ulster Covenant. Nearly 250,000 men signed it as a response to the British Government wanting to introduce the Home Rule Bill, which would have led to Ireland getting a measure of self-governance, centered in Dublin. To the Protestant majority in the north of the island, that would have inevitably meant being ruled over by the Catholic majority, with the fear that the Catholic Church would exert a dominant influence. An understanding of this is foundational to our understanding of the violence that erupted in Ireland in the late 1960s.

In the dream, I was acutely aware that this Covenant was like a supporting log in the foundations of a beaver dam. This dam was holding back a large volume of water, which I sensed was the River of God, the Holy Spirit. Only a trickle was filtering through to an otherwise parched land. In essence, the log—the Ulster Covenant—

5

and the subsequent development of the dam was an act, which not only grieved the Holy Spirit but also as a consequence quenched His capacity to flow freely through the Church into the nation. The message of Ezekiel 47:9 (RSV), resounds with the words, *"Everything will live where the river goes."* I believe that the heart cry of God is, "I want My Church back." He yearns for the river to flow!

Heal Not Lightly

This revelation led eventually, after many years of biblical and historical research and with the encouragement of some senior Church Leaders, to the publishing of a book in 2006, entitled "Heal Not Lightly." The title is taken from a verse in Jeremiah 6:14 (RSV), *"They have healed the wound of my people lightly, saying. 'Peace, peace,' when there is no peace."* As my research for the book progressed, I became aware, in a way that perhaps I had never before, of the depth of wounding in the corporate Irish psyche, and also of significant periods and events in history, which introduced some of that pain. There are layers of them, laid down over the centuries, but I draw attention to the role that people like Oliver Cromwell (a Puritan), and the Scottish Presbyterians (during the Plantation of Ulster) played in the 17th and 18th centuries. These two people groups, the Puritans and what became known as the Scots-Irish, were to reappear, within a different context!

Growing up in Ulster I knew about issues like the Ulster Covenant, but only in part. I had learned my cultures perspective—the history of the winners! Likewise, the Catholic Nationalist people had their perspective, that of the loser, the downtrodden, the oppressed and of seeking to rise up, to be free from that oppression. God gave me eyes to begin to see both of these people groups in a different light!

I was also to learn from some of my international friends, that when one group of people makes a covenant against another—using the components of deity, national identity, and land, along with a willingness to lay down their lives for a cause—that we should look out for the possibility of a mirrored response in the other. That, I believe, happened in Easter 1916, with the birth of Sinn Fein and the

Irish Republican Army! The outcome: two people groups covenanted against each other. That can set the scene for ethnic cleansing on a brutal and large scale as we saw in Rwanda between the Hutu and the Tutsi tribes.

The power of covenant

For God, "covenant" is central to all His dealings with mankind. It has legally bound God to us, ensuring that He could never walk away. Through covenant, God was committing himself to redeem us, and eventually to make it possible through the blood covenant of His Son's death on a cross, for us to have an intimate relationship with Him, and be progressively made whole.

Should we be surprised, therefore, that on the flip side, Satan, who is totally anti-God and His purposes for the nations and people groups of this world, should want to undermine this? That can be by pitching one people group against another, as I mentioned above; through the misuse of covenants, treaties, pacts, and oaths or by not delivering on them. Such misuse enables Satan to continue to exercise generationally this authority we have given him, with horrendous consequences. It also places Israel (land and people), the Church and marriage at the top of his hit-list!

We talk about having peace here in Ireland, but for me, the reality is that we are far from it. I thank God for each day that goes by without sectarian violence, but the divisions are still there. Sections of our community are still ghettoized, with "peace" walls and fences keeping them apart; paramilitary groups are still active, while sitting around the table in our power-sharing governmental Assembly the two dominant political parties are culturally and ideologically covenanted against each other. It should be no surprise, that at the time of writing this, the Assembly has not met for nearly two years!

In the light of what I have just shared, it is my understanding that the current leadership of the three major Protestant Churches in Ireland are still in need of recognizing the wrongs of their forefather's promotion of the Ulster Covenant. They need to confess/repent of it, just as the Dutch Reformed Church in South Africa did with their

Covenant, two years before the fall of the Apartheid Regime there. To that end, we sent out a copy of my book to all of the clergy in those churches. I know of many individuals who have personally cut themselves off from the personal and generational power of the Ulster Covenant. So far there has been no move at Church leadership level, from within the denominations, to do so.

A change of direction

It was during our time at the Christian Renewal Centre that I received an email invitation to participate in the first web-based Reconciliation Studies Course run by Reignbridge in Ventura, California. It is a ministry that grew out of their relationship with John Dawson and the International Reconciliation Coalition. Little did I know how much of a directional shift in my life and ministry was about to take place.

Before attending an optional week-long residential in Ventura, September 2004, one of the last questions of the course ran something like this: "Is there a people group, outside of your people group and outside of your country that you need to consider and reach out to in reconciliation?" I immediately thought of the Irish Catholic Diaspora that went to the United States because of the Irish Potato Famine of 1845. While gathering information for my answer, I discovered another diaspora from Ireland, that of the Presbyterian Scotch-Irish in the early 1700s. Reading further, I came across Andrew Jackson's name (seventh President of the United States), and his connection with the "Trail of Tears." Jackson's family were Scotch-Irish from Carrickfergus, just north of Belfast. He was born to them two years after they went to America in 1765. I found myself responding in my spirit with deep pain and weeping. I have had similar experiences from time to time as I gathered with others to intercede for Ireland, but not for something that up to then I was both historically or emotionally detached from.

The plot thickened when I went to Ventura, California, USA for the Residency. We were invited on to the land by Lew Silva, an Elder of the Chumash tribe, and once again that pain and weeping in my spirit returned as he shared with us how the land we were on belonged to his people, even though it was wrongfully taken from them through

8

colonial expansion. God was connecting me to something that I sensed was for more than just a casual visit! He was well and truly, setting me up! It was also during this time that I was given a piece of jewelry made by Lew–a silver pendant made in the shape of a turtle– a constant reminder to me that the land I stood on is known by the Native peoples as Turtle Island. Hence the symbol on the front cover of this book!

That was further compounded when a friend of ours, Daphne Swilling, from Chattanooga, visited us the following year. Standing in our kitchen, she said to me in her distinct southern drawl, "I'm here with a message from the Lord!" She felt that I should share something of my journey at a reconciliation gathering in Brentwood, Tennessee, with the representatives of the "Five Civilized Tribes" that Andrew Jackson had evicted on what became known, as I mentioned above, "The Trail of Tears": the Choctaw, Seminole, Chickasaw, Cherokee, and Creek nations.

So, that's how I got to Tennessee in August 2005! Daphne had asked me to briefly share what I had learned up to then about the Scotch-Irish/Andrew Jackson issue. Before leaving for the States, I had sensed God was prompting me to bring a map with me which I was given in Ventura; all the Native American Tribal names and land distributions were marked on it. After I shared, I also sensed that God was asking me to do an act of identificational confession/repentance. It required me to lay the map on the floor, amid those gathered; taking my shoes off, explaining that my forefathers had come into their midst, walking insensitively, all over their land with their military/pioneering boots on. I was to come in the opposite spirit and then lie on the map as an act of humility and repentance. It was a very humbling and painful experience! On prostrating myself, I once again knew this was a God moment, as my spirit connected with weeping to the pain in His heart and the hearts of the native people of the land.

You might be thinking by now, that this guy does nothing else but cry! I can assure you that this is counter to the way Harry Smith usually operates. There have been times when I wish I could turn the tears off, but it happens from time to time within the context of intercession and repentance issues. God has made it patently clear to me, "If it was good enough for Jesus and Paul, it is good enough for me!"

In September 2007, I attended another Reignbridge residential, this time on Whidbey Island, Seattle. On the way there, I stopped for a few days in Boston with Jeff Marks, who was the Director of the New England Concerts of Prayer movement. A Native American called Teresa Two Feathers, was at a meeting I spoke at, and she gave me a music CD of a ministry called RainSong, produced by Terry and Darlene Wildman (he is an Ojibwa Indian, and she is of Irish ancestry).

I was later to connect with them by email and in person when they visited us in Ireland. The following year they invited me to speak at a reconciliation gathering in Heartland Church, Fort Wayne (Kekionga), Indiana entitled "Restoring Ancient Gates." (January 2010). In one of the meetings, it was wonderful to see many of the local Church leaders showing their commitment to developing a mutual relationship of respect and honor with Chief Buchanan, the Tribal elders and the people of the Miami tribe. That was also my first experience of participating in a Christian gathering organized primarily by the Native people. Oh, I felt so much at home with them!

The following year, Dorothy and I were invited to join a ministry team on the Lakota Sioux Reservation at Pine Ridge/White Clay (South Dakota), and in 2013 I was invited by Terry and Darlene to join them in Rhode Island as we encouraged Pastor Gail Johnston and some other local Christian leaders to reach out in reconciliation to the local Wampanoag and Narragansett tribes. These are two of the tribes my Puritan ancestors first encountered when they went there in the 16th century. That was followed up by a ministry trip with Dorothy to Michigan—again with Terry and Darlene. During it, I connected with two other significant people, Dan Hawk (Professor in Old Testament, Ashland Theological Seminary) and Mark Charles (a Navajo Indian, who is committed to not only enlighten White and Native Americans regarding the Doctrine of Discovery but also how they can counter its effects). Each of these trips was such a profound experience for us.

In 2014, I was invited by Mike Berry, a friend of Alistair Petrie, to spend a few days with him in Annapolis, Maryland before attending a symposium Mike had organized in Wilmington. He carries a deep burden regarding the role the Doctrine of Discovery had played in the slave trade. In recent years, this has been extending to embrace local Native American issues. That was followed by another visit there in 2015.

November 2016, I joined Chad Taylor (Consuming Fire Ministries), and Pastor Gail Johnston for a series of meetings and prayer initiatives in Providence, Rhode Island and Plymouth, Massachusetts—some of this was connected to issues surrounding the arrival of the Pilgrim Fathers in 1620. I have a sense that this whole northeastern region (the original 13 States) of the U.S. will feature more and more for me in the coming years. In March 2017, we were again on Sioux land on the Standing Rock Reservation (North Dakota), where local Native Church leaders where receiving training on community transformation, through a "Healing the Land" Conference.

Dignity Restored
Much of the journey I have described above is tied in with us leaving the Christian Renewal Centre in 2010 to pursue God's heart further— the development of a ministry called *Dignity Restored* (www.dignityrestored.org); traveling to the U.S. researching root issues and eventually the writing of this book.

-oooOooo-

Before moving out into the main body of it, I want us to look in the next chapter at a theological issue, one that undergirds everything I write in this book—we are in a spiritual battle! As I have already mentioned in my Introduction, most, if not all the books I have read, related to the writing of this book, have dealt with our histories purely from historical and sociological perspectives. It has been my growing understanding, that we are all center stage in a cosmic spiritual battle being played out by Satan against the purposes of God for mankind— our daily living, along with the events of history, are all integral parts of that. Anything we do today that is counter to what God desires us to do has ramification, not only for ourselves individually, it can also affect those around us at societal, governmental, national and international levels today and tomorrow!

My prayer is that Christians (Native and Euro-American), as well as Christians from the UK and Ireland, will in reading this book, be open to the heart of God for all our nations so that we can embrace His ministry of reconciliation and become His agents for "the healing of the nations."

Chapter 2

Legal Footholds

As I have already mentioned in the Introduction and at the close of the last chapter, history is not just about providing a chronological record of events and happenings in a people group, nor is it just a sociological account of their culture, how they lived, etc. Over and above both, there is a spiritual dynamic. God has made us in His image: every individual and people group (Gr. *ethos* – ethnic). How we act (as individuals or parts of a people group) and in our interaction with other groups: ethnic, cultural, denominational, political, etc., can have deep, lasting and profound consequences for generations to come—for good or evil, positively or negatively! Regarding anything that is evil or negative, God's desire for us is greatly hindered! That became so apparent to me as I researched my tribes' history surrounding the Ulster Covenant in Ireland.

This dynamic has the potential for developing what the Apostle Paul calls a "stronghold" in 2 Corinthians 10:4. It can affect our thinking and ultimately our actions; which can be utilized either by God or Satan and felt by those around us or within our greater society. "Strongholds" do not always have to be negative or Satanic! They can be formed and used by God. For instance, when a husband and wife seek to follow God's will, regarding the sanctity of life, in a moral issue such as abortion, they are developing a stronghold for good in their home and society. But a nation that legalizes abortion is acting before God in an unrighteous way—a stronghold of Satan has been established. The Scriptures do not say, *"Righteousness exalts a nation,"* for nothing! (Proverbs 14:34)

I have found that our understanding of this subject, within many Churches, has not been very good. We know specific key scriptures such as Ephesians 6:13-17 regarding the necessity of us individually putting on the whole armor of God in our battle against Satan. What we tend to forget is that Paul preceded those verses with these words: *"our struggle is… against the rulers, against the authorities, against the powers of this dark world and against the spiritual forces of evil in the heavenly realms."* (v.12) We have not been great at unpacking them: "rulers," "authorities," "powers of this dark world," "spiritual forces of evil." What are they? How do they operate? What do their actions look like in our lives and the society in which we live? There is a spiritual battle going on all around us and within us, and we hardly recognize it! What Paul has been laying before us is an insight into Satan's governmental hierarchical structure. Not being omnipresent, Satan has had to organize his fallen angels into a worldwide organized system to do his bidding!

What I write here will give you helpful insights as we seek to embrace our calling by God to be His agents of reconciliation and healing in our nations (2 Corinthians 5:18-19); and to bring God's Kingdom rule *"on earth as it is in heaven."* (Matthew 6:10) I am thankful to Dutch Sheets for the insights he gives in his book "Intercessory Prayer." In this Chapter, I will draw heavily from them and on some paragraphs from my book "Heal Not Lightly."

Paul in writing to the Ephesians regarding anger (though in essence, it could be any sin) is saying, *"Do not let the sun go down while you are still angry, and do not give the devil a foothold."* (Ephesians 4:26) He is sharing something with us of immense importance. Unconfessed sin not only causes a breakdown in our relationship with each other, but it also gives Satan a legitimate, legal point of entry into that relationship. The Greek for "foothold" is *topos*, from which we get the word "topography," a geographic term related to the mapping of the earth's surface features and structures. It implies that we can give Satan a "toe in the door," or to put it more graphically, "a landing strip" into our lives.

The Scriptures are quite clear, that if I sin against someone, then I must go to them and confess that sin. This not only opens the door to reconciliation but more importantly it prohibits Satan from working in that area of our relationship and enables healing to take place. Sadly, throughout history, many "suns" have gone down on our wounded relationships with each other—at individual and corporate levels, allowing Satan to fly in and out at will! Jesus sees reconciliation as such an important issue that he says in Matthew 5:23, *"If you are offering your gift at the altar and there **remember that your brother or sister has something against you**, leave your gift there in front of the altar. First, go and be reconciled to them; then come and offer your gift."* (bold – *mine*) Note, it is not "If I have something against my brother or sister!" We are called to take the lead!

The nature of strongholds

The Apostle Paul addresses the issue of negative strongholds in 2 Corinthians 10:3-5:

> *"For though we live in this world, we do not wage war as the world does. The weapons we fight with are not the weapons of this world. On the contrary, they have divine power to demolish strongholds. We demolish **arguments** and every **pretension** that sets itself up against the knowledge of God, and we take captive every thought to make it obedient to Christ."* (Bold – mine)

In these verses, he is highlighting various issues regarding "strongholds" which we need to understand if we are going to come against these "arguments" and "pretensions" successfully. To quote from "Heal Not Lightly."

> "The first of these is **'arguments'** (Gr. *logismos*). They are the sum total of the accumulated wisdom and information learned over time. They become what we believe, our mindsets, our worldviews. Not all wisdom is godly wisdom! There is much of it around that is most certainly not of God. James tells us, *"Such 'wisdom' does not come from heaven, but is earthly, unspiritual, of the devil."* (James 3:15) These *logismos* would include philosophies, religions, racism, materialism, roots of rejection—anything that could cause us to think, act or react in wrong ways. So, if you

15

grow up being told that 'You are useless, stupid, fit-for-nothing,' or 'Home Rule is Rome Rule and hearing the slogan 'For God and for Ulster,' by the time you become a teenager they have become firmly established *logismos*."[1]

That equally applies to the words, "infidels" and "savages" used by my ancestors, regarding both the Irish and the Native Americans they encountered.

In describing a mindset, author, and pastor, Robert Heidler writes,

> "[It is] a set of assumptions and methods which is so firmly established that it creates a powerful incentive to behave in a certain way… whether you attain your destiny will largely be determined by your mindset. How you react to the world is determined by your mindset."[2]

I continue to quote from "Heal Not Lightly,"

> "The second aspect Paul mentions is **'pretensions'** (Gr. *hupsoma*), which means 'any elevated place or lofty thing that sets itself up against the knowledge of God.' The Living Bible calls it *'every wall that can be built to keep men from finding Him.'* It came to humanity at the Fall, when Adam and Eve bought the lie, *'You will be like God.'* (Genesis 3:5) These words carried with them the possibility of being able to be on equal footing with God himself. At that point, we become 'not the Most High, but our own most high - filled with pride.' So 'pretensions,' encompass all mind-sets that exalt themselves against the knowledge of God. Pride!"[3]

Paul is speaking here to Christians. The scary reality for me is that I can be a follower of Jesus and still have these undealt with 'arguments' and 'pretensions' in my life! Cromwell, for instance, was living not long after the Reformation. As we say in Northern Ireland, "a Bible-believing **Christian**" and yet could commit horrendous acts of genocide in Ireland and then thank God for His assistance! The Puritans in New England also did so, in a similar fashion! They were living out of centuries-old 'arguments' and 'pretensions.' Now, that is scary. Real scary!

—oooOooo—

In my involvement in reconciliation over many years in Ireland and internationally I have increasingly recognized that there are many parallels between the Protestant, Unionist/Catholic, Nationalist issues in Ireland and the Native issues in North America. As you will see in the chapters following this one, on the Doctrine of Discovery, many of the belief systems and actions formed over centuries in Western Europe, both in the Roman Catholic and Protestant Churches, fed directly into the foundations of what became the United States of America. This is the stuff from which negative "strongholds" are made!

—oooOooo—

Revelation needed
In his book, "The Powerhouse of God," Johannes Facius writes:

> "There is one major problem that stands in the way of healing the land. That is the unconfessed historical sins of the nation. Unconfessed sin is the foothold of satanic forces, whether we speak of the individual or the nation. Unconfessed sins constitute a basis for satanic rule. We must, therefore, find a way of dealing with it, if we are to see our people delivered from demonic strongholds."[4]

John Dawson in "Taking Your Cities for God" gives us another insightful perspective:

> "The problem is not the presence of the enemy, but the absence of the glory. When our sin causes God's

revealed presence to depart, the demonic swarm to fill the vacuum. Therefore, our focus should be on repentance and priestly mediation rather than on becoming experts on the satanic hierarchy."[5]

And the Apostle Paul in 2 Corinthians 4:3-4 writes:

*"And even if our gospel is **veiled**, it is veiled to those who are perishing. The god of this age has **blinded** the minds of unbelievers, so that they cannot see the **light** of the gospel that displays the glory of Christ, who is the image of God."* (emphasis – *mine*)

Dutch Sheets, in "Intercessory Prayer"[6], shares some valuable insights on this issue, as he explains several New Testament passages and unpacks the meaning behind some of the keywords in them.

In the first of these, the word "**veil**" (Gr. *kalupsis*), means "to hide, cover up, wrap around," just as bark veils the inside of a tree. Interestingly, the word "**revelation**" is *apokalupsis*: *apo* means "off or away." So, a revelation is quite literally an unveiling, an unwrapping, an uncovering. That is a helpful insight when it comes to sharing the gospel message with people. Sometimes we find that people don't grasp the message and according to this verse, they don't see the light because they can't! What was shared with them was heard through the filter of their belief system or worldview, which can mean that they interpret it in a very different way.

Another example of this is related to someone who is told that God is a heavenly Father who loves them. If, however, that person's only experience of a father is one of being physically abused by him, such a message regarding God is not understood by them. In both examples, they need to have an unveiling—a revelation.

It also has another application. For many Native Americans, their worldview regarding Anglo-Saxon Christianity has been shaped by three or four centuries of victimization, genocide, broken covenants/treaties, forced land removals, and Residential Boarding Schools. While, on the other hand, many whites have lived out of a worldview of superiority, exceptionalism, of being in America by Divine right, a view shaped, albeit unknowingly for many, by the Doctrine of Discovery and Manifest Destiny.

That is also true of other wrong mindsets that we hold on to as Christians:

- Denominationalism, which impeded us in our working with other denominations for the kingdom of God
- Replacement theology, which hinders our capacity to fully embrace God's covenant purposes for Israel as a people and land
- Cessationism, the gifts of the Holy Spirit are not for today, etc.

All of which sadly send out a message to the world of a divided Church, counter to the prayer of Christ in John 17:22-23, *"... that they may be one as we are one... then the world will know that you sent me."* And perhaps it is not so much the fact that we hold different views but how we hold them in adversarial ways!

Letting in the light

Let's turn to another of Dutch's passages, Ephesians 1:18. It is worth reminding ourselves that Paul is addressing followers of Jesus when he writes, *"I pray that the eyes of your heart may be **enlightened** in order that you may know the hope to which he has called you..."* (emphasis – *mine*) The word "**enlighten**" (Gr. *photizo*), means "to let in the light," and is closely related to the word for light (Gr. *photismos*) meaning "illumination."

The obvious illustration of this is found in the cameras I knew in my childhood. When we took a photograph, a shutter opened to let the light in and enable an image to be captured on the film loaded inside. If the camera shutter did not open, there would be no image. The same applies to the human soul. It makes no difference how great Jesus is, or how wonderful the message is that we communicate; if the veil is not removed (i.e., the shutter doesn't open) there will be no actual image of Christ made in us.

John alludes to that in the opening of his gospel, when he proclaims, *"In Him [Christ] was life, and that life was the light of men. The light shines in the darkness, but the darkness has not understood it."* (John 1:4-5)

That is what Paul is saying in Acts 26:17-18, in his defense before King Agrippa. God had told Paul, that He was sending him *"to them [the Gentiles] to open their eyes and turn them from darkness to light, and from the power of Satan to God..."* He was called *"to open their eyes"* to enable them to experience an unveiling, revelation, repentance, *"so that they may turn (epistrepho) from darkness to light."*

Regarding this, Dutch Sheets points out that the word repentance— counter to common thought—does not mean to "turn and go another way, to change direction." Repentance (Gr. *metanoia*) means to have "a new knowledge or understanding of something," "a change of mind." Light has been let in, and revelation has come, we positively respond! The Greek word *epistrepho* mentioned above means "converted," which is the result of repentance.

Paul is talking here about bringing the gospel to people who had previously not heard it. This can, however, be equally applied to the process of a Christian experiencing revelation, insight, and understanding into areas of their own life that need transformation, e.g., the tearing down of cultural strongholds about Native Americans that are contrary to how God sees them.

Blinded by pride

Lastly, in 2 Corinthians 4:4, Paul gives further insight into this issue of "being veiled." He tells us that *"The god of this age has **blinded** the minds of the unbeliever..."* (emphasis – mine) The Greek word for "**blinded**" is *tuphloo,* which means "to dull the intellect; to make blind." It comes from the root word *tupho*, which has the meaning "of making smoke." The blindness referred to in this passage is like smoke filling a room, impairing a person's vision so that they may even find it difficult to locate the door.

Such smokescreens can be made up of historical events in our culture which cloud how we see another people group; a negative personal experience about something; stereotypes—e.g., All Catholics are scroungers/all Indians are lazy. The antidote to these is to begin the journey of embracing "the mind of Christ," not only about ourselves but also in how Christ sees the other person(s) or situation.

From this root word comes the word *tuphoo,* meaning to be high-minded, proud or inflated with conceit. That connects the words blindness and pride. It was, after all, the sin of pride that caused God to expel Satan from this immediate presence. It was this same sin that Satan passed on to mankind in the Garden, and which he has continued to use as he seeks to keep us blind; from seeing the truth.

When people choose to reject Christ, it can be based on the simple fact that they don't want to give the lordship of their lives to Him… this is pride. It is the ultimate enemy of Christ and will finally be dealt with when every knee bows and every tongue confesses that Christ is Lord.

This understanding of pride being capable of blinding us, along with the other dynamics mentioned in this chapter, gives us an important pointer when we pray for people locked into a stronghold. It was most certainly a key for me as I talked with people about the Ulster Covenant. Often, they were not able to understand or grasp what I was sharing. I was finding out that many of them were, unconsciously, under the control of the Ulster Covenants' generational stronghold. They were incapable of either understanding or responding positively to what I was sharing with them. When we are under the influence of a stronghold, it is not a matter of not wanting to see—we can't see! Just as a non-Christian is unable to understand and respond to the gospel, because a spiritual blindfold is in place (2 Corinthians 4:4), they likewise could not see! You can argue with and try to persuade such a person until you are "blue in the face," but nothing will change. Prayer for revelation is needed!

It is one of my major desires in writing this book that both Native and White Americans, along with my own people, can have many mighty "unveilings," blindfolds removed so that we can recognize what truly is in the heart and mind of God for us. Every Native American tribe has a specific calling from God to be embraced, and that is equally true of Euro-Americans in the multiplicity of their ethnicities. The challenge is to recognize what God has put into each and to work towards honoring, helping and respecting one another. In so doing we can weave a rich tapestry with our different colors to bring glory and honor to God. It is truly only possible in Him.

Not just theory

Let me anchor what I have been sharing here with a personal story, which is printed indelibly in my mind. It is related to an annual event in Northern Ireland, held on the 1st Sunday of July when the Orange Order[7] parades to a Church in Drumcree on the outskirts of Portadown, Northern Ireland. To put it in context, here is a bit of the history surrounding it:

> "The Orange Order was instituted in 1795, just a few miles from Portadown. That placed the Order there in something of a special position, leading many to hold a view that they are "in the vanguard of defending the Protestant faith."

> Before the unrest that erupted in Northern Ireland in the late 1960s (often known as 'the troubles'), the Orange Order returned [from its annual Service at Drumcree Parish Church], uninhibited, to Portadown via the Garvaghy Road. However, things were set in place for conflict when many Catholics were driven out of sections of the town in the early 70s to be re-housed into single identity housing estates, one of which was to straddle Garvaghy Road.

> In 1995, when the annual Orange Parade had been re-routed away from the Garvaghy Road because of civil unrest the previous year, mass protests were staged at the Drumcree Church. Throughout Northern Ireland, Protestant rioters in support of their Orange brothers attacked and destroyed property, set up illegal

roadblocks, bringing many parts of Northern Ireland to a standstill.

That led to the Orange Parade being forced down the Garvaghy Road—under a massive security operation—against the wishes of the people living there, leading to serious civil disturbances in republican/nationalist areas. Since then there had been a yearly stand-off, with neither side being willing to back down. The Portadown Lodges then continued with a new 'tradition' of leaving the Drumcree church, marching a few hundred yards down the hill, before being brought to a halt by the police and army barrier blocking their route."[8]

The last parade down the Garvaghy Road was in 1997.

Keep that in mind, as I continue to share the unfolding of events. In the year following the ban, this parade was to produce a massive "stand-off," which lasted for several days, between the Orangemen and their supporters against the Police and the British Army. A very ugly scene was developing, as a new level of civil unrest was spreading throughout Northern Ireland. On the 11th of July, the "pressure cooker" atmosphere needed to be eased, as the day of Orange parades was the following day. It was to take the burning to death of three young Catholic boys (aged 8-10) of the Quinn family, when their house was petrol bombed, to shock at least some to come to their senses.

In January 1999, during a Prayer Gathering at the Renewal Centre, we had the sense that God wanted to call a "solemn assembly." The key scripture for this was Joel 2:12-17:

> " 'Even now,' declares the Lord, 'return to me with all your heart, with fasting and weeping and mourning.' Rend your heart and not your garments. Return to the Lord your God, for he is gracious and compassionate, slow to anger and abounding in love, and he relents from sending calamity. Who knows? He may turn and

relent and leave behind a blessing—grain offerings and drink offerings for the Lord your God.

*Blow the trumpet in Zion, declare a holy fast, **call a sacred assembly**. Gather the people, consecrate the assembly; bring together the elders, gather the children, those nursing at the breast. Let the bridegroom leave his room and the bride her chamber. Let the priests, who minister before the Lord, weep between the portico and the altar. Let them say, 'Spare your people, Lord. Do not make your inheritance an object of scorn, a byword among the nations. Why should they say among the peoples, 'Where is their God?''"* (emphasis – *mine*).

Not long after that, a prayer partner in the United States wrote and shared something similar with us. And then a few months later a church in Weymouth, England, had felt that God wanted them to come to the field at Drumcree, to set up a tent and pray and fast for the week preceding the next parade on Sunday 4th of July. They also sensed that the last day should finish with a "solemn assembly."

And so, on the 3rd of July, we met in a tent at Drumcree: a group from the church in England; members of the inter-church prayer group in Portadown; other leaders and praying people from across Ireland. What a scene! There was a heavy military presence, as they were preparing for the worst, soldiers had put up rows of razor wire; others plowed up the bottom of the field and turned it into a quagmire; helicopters circled overhead. Inside the tent, we laid down our personal agendas for the day, along with the British and Irish flags at the foot of a cross. And then we worshiped. Flowing out of that time of worship came a time of deep repentance. I don't think I have ever been at a gathering where we experienced such a "spirit of repentance." And then it was over, a tangible sense of peace settled on us and, in keeping with the wishes of the military, we packed up and went home.

The following day the Orangemen paraded to Church, the military and police were on high alert, the crowds had gathered, and the world's media looked on. With the service over, the Orangemen lined up, paraded to the security cordon, handed in a letter of protest and then turned around and marched off: the crowd dissipated with them. This annual event has never been the same since and I believe that many people, including the Orange Order, didn't understand why. But I did, along with everyone else who had gathered in that tent. That day, as we met there in obedience to God to hold a "solemn assembly," He showed up, and something dynamic happened in the heavenly realms over Northern Ireland in general and Drumcree specifically. A stronghold of Satan was broken!

Closer to home

What I have described here is just as applicable to personal issues closer to home. If two friends have fallen out due to an argument, then pastorally someone has to help them unpack the point of breakdown. Where there has been no ownership, repentance and reconciliation cannot follow, and consequently, Satan has been allowed to maintain a "foothold," sometimes over a lifetime! Ownership and repentance automatically break Satan's hold—the relationship can now start a process of restoration.

It also leaves me with many questions. What is going on in the heavenly realms over our communities? How is Satan engaged in this battle, to hinder the purposes of God for them? Is this connected in any way with the divisions in the Church? In the United States, is it related to its historic and current Indian Policies:

- The Doctrine of Discovery
- Manifest Destiny
- Residential Boarding Schools
- Reservations
- Broken treaties
- Federal and state non-recognition of some tribes
- As to why the blood continues to cry out at places such as the Wounded Knee massacre site.

Somehow, I think I know the answers!

—ooo0ooo—

As I mentioned at the beginning of this chapter, a fuller researched understanding of an issue is of extreme importance when it comes to dealing with the past—things that have become so deeply embedded into our present cultures, that we unknowingly continue to live out of them. This gives us insights and clues as to how the Church in North America (and in the UK and Ireland) needs to face up to and remove these strongholds in the Church and society. For the Church in the United States to come against the stronghold of the Doctrine of Discovery within it and reach out in reconciliation to the Native Americans, this is essential!

The big question is, are we up for it? It is clear to me that some sections of the Church are—Native and White! What if others, especially the leadership of the historic predominantly white Churches joined them, to pray for such a breakthrough, for such a work of the Holy Spirit? Is it willing to pay the price? Desperation has time and time again proven to be a key! History also shows us that such a move of God may only require a small body of people to begin a committed engagement process with Him. Ask Him, to reveal his heart to you!

So, armed with these insights, let us now move on to look at the Doctrine of Discovery and then, how it influenced the Anglicans/Puritans as they came to North America to unwittingly establish something very much counter to the Kingdom of God, to what they thought they were.

References:

1. Harry Smith, *"Heal Not Lightly."* Pub. New Wine Ministries, 2006. Pgs. 117-118.
2. Here is a partial quote by Heidler. The full quote: "A mindset is a set of assumptions, methods, or notations held by one or more people or groups of people that is so established that it creates a powerful incentive within these people or groups to continue to adopt or accept prior behaviors, choices, or tools." is found in various places.

E.g.,
https://scrumalliance.org/community/articles/2015/june/fixed-mindset-versus-agile-mindset

3. As 1 above.
4. Johannes Facius, *"The Powerhouse of God."* Pub. Sovereign World (1995), Pg. 44.
5. John Dawson, *"Taking Your Cities for God."* Pub. Charisma House, Pg. 119.
6. Dutch Sheets, *"Intercessory Prayer."* Pub. Gospel Light, Regal Books (1996), Pgs. 160-177.
7. Source: https://en.wikipedia.org/wiki/Orange_Order
8. Adapted from Mervyn Jess, BBC News, 4th July 2002. Source: http://news.bbc.co.uk/1/hi/uk/2092771.stm

Chapter 3

The Doctrine of Discovery: Laying the Foundations

Jesus: *"The one who hears my words and does not put them into practice is like a man who built a house on the ground without a foundation. The moment the torrent struck the house, it collapsed..."* Luke 6:49.

Before we look at the historical, social and spiritual journeys of the Puritans and Scotch-Irish and catch a glimpse of what made them into the people they were before going to America, I want us to look at a subject that is foundational to the overall content and flow of this book. I think it is best that I introduce this here, as it will appear in Chapter 7 without a context if I don't!

For years, I had asked myself the questions, "What lay behind the English Crown and Churches thinking (and also that of the Scotch-Irish Presbyterian following the Plantation of Ulster), to do what they did to the Catholic Irish?" "How could they justify what they did, as followers of Christ?" "What ideas were empowering their actions?" The more I read about their conduct in Ireland and then subsequently what they did in America to the Native Americans and asked myself those questions; I knew that I would have to hit the research trail hard! Little did I know the terrain I would cover during the journey I was about to undertake!

It all started with the phrases "Doctrine of Discovery" and "Discovery Discourses" leaping off the pages at me from one of the books on the Puritans that I had obtained in the United States! These were terms that neither I, nor several of my colleagues I asked within the UK reconciliation movement, had ever heard of before! Though granted, some had heard of a few of its components.

So, get a coffee, tighten your seatbelts, we are in for a roller-coaster of a journey!

The Doctrine defined

In a nutshell, the Doctrine of Discovery (DOD) is one of the earliest examples of international law. It encapsulates a gradually developing and evolving process over many centuries, which became the accepted legal principle being applied by the Catholic Church to "Christian" European nations as they related to each other regarding the control of trade, exploration, and colonization of non-European countries. It was also used to justify the domination of non-Christian peoples. Following the Reformation, England continued to use it in the North American colonies and further afield in Australia and New Zealand as the British Empire grew. With regards to Ireland, England's oldest colony, attempts at subjugating it had been going on for centuries without any direct mention of the term in the history books (though back then the DOD was very much in the early stages of its development)!

Perhaps there was no need to! England's presence there was already well established! The closest I got to finding something in writing, any way related to this, is a Papal Bull entitled the *Laudabiliter*. While some historians would question its validity, others would support it and even key legal figures of the day referred to it. It is believed to have been issued by Pope Adrian IV in 1155, granting King Henry II of England the right to invade Ireland, govern it and bring the pre-Catholic Irish Celtic Church under Papal authority. It took approximately another 450 years before it would appear in the format of Queen Elizabeth I's granting of Charters for the colonization of North America.

Though not a remit of this book, I nevertheless want to note that the development of the black African slave trade, within the original 13 American colonies, was also very much connected to the Doctrine. It became a vital part of the economic growth both there, and in England e.g. regarding the cotton and rice production in the Carolinas and the tobacco crop of Maryland and Virginia. Even Belfast in its early developmental days benefited financially from the lucrative trade of producing and exporting shoes for the slaves and linen for their owners.

In the Preface to his book, "*Native America Discovered and Conquered*," Robert J Miller (a law professor, and a member of the Shawnee Tribe of Oklahoma), explains that from 1492 it was understood and variously applied by Spanish, Portuguese, French and English explorers and colonists. They used it to limit "the human and property rights of indigenous people."

It was subsequently taken and used by "the American state and federal governments to dominate Indian People and nations and to dispossess them of much of their sovereignty, self-determination rights, and their property rights." He would believe that it "still has a major impact in federal Indian law and the lives of Indians and their tribal governments today."[1] I am indebted to him for his many helpful insights.

Our understanding of the Doctrine of Discovery is crucial, not only as an answer to my questions but ultimately to get to grips with the reasoning behind the westward expansion of European Empires into America and beyond. Such a powerful concept could not just have been "tailor-made" to fit the current needs of the day in Europe as it dramatically emerged center stage in the fifteenth and sixteenth centuries. It was as I have already mentioned part of a gradually evolving process.

In coming across the term "Doctrine of Discovery," My research began to move in two directions: one backward in time to 313AD and Emperor Constantine, the other forward from the mid-eleventh century in Europe (and ultimately to America). So, do bear with me as I try to unpack this. It will mean names, dates, quotes and some legal technicalities, but, to the relief of many, it will certainly not be to the depth I have found others, such as Robert Miller, have gone to when sharing their research! It will, I trust, give a broad overview, looking at what I sense are a few key landmarks on the road, a laying of the foundations of the developing Doctrine of Discovery and Empire expansion! I warn you; this is mind-boggling stuff! The lengths that men went to, to bring God onside, as they sought to justify their empire expansion actions, is incredible!

Moreover, it is again, my desire that we will hear the heart of God and what His Spirit wants to impart to us. In Revelations chapter 2 we read these words of Christ to the seven Churches mentioned, *"Whoever has ears, let him hear what the Spirit says to the Churches."* They are just as significant for us in Europe and North America today. We are being called to be God's reconcilers and healers regarding the deep hurt our forefathers inflicted upon the Native American peoples—wounds that have kept so many of them from coming to the full revelation of Creator through His Son.

Constantine and Theodosius I

One thing became very apparent to me at the beginning of this specific research journey, was that without the control of the Holy Spirit, Emperor's Constantine and Theodosius I by embracing the Church into the Roman Empire, effectively sowed the seeds of the "spirit of Empire" into it. Consequently, the Church, through never repenting of that, continued to develop and act out of that spirit to become of itself, a powerful hierarchical, controlling, manipulative institution— Christendom was born! A legacy, I believe that we continue to live with to this day!

In 313, Emperor Constantine issued the Edict of Milano, which stopped the persecution of the Church and began the process of the Roman Empire's incorporation of Christianity. That was followed in 380 with Theodosius I, who issued the Edict of Thessalonica, which not only forbade the practice of pagan religions but also proclaimed Christianity to be the religion of the Empire.

The relationship, in those early days, between Church and State was a tense one, as popes diplomatically sought to develop and maintain their authority. On the one hand, as Robert A. Williams Jr. puts it in his book, *"The American Indian in Western Legal Thought: The Discourse of Conquest."*

> "By virtue of the papacy's asserted history, origins, and mandate (according to scripture, Christ had declared: *'Thou art Peter, and on this rock, I will build my Church'*), the Roman pontiff represented the one

institution within the Church that could conceivably assert any type of primatial claims in opposition to imperial prerogatives. As St. Peter's divinely elected successor, the pope was posited in early Church legal and political discourse as possessing a universally-recognized supreme position in the spiritual life of all Christians within the empire."[2]

However, Williams recognizes that Pope Gelasius I was walking something of a tightrope in his dialogue with the Emperor Anastasius I. He had sent a letter to him in 494, using the argument of his Petrine succession to challenge the support that Emperor Anastasius I was giving to the divisive Byzantine patriarch of Constantinople, in the Eastern Roman Empire. He argued that while accepting that two powers were ruling the world—secular and ecclesiastical—the sacred authority given by God to the priesthood was superior to the royal one. Brian Tierney in, *"The Crisis of Church and State, 1050-1300,"* writes:

> "[In his] letter, he gratuitously conceded limited priestly obedience to the secular power, as long of course as the emperor conceded the Church's hierarchical (i.e., ecclesiastical authority/rule – *mine*) position respecting the spiritual sphere. "For if the bishops themselves... obey your laws so far as the sphere of public order is concerned lest they seem to obstruct your decrees in mundane matters, with what zeal, I ask you, ought you to obey those who have been charged with administering the sacred ceremonies?"[3]

> Gelasius's magnanimous recognition of secular imperial prerogatives was wise political practice, given the fact that too aggressive an assertion of papal primatial authority would throw the Roman Church's constitutional theory into a perilous open conflict with Byzantium's assertion of imperial rights. Gelasius' concessionary dualism reflected an acknowledgment of the papacy's inability to enforce its Petrological thesis and to impose spiritually hierarchizing logic on

32

the empire during this early period in the Church's institutional history... this explains in part why the early popes focused so much of their energies on the task of enforcing the Petrological hierocratic viewpoint within the institutional church itself."[4]

Pope Gregory and the Leo's

During the Pontificate of Pope Gregory I (590-604), we see a shift in focus from the east to the west, as he, through his order of the Benedictines, reached out in mission to convert the barbarians of Spain, Portugal, and Britain. Whether or not, this was an intentional way of diverting his attention away from sensitive Byzantium issues, it nevertheless enabled him to implant something of the Church's influence and ecclesiastical structures into the secular society of a rising and distinctly different Western European worldview.

Moving on two hundred years, another key development on this journey took place when Pope Leo III (800) crowned Charlemagne as monarch of the Carlovingian Dynasty—The Holy Roman Empire. By doing this, we have one early example of the process by which the destinies of the secular, political West and the Roman Church's hierocratic claims to primacy, were increasingly becoming intertwined. That eventually caused the Church to enter a very dark time due to compromises, which left the door open for corrupt practices such as Bishoprics, and other church offices being sold or bartered by kings and lay lords demanding the right to have a say in the appointments of principal ecclesiastical positions within their jurisdictions.

It took Pope Leo IX to begin the process of purging the church of these sins of simony. At the Council of Rheims (1049), the reformers within the College of Cardinals sought to reinstate the separateness between the priestly and the secular, decreeing that no layperson could hold an office in the church and that the buying or selling of church offices was not allowed to continue. These reforms were to continue after his death through the ongoing activities of the church lawyers and canonical scholars within the curia, who showed utter contempt for any secular privileges given to people in the affairs of the church, even those claimed by the emperor!

Humbert of Silva Candida

One of the most influential reformists was Humbert of Silva Candida (d. 1061). In the light of all the negatives that had taken place within the church, he reasoned that there needed to be a restoration of its hierarchical functions to enable the papacy to practice the mandate of shepherding all of God's flock. That had been hinted at by Gelasius as far back as the 490s, when he wrote to the Eastern Emperor, "The responsibility of the priest is weightier, in so far as they will answer for the kings of men themselves at the divine judgment."[5] However, the reality was, the relationship between pope and emperor, ended up as being one of equals.

Humbert wanted to change that, to move it from theory into practice, which required undoing some things, and the practice of simony, which lay investitures made possible. He openly declared, that if an archbishop had not canonically elected a bishop, he was "a pseudo-bishop." From Humbert's perspective, all grace was to be mediated through the church, as God directed the papacy, and all the secular functions of the emperor were being subordinated, resulting in him becoming subservient to the pope.

To enforce this radical position, would, strangely enough, require military support. It was Archdeacon Hildebrand (soon to become Pope Gregory VII) who, having the responsibility for the military defense of the Papal State, led negotiations to form an alliance in 1059, between Pope Nicholas II and Robert Guiscard (Norman conqueror of Southern Italy). That conveniently suited both parties—the Church, as it sought to distance itself from Germanic imperial control, found an ally to protect the Pope, while Guiscard got papal recognition for his recent land seizures (arguably from the German Holy Roman Empire). What brought about Guiscard's acceptance of papal favor i.e., land given in exchange for a pledge of service, is not clear, but the outcome was significant. He defended the legality of the alliance and his feudal grant from the pope by submitting himself to the strictures that came along with it:

"In order to obtain God's help and the intercessions of Sts. Peter and Paul, to whom all kingdoms of the world are subject, I have subjected myself with all my conquered land to the vicar, the pope, and have received it from the hand of the pope, so that, by God's power, he might thus guard me from the wickedness of the Saracens and I might overcome the insolence of the foreigners. The Almighty has given me victory and subjected the land to me. This is why I must be subject to Him for the grace of the victory, and I declare myself to have the land from Him."[6]

This idea that the spiritual legitimated authority in the secular realm would ultimately permeate the literature of the Crusade-era, making way for the legal position that the heathen and infidels had no right to property.

The plot thickens

While not anticipated, probably the most significant aspect in all of this was how the papacy embraced the political and legal forms of the feudal period to its advantage. By taking on an increasingly dominant role, it gradually became the largest feudal ruler in medieval Europe. In so doing, it made possible the development of the structures that would enable Rome to later assert itself in the Discovery-era through Portugal and Spain's Renaissance monarchs, in the New World lands of the American Indians. Though not a reality for a few hundred years, the notion that the pagan nations of the Americas should also be subservient to Rome's jurisdictional authority would clearly have harmonized with this eleventh-century absolutist legal vision.

One of the things Gregory VII (1073-85) did when he ascended the papal throne was to make the declaration, that as successor to St. Peter he had been given universal rulership over Christendom, which included the secular rulers of his day: kings and emperors. That was contested by the German monarch Henry IV, a successor to Charlemagne, who at one point chose to openly defy Pope Gregory by naming his own candidate to the Bishopric of Milan. What followed was a protracted and heated dispute, which became known as "the investiture controversy."

Gregory's response was to make several attempts at asserting his position that he was above the authority of the emperor. In one of his letters to Henry IV, he reaffirmed his stance regarding his papal authority, as handed down to him through Peter:

> "It would have been becoming to you, since you confess yourself to be a son of the Church, to give more respectful attention to the master of the Church, that is, to Peter, prince of the Apostles. To him, if you are of the Lord's flock, you have been committed for your pasture, since Christ said to him: *'Peter, feed my sheep.'* (John 21:17), and again, *'I will give you the keys of the kingdom of heaven; and whatever you bind on earth will be bound in heaven and whatever you loose on earth will be loosed in heaven.'"* (Matthew 16:19. NASB.[7]

Henry's response was a defiant one! He brought together his German bishops, who, having put forward several charges regarding crimes and abuses in Gregory's papal authority, deposed him as pope. Gregory, in turn, responded by excommunicating Henry and prohibited the exercising of his royal authority.

In his book, Williams, comments on the significance of the Pope's response:

> "Although previous popes had threatened to excommunicate and depose a rebellious ruler, no pontiff wielded this potent weapon and with so profound an effect on secular political and legal theory and practice as Gregory VII. Being the most serious of all sanctions in a universally conceived, hierarchically structured society, excommunication meant exclusion from participation in the divinely willed Christian commonwealth. All intercourse with an excommunicant was prohibited. Vassals tied by oath

to an excommunicated king… were, in theory, released from their feudal obligations. Unable to issue binding orders to his royal subjects, an excommunicated ruler was denied all means of governance.

Excommunication was thus employed by the papacy as an effective reminder of Rome's hierocratically conceived, absolutist perspective. Pope Gregory used the instrument of excommunication to underscore his own innovative elaboration on the subservience of royal secular power to papal hierocratic goals."[8]

In no uncertain terms, Gregory was putting down a clear marker that his jurisdictional authority had no boundaries when it came to exercising authority over the *Societas Christiana*, the Christian body politic.

King Henry's response was a defiant one, as he ended up electing an antipope, marching on Rome, where after a three-year siege he caused Gregory to flee… never to return. Whichever way one may view his demise, one thing is sure: Pope Gregory's influence in laying down a legal and political discourse cannot be underestimated. It would be continually developed and played out in Europe and the Holy Land during the time of the Crusades (1095-1291), and in the Americas for centuries to come.

The *Concordia discordantium canonum*. The what?

Another key development in the twelfth-century church was the publication of the Camaldolese monk Gratian's, "*Concordia discordantium canonum*"—a concord of discordant canons—or *the Decretum* for short. In it, he brought together most of the significant documentation of the first one thousand years of the Church history. He was seeking to line up a number of texts surrounding various issues; look at the pros and cons and determine whether they could be reconciled to each other or make a case as to why one position had superior reasoning over another.

That was to have a growing authoritative significance throughout Europe regarding Church law, as Brian Tierney comments:

> "[T]he use of a single, universally accepted code of canons made possible an unprecedented growth of administrative unity in the Church... New legal procedures often borrowed from Roman [Empirical] law, were adopted in order to facilitate appeals to Rome, and as appeals flowed in by the thousands from every corner of Christendom, the necessary apparatus of papal courts, bureaucratic administrators, and delegated judges were developed to cope with them."[9]

In Chapter 1 of Gratian's text we find what is known as the *distinctio*:

> "The Roman church established the dignities of all other churches of every rank, the eminence of each patriarch, the primacy of metropolitans, the sees of bishops. But she herself was founded and built on the rock of the dawning faith of Him who conferred simultaneously on the blessed key-bearer of eternal life the rights over the heavenly and earthly empire."[10]

Once again, we see that the papacy is unequivocally seeking to assert its right to hold total authority over both the ecclesiastical and secular.

The *distinctio* raised a fundamental question: If the emperor received his imperial power from the pope, could he not only depose the emperor but also assume his temporal jurisdiction? That was not just a theoretical question, but one that had enormous implications regarding the popes' relationship with the German Emperors.

During Pope Hadrian IV's primacy (1154-1159), which was marked with open hostility between himself and the German Emperor Frederick Barbaross, this precise point was to be picked up by Rufinus of Bologna in his commentary on the *distinctio*. He conjectured on Gratian's words quoted above, "rights over a heavenly and an earthly empire" as follows:

"He calls the heavenly militia, that is, the whole body of the clergy and the things that pertain to them, a heavenly empire. He calls secular men and secular things an earthly empire or kingdom. From this, it seems that the supreme pontiff, who is vicar of the blessed Pater, holds rights over the earthly kingdom."[11]

Rufinus's commentary also highlighted the significance of two concepts, "authority" and "administration," taken from Roman jurisprudence. "Authority" had with it an inbuilt claim to exercise power, while "administration" is likened to a "steward, for he has the right to administer, but he lacks the right to rule." From this he argued that the pope held "rights over the earthly kingdom as regards authority," while the emperor was rather like a steward, administering the secular, but only because he was enabled to do so through the pope ceremonially conferring it upon him. The pope ultimately held both direct and indirect authority in both the sacred and secular realms!

Pope Innocent IV
As we pick up the trail once more, we see these ideas being further developed and articulated by Pope Innocent IV (1243-1254), albeit, without much immediate success.

He has often been described as one the greatest legal minds to ever become a pope, as well as a distinguished canonist and lecturer at the University of Bologna—also famous for producing men such as Thomas Aquinas (1225-1274), who is attributed to having laid the foundations of what would later become known as the law of nations (*ius gentium*). It would have increasing significance as issues concerning the ownership of newly discovered lands by European nations in the 16th and 17th centuries would come to the fore.

Law of Nations (*ius gentium*)
This is a concept of international law within the ancient Roman legal system and the Western Law traditions which are either based on or influenced by it. The *ius gentium* is not a body of statute law or legal code, but rather customary law which is thought to be held in common

by all *gentes* (people or nations) in "reasoned compliance with standards of international conduct."[12]

> "We must therefore apply to nations the rules of the natural law to discover what are their obligations and their rights; hence the Law of Nations is in its origin merely the Law of Nature applied to Nations... Since men are by nature equal, and their individual rights and obligations the same, as coming equally from nature, Nations, which are composed of men and may be regarded as so many free persons living together in a state of nature, are by nature equal and hold from nature the same obligations and rights... From this equality it necessarily follows that what is lawful or unlawful for one Nation is equally lawful or unlawful for every other Nation."[13]

Innocent IV was to play a significant role in the production of a commentary on the rights and duties of pagan nations under natural-law (*ius naturale*). That was a by-product of the decree "*Quod super his*" made by his predecessor Innocent III, which legitimized the Crusades.

Natural-law (*ius naturale*)[14]

> "Classically, natural law refers to the use of reason to analyze human nature—both social and personal—and deduce binding rules of moral behavior from it." It is a view that "certain rights or values are inherent in or universally cognizable by virtue of human reason or human nature." Other nations will, however, have different conceptual understanding and applications of natural law. E.g., Marxism and Islam.

From a Christian perspective, the Apostle Paul's letter to the Romans has been used in support of this:

> *"Indeed, when Gentiles, who do not have the [Jewish] law, do by nature things required by the law, they are*

a law for themselves, even though they do not have the law. They show that the requirements of the law are written on their hearts, their consciences also bearing witness, and their thoughts sometimes accusing them and at other times even defending them" (Romans 2:14-15).

In this commentary, he defended the position that the church had a right to protect the Holy Land against the attacks of the infidel Saracens, by it being a just war—something that was already well established by Augustine.[15]

Another significant component of his commentary addressed the question, "Did infidel societies possess natural-law rights to hold property and to rule themselves (their *dominium*), or could Christians legitimately dispossess infidels of their lordship and property on the sole basis of their non-belief in the Christian God and the papacy's mediating position in relation to that divine power?"[16]

His answer in part was an attempt to synthesize the polarized views of people like Alanus and Aristotle. The former held that all *dominium* is entrusted to the church and that the pope "reserved an indirect right of intervention in the secular affairs of all the Church's subjects, actual and potential" and the later held the view that infidels and heathens did "have natural-law right to hold property and exercise lordship."

Robert Williams writes that

> "Innocent readily accepted that infidels and heathens possessed the same natural-law rights as Christians to elect their own leaders and to exercise *dominium* over property. But while he appeared to reject outright the position of Alanus that all *dominium* is held through the Church, he qualified the infidel's natural-law rights by reference to the Pope's own universalized Petrine mandate... [that he] possessed both direct and indirect authority. Thus, the papal office necessarily reserved an indirect right of intervention in the secular affairs of all the Church's subjects, actual and potential... [that

he] had been entrusted by Christ through Peter with the care of the spiritual well-being of infidel and heathen nations."[17] He had "jurisdiction over all men and power over them in law but not in fact."[18]

One application of this can be seen regarding idolatry: If an infidel ruler and (therefore an infidel nation) was guilty of worshipping an idol, was he then in serious violation of natural law and therefore standing in need of correction? In the light of that, Innocent's argument went as such: Because every man was "made for the worship of God" it was therefore natural for man to worship the one and only God. That threw up a challenging question: "If God, the creator of all, had intended that heathens and infidels were to be sheep of his universal flock (e.g., Muslims in the Holy Land or [later] Native Americans in the Americas), how could their rejection of the Christian God and his papally interpreted and revealed divine plan for their salvation be explained?"[19]

In the end, it all came down to his European-defined reasoning regarding natural law—God's will, as interpreted through his pontifical office, was far above any reasoning held by any imperfect human being. Therefore, anyone who couldn't recognize that was simply, clearly in error. According to this logic, "there was only one right way of life for mankind, and… the papal monopoly of this knowledge makes obedience to the Pope the only means of salvation."[20] Therefore anyone who rejected the pope's position was clearly in need of corrective intervention by the papacy. The intervention of choice in situations like the Crusades and later, during Spain and Portugal's empire expansion into the Americas, was to call on Christian princes to send out armies to punish any serious violations of natural law by the heathens or infidels. These armies often accompanied missionaries to heathen lands to assist in this conversion process.

Pope Boniface VIII (1302) was to add his "penny's worth" to the debate in the conclusion of his *Unam Sanctum* with the words, "[it] is altogether necessary to salvation for every human creature to be subject to the Roman pontiff."[21] As Williams puts it, "Only by the pope's implementation of a Christian government on a world scale,

using Christian princes and armies, would the ecclesiastical society…
be realized. That of course, was the idea of the Crusades, grounded in
the universal Church's assertion of a divine right to enforce its vision
of truth in all lands and cultures, Christian and non-Christian alike."[22]

The Council of Constance (1414)—*Dominium* Natural Law and the Law of Nations

In 1414, a further, yet key, clarification was required. There had been
an ongoing conflict between Poland and the Order of Teutonic
Knights, as to who had control over the non-Christian Lithuanians.
"The Order was originally established in 1196 in Palestine as a
German religious confraternity of monks devoted to good works.
Under German imperial influence and benefice, however, the monks
were quickly transformed into a military order with a constitution
modeled on other Crusading orders such as the Knights Templar."[23]
They had obtained the blessing of a former pope (Gregory IX), on the
basis that the Lithuanian pagans could be attacked by them (a
Christian army) and dispossessed of their *dominium* (i.e., their
sovereignty and property rights). The Polish King, on the other hand,
had entered an alliance with the Lithuanians to help protect them from
further attacks by the Knights—who had only one real goal in mind—
empire expansion! Following a series of unresolved conflicts, a papal
legate was able to persuade both parties to submit what was an
extremely complex issue to the Council of Constance.[24] The question
of the legal rights or wrongs of seizing "infidels" lands by papal
sanction was being raised: Who had *dominium*—Church or State?

At the Council both sides of the case were considered: The Poles
called on the writings of Pope Innocent IV (1243-1254), arguing that
while the infidels had the same "natural law" rights to sovereignty and
property as they had, the Pope could order an invasion to punish their
breaking of natural law or to enable the spread the gospel. The
Teutonic Knights, however, claimed that they had outright authority,
based on a papal bull from the time of the Crusades, which allowed
them to not only take the property but also the sovereign rights of
heathen nations. The Council came down on the side of Poland. In so
doing, it was affirming that Papal authority was superior to the
Teutonic Knights authority!

That was a landmark decision because it meant that all future crusades, conquests of heathen land and discoveries would be governed by Innocent IV's legal ruling (as we shall see early in the next chapter), that while pagans had natural law rights, they had to adhere to the church's position/interpretation regarding those rights. To do otherwise, they would run the risk of conquest and suppression by "just war." The crucial outcome of The Council of Constance was that a formal definition on the Christian Doctrine of Discovery had been established: both the Church and secular Christian princes had to respect the natural law rights of pagans, but only if the pagans/infidels did not stray from the European definition of it.

Throughout Europe, the stage was being set for the big move west, and with it would come all the baggage of Church and Empire regarding discovery.

Congratulations, you made it! As we move on, the implications, the ramifications, of what you have been reading here may possibly be even harder to get your head around—for very different reasons!

References:

1. Robert J. Miller, *"Native America, Discovered and Conquered-Thomas Jefferson, Lewis and Clarke, and Manifest Destiny."* (University of Nebraska Press, 2008), Introduction, pgs. xiv, xv.
2. Robt. A. Williams Jnr., *"The American Indian in Western Legal Thought: The Discourse of Conquest."* Oxford University Press, 1990, Pg. 16.
3. B. Tierney, *"The Crisis of Church and State, 1050-130."* Supra note 2, Pg. 14.
4. *Ibid*, supra note 2, Pg. 11-13.
5. C. Erdmann, *"The origin of the idea of Crusade."* (M. W. Baldwin & W. Goffart trans. 1977), supra note 18, Pgs. 150-60.
6. Ibid, supra note 18, Pg. 167.
7. J. A. Brundage, *"The Crusades: Motives and Achievements."* (1964), Pg. 149.
8. Williams, Pgs. 22, 23.
9. Tierney, supra note 2, at Pg. 98.

10. Gratian, Dist. 22 c.l. (c. 1140) ed. E. Friedberg, Corpus Iuris Canonici (1879), col. 73. B. Tierney, *The Crisis in Church and State, 1050-1300.* Supra note 2, at Pg. 117.
11. Rufinus, Commentary on Dist. 22 c.l. (1157), reprinted in B. Tierney, *The Crisis in Church and State, 1050-1300.* Supra note 2, at 119-20.
12. Source: http://en.wikipedia.org/wiki/Jus_gentium
13. Ideas and General Principles of the Law of Nations – www.pixi.com/~kingdom/lawintro.html
14. Source: http://en.wikipedia.org/wiki/Natural_law
15. Source: http://savagesandscoundrels.org/events-landmarks/1243-1254-pope-innocent-iv/
16. Williams, Pg. 45.
17. Ibid.
18. J. Muldoon, *The Expansion of Europe.* ed. 1977, Pgs. 191-192.
19. Williams, Pg. 46.
20. M. Wilks, *The Problem of Sovereignty in the Later Middle Ages.* Pgs. 413-14.
21. Williams, Pg. 29.
22. Ibid.
23. Ibid, Pg. 61.
24. Ibid, Pgs. 60-67. The text of these pages can be found at: https://books.google.co.uk/books?id=KmIqnHquHhIC&pg=PA60&lpg=PA60&dq=council+of+constance+and+the+Teutonic+Knights+controversy&source=bl&ots=LHbCC97KBh&sig=32jpJ4pD8Bv8ylXS65zioQYmG9Q&hl=en&sa=X&ved=0ahUKEwi-t7myz-PVAhVGUlAKHe2GBOcQ6AEIPTAC#v=onepage&q=council%20of%20constance%20and%20the%20Teutonic%20Knights%20controversy&f=false

Chapter 4

The Doctrine of Discovery Moves West

By the mid-1400s, both Portugal and Spain had been developing the means to make long distance sea travel possible, and a clash of interests soon became inevitable when the Canary Islands were "discovered" in the mid-Atlantic. As a means of 'protecting' the islanders—converts, and infidels—the Church got involved, with Pope Eugenius IV issuing a papal bull in 1434, which banned all Europeans from further involvement there. This decision was contested by King Duarte of Portugal in 1436, arguing that their explorations were conquests, done on behalf of Christianity and that the Church now had a role of being a guardian to the infidels.

As Robert Miller puts it:

> "The conversion of the infidel natives was justified… because they allegedly did not have a common religion or laws; lacked normal social intercourse, money, metal, writing, and European-style clothing and lived like animals. The king claimed that the Canary converts to Christianity had made themselves subjects of Portugal and had now received the benefits of civil laws and organized society. Moreover, the King argued that the pope's ban interfered with this advance of civilization and Christianity that the king had commenced out of the goodness of his heart, 'more indeed for the salvation of the souls of the pagans of the islands than for his own personal gain.'"[1 & 2]

With the papal acceptance of Portugal's appeal, a revision of the Doctrine of Discovery was on the cards. When his legal advisors recalled the deliberations of Pope Innocent IV in 1240, Eugenius confirmed under the Law of Nations (*ius gentium*), that while the Islanders had a right to *dominium* (governmental sovereignty and property), the papacy would keep a supervisory control over their secular activities. He would only step in if he thought that they violated European defined natural law (*ius naturale*) or didn't want to have Christian missionaries among them. That was concretized by the Pope issuing another bull in 1436—*Romanus Pontifex*—which gave Portugal the authority to not only convert the people of the Canary Islands but also to oversee the islands on his behalf.

Another Bull—*Dum Diversas*—was issued by Pope Nicholas V in 1452. It was decidedly aggressive, giving Portugal authority "to invade, search out, capture, vanquish, and subdue all Saracens and pagans"[3] and to place them into perpetual slavery and to take all their property. A further rendition of *Romanus Pontifex* was made by him in 1455 (some sources give 1454), enabling Portugal to expand its empire along the west coast of Africa. These papal bulls demonstrated the developing meaning of the Doctrine of Discovery at that time. They recognized the pope's interest to bring all humankind to the one true religion; authorized Portugal's work towards Christian conversion and civilization and recognized Portugal's title and sovereignty over lands "which had already been acquired and which shall be in the future."[4] and to accumulate enormous wealth through the extractions of precious minerals, by mining in them. Sadly, it would also lead to the eventual development of the black African slave trade.

How was Portugal's neighbor—a recently united kingdom of Spain under King Ferdinand of Aragon and Queen Isabella of Castile—going to respond to all of this, knowing for sure, that to violate the Pope's rule would undoubtedly incur the threat of excommunication? Following Christopher Columbus' suggestion, they commissioned him to discover new lands beyond Portugal's geographical remit. He initially thought that he could find a westward route to the Indies. Having studied the scriptural and legal basis for such an undertaking, he set out with a contract that would make him Spanish Admiral of any lands *en route* that he would "discover and acquire."

When he came across already inhabited islands in the Caribbean, they were claimed for the Spanish crown, with Ferdinand and Isabella quickly seeking papal endorsement regarding them. In 1493, Pope

Alexander VI not only issues three bulls confirming these discoveries, but he also issued *Inter caetera divinai*, which further granted Spain any other lands it might discover in the future, with the understanding that they were "not previously possessed by any Christian owner."

The Doctrine of Discovery arrives in the New World

Under international law, European monarchs now had gained ownership rights in the New World, giving them sovereignty and commercial rights over its people.

During that same year, Pope Alexander VI was to issue *Inter caetera II*, which drew a north-south line, approximately 300 miles of the Azores, granting Spain all the lands discovered or to be so, west of it. That was to be modified a year later in the Treaty of Tordesillas, as a means of reducing tensions between Spain and Portugal. In it, a new line was drawn up further west, giving Portugal discovery rights to a part of the New World, and what is now Brazil. That, simply put, is why Brazil is the only Portuguese-speaking country in South America!

Miller drew on Anthony Pagden's book, "*Lords of all the World: Ideologies of Empire in Spain, Britain and France c.1500-c.1800,*" to bring together four firmly established aspects of the Doctrine of Discovery by 1493:

> "First, the Church had the political and secular authority to grant to Christian kings some form of title and ownership rights in the lands of infidels. Second, European exploration and colonization was designed to assist the pope's guardianship duties over all the earthly flock, including infidels. Third, Spain and Portugal held exclusive rights over other European, Christian countries to explore and colonize the unknown parts of the entire world. Fourth, the mere sighting and discovery of new lands by Spain or Portugal in their respective spheres of influence and the symbolic possession of these lands by undertaking the Discovery rituals and formalities of possession,

such as planting flags or leaving objects to prove their
presence, were sufficient to pass rights in these lands
to the discovering European country."[5]

This was understandably not particularly welcomed by other
European countries like France and England!

One of the most significant regulations regarding the actual
outworking of Spain's natural law rights in the New World was a
document developed by King Ferdinand in 1513, entitled the
Requerimiento.[6] It was to be read out to the natives (or at least in their
hearing, even from the deck of a ship) before any hostilities or "just
war" could have legally ensued. It informed them that their lands had
been "donated" to Spain by the Pope and that they should, therefore,
acknowledge, the Spanish King, the Church, and the gospel
proclaimed to them by its priests. A refusal was enough for "just war"
to be waged on them—which amounted to genocide by the
conquistadores! How's that for respecting and honoring the free will
of the natives who didn't even know Spanish?

Las Casas and Vitoria

As I mentioned earlier, the Doctrine of Discovery was a constantly
evolving Doctrine. This was a time when the increasingly centralized
control by the Roman Curia was being challenged both by the Spanish
bishops and the Renaissance influences of Secular Humanism which
were being felt all over Europe.

By 1532, major challenges regarding this would be on the cards, as
two Dominican priests strongly criticized Spain's policy of
engagement with the Indians. For them, "Spain's imperial institutions
were 'perverse, unjust, and tyrannical,' designed to mask Spanish
barbarity."[7]

One of these was Bartolomé de las Casas, who urged Charles V to
radically reform the way they dealt with the Indians. He held the view
that they possessed the same natural rights as the Spanish; therefore,
any legal justifications for conquest was illegitimate; and the taking
of land, property, etc., from the Indians, was wrong. As a result, it was

49

now the duty of the conquistadores and encomenderos (grant holders) to restore to the Indians everything that was by natural right, theirs.

In 1556, the legitimacy of the *Requerimiento* was also being contended, and moves were being made, to see Spain's colonial expansion in terms of a "missionary enterprise" rather than a military conquest. Christianity, they were saying, should not be coercively imposed on the Indians; if they did not have the freedom to choose Christianity, then any profession of faith was meaningless.

Williams writes:

> "This growing body of dissenters based their opposition to Spanish rule in the New World on the central tenant of Thomistic-Humanist philosophy (see Reference 8) that all humans possessed the common element of reason. This divine gift gave all individuals, Christians and non-Christians alike, the natural-law right and duty to order their political and social lives by rational means. Spanish colonial law in the New World, however, steadfastly denied the Indians any effective right to self-rule and autonomy. To Humanist-inspired radical reformers, therefore, Spain's colonial regime in the Indies appeared irrefutably opposed to natural and divine law. Dubiously legitimated by papal grant and violently sustained by Indian enslavement..."[9]

Through applying continued pressure, the Dominicans could attempt various experiments, to see if, given the right conditions, Indians could be civilized to live like an average Spanish laborer. One such experiment was called *reducción*—"the establishment of isolated missionary communities to protect the Indians from slavery... [it] was to become the principal vehicle by which the priestly missionaries pursuing the Church's own peculiar will to empire sought to frustrate the self-fulfilling prophecy of Indian degeneracy that legitimated Spanish American slave colonialism."[10] While it may have been a humanistic approach, it was, however, an experiment that "failed to resolve definitively the issue of whether the Indians were slaves by nature" or not, because of their lack of corporation.

One of the foremost Dominican reformers was the Spanish priest, Franciscus de Vitoria. He was an influential theologian at the University of Salamanca and was one the earliest writers regarding international law. As a leading advisor to the King, he was asked to make some deliberations, because of the heated debate that had flared up in Spain's religious and legal circles, especially around the issue of the Papal claim to having sole authority to its land titles in the New World. The Crown along with the Spanish episcopate were seeking to develop "an autonomous right of existence, related to, but jurisdictionally separate from, pontifical authority." The "application of Thomistic natural-law principles to all human relationships," was tailor-made for this to happen![11]

The outcome was a series of lectures entitled *"On the Indians Lately Discovered,"* in which Vitoria set forth three fundamental arguments: Firstly, he declared that indigenous people were free and rational people and that their rightful ownership of the land should not be relinquished to Europeans by Discovery alone. Secondly, the granting of the Americas to Spain, by the pope, was "baseless and could not," therefore, "affect the inherent [natural law – *mine*] rights of the Indian inhabitants." Lastly, if the Indians violated any natural law principles of the Law of Nations (as defined by European Christian nations) it could justify a Christian nation making conquest and expanding its empire among them.[12] It is worth noting here that Vitoria drew much from the writings of St. Augustine (founder of the Just War theory) in support of this third point.

While it might look like his first two points were verging on treason, undermining the authority of the king and the pope, what Vitoria sought to do was to strengthen the justification for Spain's empire and its rights against other Europeans and the indigenous peoples in the New World from being solely based on papal authority. He argued for placing them on a firmer Thomistic-Humanist foundation based on the "universal obligations of a Eurocentrically constructed natural law. The savage could be conquered and colonized by Christian European nations seeking to enforce or inculcate the rational norms binding on all humankind under a natural Law of Nations."

Miller sums it up with the following:

> "In applying this understanding of European natural law to the New World, he reasoned that natives were required to allow Spaniards to exercise their natural law rights in the New World. These rights included Spanish travel to foreign lands; Spanish trade and commerce in native lands; the taking of profits from items the natives apparently held in common, such as minerals for example and the Spanish right to send missionaries to preach the gospel. Vitoria's conclusion… was that if infidels prevented the Spanish from carrying out any of these natural law rights, then Spain could 'protect its rights' and 'defend the faith' by waging lawful and 'just wars' against the natives."[13]

The bottom line appears to be that nothing much changed for the Indians. As William's says, "The Dominican's famous defense of Indian's rights under the natural law did not emancipate the Indians from the guardianship of Christian Europeans."[14] However, Spain was now operating out of a new framework for doing Empire!

Unknowingly, the developing discourse on discovery described above would also serve as a link to England legitimizing its move into North America. In the England of the Elizabethan/Stuart reigns there arose two of its most prominent legal theorists: Alberico Gentili and Sir Edward Coke. "They illuminate[d] the nature of the conceptual bridges that were being constructed between medieval and modern forms of Western legal thought throughout the Renaissance Discovery era… [they were] two of the principal architects of the process by which reason and enlightenment gradually opened itself up to English legal thought and process."[15] I will pick up on Gentili and Coke in Chapter 7.

Other components of the Doctrine of Discovery

Regarding Discovery, there were two other significant components. One was called *terra nullius* (meaning land or earth that is empty or void), which would be added by France and England to justify their "right" to native lands. It claimed that any land not inhabited by any person or nation, or if occupied, was not used in a way that European legal systems approved, it was considered empty and waste and therefore available for Discovery. The bottom line was, Europeans and later the American colonies and the United States did not recognize the sovereign, commercial and property right these "non-civilized" peoples had to the land they occupied. They argued that the Natives only used it for hunting, beyond that it was a vacant land waiting to be claimed, despite early evidence to the contrary in New England!

The second one, which is closely associated with this, is the concept of **Contiguity**. The dictionary defines this as being contiguous to, to have proximity to, or to be near to. Within the context of Discovery, it meant that a European country on discovering the mouth of a river had the legal right to claim all its hinterlands. E.g., The mouth of the Mississippi River would have given them thousands of square miles of territory (the Louisiana Territory). Initially, all that countries like Spain were required to do was to plant their countries flag at the mouth of the river and claim it, along with its entire drainage system for their King and the Catholic Church.

The term also applied to European countries, which had settlements that almost adjoined each other. In which case a line was drawn halfway through the unoccupied territory between them, giving each an entitlement to the stretch of land on their side of it.

—oooOooo—

England and France

At the time of Alexander VI's papal bull in 1493, England and France were both Catholic countries, and as such, they ran the risk of excommunication if they were to infringe Spanish or Portuguese Discovery rights—they could explore and trade but not claim any lands for Crown or Church. That would lead them to examine their legal position and develop a modified version of Discovery theory that enabled them to both explore and colonize in the New World. In England, Henry VII's (a Catholic, who reigned from 1485-1509) legal scholars were to put forward the idea that they would not be in violation of a papal bull if their explorers limited themselves to only claiming lands that were not yet discovered by other Christian sovereignties. In the light of that, Henry VII granted a patent to the Italian navigator and explorer John Cabot and his son Sebastian in 1497. It reads in part:

> "We… give full and free authority, faculty and power to sail to all parts, regions and coasts of the eastern, western and northern sea, under our banners, flags and ensigns, with five ships or vessels of whatsoever burden and quality they may be, and with so many and with such mariners and men as they may wish to take with them in the said ships, at their own proper costs and charges, to find, discover and investigate whatsoever islands, countries, regions or provinces of heathens and infidels, in whatsoever part of the world placed, which before this time were unknown to all Christians… And that the before-mentioned John and his sons or their heirs and deputies may conquer, occupy and possess whatsoever such towns, castles, cities, and islands by them thus discovered that they may be able to conquer, occupy and possess, as our vassals and governor's lieutenants and deputies therein, acquiring for us the dominion, title and jurisdiction of the same towns, castles, cities, islands, and mainlands so discovered…"[16]

Both the Canadian and United Kingdom governments hold that Cape Bonavista in Newfoundland is where Cabot landed. It is believed that he only set foot on it once, with the crew staying long enough to obtain fresh water; raise the Venetian and Papal banners; claim it for the King of England and recognize the authority of the Roman Catholic Church over it.

Thus, England's interests in furthering its colonial empire there were launched. This discovery was further endorsed in the mid-1500's when Elizabeth I (a Protestant) argued that the Doctrine of Discovery should require any European country to show that they had current occupancy of a claimed possession (*terra nullius*)—see also Hakluyt's Discourse in Chapter 5. That, along with contiguity, would be employed by England and France in future encounters they had with Spain, Portugal and between each other.

The post-reformation period

From the time of Henry VIII (reigned 1509-1547) onward, with the formation of the Church of England and its separation from the Roman Catholic Church, fear of excommunication was no longer an issue. Nevertheless, explorers were still instructed to only colonize land that was unknown to all Christians or was not in actual possession by any Christian Prince.

A few years after Henry VIII's death, Richard Eden, a Cambridge University graduate, published an abridged version of Amerigo Vespucci's experiences in the New World, followed by further shortened versions of works by Pietro Martire and Gonzalo Fernández de Oviedo, historians of the Spanish conquests in America. These were to bring the New World into clearer focus for his English audience.

He also pressed for them to "emulate the genius of the Spanish by pursuing Christianity's trade-facilitated divine mandate in regions not yet conquered by that Christian country: 'there yet remaineth another portion of that mainland, reaching towards the northeast, thought to be as large as the other and yet not known but only by the sea coasts, neither inhabited by any Christian men.'"[17]

Having been educated in Cambridge University, an institution aligned with radical Protestantism, it would appear that Eden saved his life during Catholic Mary Tudor's reign by writing in a rather complimentary way about the conquests of her husband Prince Philip II and his father King Ferdinand of Spain who instigated the Spanish conquest of America. In it he wrote:

"God hath fulfilled in him (Ferdinand)... the promise and blessings of Abraham. As to make him the father of many nations, and his seed to grow great upon the earth... He saved not only the bodies and souls of innumerable millions of men inhabiting a greater part of the world heretofore unknown and drowned in the deluge of error."[18]

In his writings, he also defended Spain's conquests. He did not mention its butchery of the Indians and its "possess and inhabit" policies but rather called on the now familiar reasoning of the European colonizing discourse of the necessity to convert and assimilate the natives into European ways, if needs be, by conquest and enslavement. For those who claimed that the Spanish desire for gold was the primary motivation for conquest, Eden was to argue that there was no reason why the Spanish conquerors could not be merchants as well as Christians!

Within English Protestant society, such an expansion of colonizing interest and discourse was both urged and readily accepted. Williams concludes that it "elevated merchant trade with the American savages to the level of a divinely mandated imperative, the worldly means by which Indians' souls would be saved."[19]

The climate had now sufficiently changed, enabling men like James I to grant charters to Trading Companies in Virginia in 1601 and the Council of New England in 1620. With the granting of these charters, other aspects of Discovery would also be embraced. That included the introduction of Christianity and civilization to the American Indians as means of "propagating Christian Religion to those [who] as yet live in Darkness and miserable Ignorance of the true Knowledge and Worship of God, and [to] bring the Infidels and Savages, living in those Parts, to human civility, and to a settled and quiet Government."[20] Back home in England the Companies most certainly expected financial returns from the colonists' engagement with the Indians.

So, with this as a foundation, let us look further at the outworking of the Doctrine of Discovery and its Protestantization, as it crossed the Atlantic from England to America.

For an overview of the various components, which Miller considers makes up the Doctrine of Discovery, see Appendix I.

References:

1. Robert J. Miller, *"Native America, Discovered and Conquered – Thomas Jefferson, Lewis and Clarke, and Manifest Destiny."* (University of Nebraska Press, 2008), Pg. 13.
2. Miller, quoting Williams, Pg. 7.
3. Source: http://en.wikipedia.org/wiki/Romanus_Pontifex
4. Williams, Pgs. 71-72.
5. Anthony Pagden, *"Lords of all the World: Ideologies of Empire in Spain, Britain and France c. 1500-c.1800."* (New Haven, CT: Yale University Press, 1995), Pgs. 31-33.
6. Williams, Pgs. 91-93.
7. Ibid. Pg. 93.
8. Note on Thomistic-Humanist philosophy:

    "The Christian-Humanist synthesis, while respecting the unitary aspects of traditional Christian ideology, acknowledged the more appealing elements of the naturalistic thesis on human nature in a form acceptable to secular and ecclesiastical moderates reluctant to abandon their theocratic moorings. In ceding to the state (and derivatively to an increasingly independence-minded episcopate) a natural and autonomous right of existence, related to but jurisdictionally separate from pontifical authority, the Thomistic synthesis responded to criticisms directed at the more extreme versions of papal hierocratic theory.

    Thomas's notion of a "double ordering of things," by the natural and the supernatural, argued that the state "had nothing to do with faith or grace regarding its origin or operation, but for its better working, grace, and faith were necessary complements." The laws of the human state could thus be valid in their own right, but in order to be more perfect (for perfection in all things human were universally recognized in the Middle Ages, even by the secular party, as humankind's ultimate goal), the laws should find their orientation in those traditional tenets of fundamental justice directing civilized—that is, Christian—society.

Thus, while the spiritual power, which in Thomistic discourse ultimately referred to the pope, did not possess direct power in secular affairs, papal authority did imply a regulative, indirect authority over the secular sphere. But it was an authority of limited scope, exercisable only in certain narrowly defined instances," i.e., issues that are connected to the salvation of the soul rather than with the secular. Source: *"The American Indian in Western Legal Thought."* Williams, Pg. 56. Note 90.

9. Ibid. Pg. 93.
10. Ibid. Pg. 95.
11. Ibid. Pg. 96.
12. *Ibid.* Pgs. 96-108 for more detail.
13. Miller, Pg. 16. See also Williams, Pgs. 98, 101-03.
14. Williams, Pg. 98.
15. Ibid. Pg. 194.
16. Source: http://www.bris.ac.uk/Depts/History/Maritime/Sources/1496cab otpatent.htm. First Letters Patent granted by Henry VII to John Cabot, 5 March 1496.
17. Williams, Pg. 131. Quoting from H. C. Porter, *"The Inconstant Savage."* 1979, Pg. 29.
18. Ibid. Pg. 129. Quoting from H. C. Porter. Pgs. 25-26.
19. *Ibid*, Pg. 131, quoting from H. C. Porter *"The Inconstant Savage: England and the North American Indian, 1500-1660."* (Duckworth Publisher, 1979).
20. Robert J. Miller, *"Discovering Indigenous Lands: The Doctrine of Discovery in the English Colonies."* Oxford University Press, Pg. 19.

Chapter 5

The Doctrine of Discovery in North America

Writing on the Doctrine of Discovery in America, Robert Miller states,

> "It is no surprise that the North American colonists and colonial governments, considering their European ancestry and legal history, also adopted and applied Discovery in their interactions with the American Indians and their governments."[1]

Keeping that in mind, I want to share with you some further insights regarding the early days in the colonial development in North America. How the dynamics within the Doctrine of Discovery, which were well embedded into British Church and political life under Catholicism (albeit, initially clearly determining what they could not do), appear to have traversed both the Reformation and the Atlantic more-or-less intact!

Many of these early colonists, such as the Puritans, may have had the Scriptures and understood afresh the need for a personal encounter with God through what Jesus had done on the cross and the call to lead a sanctified life, but they appear to have fallen short in their love, mercy, and grace towards others. These were integral aspects of the Christian life as taught by Christ and the early apostles, but they appear to be not so apparent in Protestantism, and expressions of it such as Calvinism! They embraced something of an Old Testament perspective which was prevalent in those days: they were the chosen people of God and America was their new "promised land." The native people were likened to the Amalekites, infidels to be conquered (and yet continued to be a thorn in their side. (Genesis 14:17) The bottom line is, there was a profound clash of worldviews, with the Europeans always seeing themselves as being superior and having

God on their side! Little wonder, that I have heard Native Americans say, "Calvin, is no friend of ours!"

—ooo0ooo—

Following Queen Elizabeth I's excommunication from the Catholic Church in 1570, it was no surprise that her reign was rife with strong anti-Catholic and anti-Spanish feelings. By rejecting Spain's papal entitlement to America, the impetus was there for England to go for its "piece of the cake."

In effect, because of the Reformation, Elizabeth—as both sovereign monarch and head of her own reformed church—changed the way Europe was to approach the future of discovering territory in the New World, by enabling the Protestantization of the Doctrine of Discovery! Rome's sole mediating role in European colonization was no longer valid, and as I have already mentioned at the end of the last chapter, the useful occupation, not just discovery of these newly discovered territories, was being introduced as a primary test for the right of a European sovereign to be there. Not surprisingly, the rights of the Native American people would still be disregarded, just as those of the Native Irish had been for centuries before.

In this new phase in the development of the Discovery-era doctrine of European rights in non-European lands, the Indians and their lands would be the new arena in which the now ever-expanding sectarian fueled aspirations of competing Catholic and Protestant "Christian" dynasties were to be played out.

Sir Humphrey Gilbert
Queen Elizabeth's first attempt at establishing a colony in America was through the appointment of Sir Humphrey Gilbert, one of her most decorated veterans in her ruthless wars of suppression in Ireland. James Wilson in "The Earth Shall Weep." quotes historian Nicholas Canny who observed that Gilbert's "years in Ireland were years of apprenticeship."[2]

With regards to his military exploits in Ireland, Williams notes:

"Once Gilbert had conquered a region, he engaged in a gruesome ceremony with the surviving inhabitants, who received a pardon only on marching to Gilbert's tent and pledging loyalty. According to a contemporary, the path to Gilbert's tent was lined with the heads of the rebels—dead fathers, brothers, children, kinsfolk, and friends - who had recently been killed or executed.[3]... Fear rather than love, Gilbert opined, was the emotion that the victor should instill in such detestable vanquished peoples."[4]

He was also known to have included the slaughter of farmers and herders, so that food supplies to their armies were inhibited.

In July 1578 Gilbert was granted a six-year exploration license by the Queen which empowered him "to discover, search, find out, and view such remote heathen and barbarous lands, countries, and territories not actually possessed of any Christian prince or people... to have, hold, occupy and enjoy to him his heirs and assigns forever."[5] Authority had also been given to him, to repel anyone who made an attempt to settle within a 200 leagues (approx. 450 miles) radius of any colony he would establish.

And so, in November that same year, Gilbert, with a fleet of 7 ships, 440 men, and 122 guns set sail, only to be thwarted by inclement weather. In the spring of 1580, he set sail again, this time with only one ship to explore the North American coastline. He was to set out for a third time in June 1583 from Plymouth with five ships under his command. Edward Hayes (owner and captain of the Golden Hind), one of his closest associates, chronicled the expedition. In it, he gave a detailed description of their arrival in St. John's, Newfoundland, that August. Gilbert, he said, made an announcement to the crews of the various fishing vessels anchored in the harbor that he was claiming the territory for the Crown of England so that he could advance the "Christian religion in those Paganish regions."[6]

He then gathered together the captains of those ships and read to them his commission from the Queen. Gilbert continues, "by virtue whereof, he took possession in the same harbor of St. John, and 200 leagues every way."[7] Gilbert then "had delivered unto him (after the custom of England) a rod and a turf of the same soil entering possession also for him, his heirs and assigns forever."[8]

He was also equipped with the written advice of lawyer Richard Hakluyt, entitled *"Notes on Colonization."* in which he argued for an "initial policy of self-serving amicability"[9] as the wisest way forward:

> "Nothing is to be more endeavored with the inland people than familiarity. For so may you best discover all the natural commodities of their country, and also all their wants, all their strengths, all their weaknesses, and with whom they are in war... which known, you may work great effects of greatest consequences."[10]

Not something, as we have seen, that Gilbert was readily known for!

The ploy of an initial peaceful course was nevertheless only a means to an end—that of establishing the Crowns authority and control in the New World:

> "[A]ll humanity and courtesy and much forbearing of revenge to the inland people [must] be used, so shall you have firm amity with your neighbors, so shall you have their inland commodities... and so shall you wax rich and strong in force."[11]

Gilbert was never to return home to England, presumably because his vessel sank on the homeward journey. The following year his half-brother, Sir Walter Raleigh, would inherit these patent rights.

Edward Hayes

In his biography of Gilbert, Edward Hayes referred to John Cabot the Italian navigator, explorer and reputed discoverer of Newfoundland in 1497.[12] That discovery, Hayes writes, gave them the unquestionable obligation to plant "a Christian habitation and regiment" there. Something that was now the responsibility of Protestant England to embrace, without delay. It would appear that he felt that time had been wasted regarding this, when he strongly charged them not to neglect their Christian duty any further:

> "And which is more; the seed of Christian religion had been sowed amongst those pagans, which by this time might have brought forth a most plentiful harvest and copious congregation of Christians."[13]

The idea of the "seed" pertaining to the Christian faith being planted in the human soul, was very much associated with his hometown of Cambridge at that time. It was a focal place for radical ideas of faith such as John Calvin's teachings on predestination and grace, which were to be developed there into the unique and radical brand of theology, known as Puritanism.[14]

Another one of Cambridge's most influential Calvinist teachers and writers of the time was William Perkins. He was, according to historian Perry Miller, a "'superb popularizer' of Calvinist doctrine throughout Protestant England and in early colonial America and one of the outstanding pulpit orators of the century."[15]

Through embracing such teaching, Hayes would have believed that God had foreordained, irrespective of the earlier failure of others, that the English should bring Christianity to the heathen of North America:

> "… events do show that either God's cause hath not been chiefly preferred by them, or else God hath not permitted so abundant grace as the light of his word and knowledge of him to be yet revealed unto those infidels before the appointed time."[16]

England's conquest of America and the planting of the seed there were certainly seen by Hayes through that "foreordained" lens:

> "But most assuredly, the only cause of religion hitherto hath kept back, and will also bring forward at the time assigned by God, an effectual and complete discovery and possession by Christians both of those ample countreies and the riches within them hitherto

concealed: whereof not withstanding, God in his wisdom hath permitted to be revealed from time to time a certain obscure and misty knowledge, by little and little to allure the minds of men that way (which else will be dull enough in the zeal of his cause) and thereby to prepare us unto a readiness for the execution of his will against the due time ordained, of calling those pagans unto Christianity."[17]

Williams makes the comment[18] that,

"Any seventeenth-century New England Puritan worth his theological salt could trace in Hayes's 1583 narrative the emergence of themes that their own preachers constantly declaimed as the Puritans' errand into the wilderness: the colonization of America was the elect's obligation in fulfillment of the covenant of grace with God.

Hayes expressly declared that those who pursued the task of American colonization with motives 'derived from a virtuous and heroical mind, preferring chiefly the honor of God' and 'compassion of poor infidels captived by the devil, could confidently repose in the preordinance of God, that in this last age of the world (or likely never) the time is complete of receiving also these Gentiles into his mercy, and that God will raise him an instrument to effect the same.'"[19]

Hayes's, one feels, held the view that the Puritans should appropriate the discourse of discovery and conquest into England's intent to further its empire in the New World "wilderness," as something predestined by God.

Sir Walter Raleigh
Born in 1554, Raleigh, like his half-brother Sir Humphrey Gilbert, participated with distinction in the various conquests and massacres of Elizabeth's Irish Wars. In 1584, he inherited Sir Humphrey's charter from Queen Elizabeth, authorizing him to "claim, conquer,

and plant colonies in America in regions not already held by any other Christian prince or people."[20]

He initially sent two vessels on a reconnaissance trip, led by Arthur Barlowe (another veteran of the wars in Ireland) and Philip Amadas. They reported to Raleigh that having sighted land (on what is now the Georgia coast), they sailed north to disembark off Hatteras Island (North Carolina).[21] Having claimed it for the Queen "[they] delivered the same over to your [Raleigh's] use according to her Majesty's grant, and letters patents."[22] History records for us that everything was done "according to the ceremonies used in such enterprises."[23]

Moving on, he came to Roanoke Island, were having met a few natives there, he and the entire crew were introduced to and fed by Algonquin Indians in their palisaded village. There, they discovered that the tribe's Emperor Powhatan ruled over a confederacy of over thirty tribes which spread over an area covering more than 900 square miles. After spending six weeks living among the Indians, which Barlow described as "the kindest people in the world," they returned to England, having taken on board two of the tribe's members, Manteo and Wanchese.

Hakluyt's Discourse

Not long after Barlowe returned from Roanoke Island in September 1584, Raleigh brought before the Queen a treatise entitled, *A Discourse on Western Planting*,[24] which he had asked Richard Hakluyt (the younger) to write for him. In it, he reasoned that the Queen should give her backing to the establishment of colonies in the New World to counteract the abhorrent economic and religious influence that Catholic Spain had there.

In doing so, these colonies would plant the seeds of faith and good manners among the "simple people," which would lead them out of "error" and "into the right and perfect way of their salvation." The other more political motive behind this (and likely the primary one) was that this would be most beneficial in not only strengthening England's economic and political interests in the New World but also in weakening Spain's.

Hakluyt reasoned that through the wealth that Catholic Spain had accrued in the Indies, it had been able to strengthen its military control and influence in Europe. England, on the other hand, by developing several fortified colonies between Florida and Cape Briton, could use them as a launch pad, along with their Indian allies, to attack the distant and therefore hard to defend Indies—the apple of King Philip's eye. In so doing, England would severely weaken Philip's Spanish Empire. Another spin-off from this would be felt closer to home, as it would "trouble the king of Spain more in those parts than he hath or can trouble us with Ireland and hold him at such bay as he was never yet held at."[25]

Hakluyt's "Discourse" intertwined the two key elements of Elizabethan colonizing or Discovery thought together: that of not only converting the Indians to English Protestantism and civilization but also in the process, to so severely weaken the Spanish Empire that it would, along with their papistry be purged from the New World. It also shows that he had a clear understanding of the Doctrine of Discovery.

In the closing section of his "Discourse," Hakluyt laid out in detail his thinking behind England's claim to North America, using a variety of reasons for it:

- He challenged what has been called "medieval hierocratic theology." It was developed by Pope Gregory VII (1073-1085), in which he stated that the pope was officially, divinely inspired; his judgment was that of the Holy Spirit, and he who obeys the Pope obeys God. From the divine command that God rather than man is to be obeyed, Gregory drew the conclusion that it is the pope rather than the King who is to be obeyed by all Christians. Hakluyt pointed out that the popes themselves had admitted that their meddling with worldly kingdoms was done by their "indirect" power. "Such indirect dealing is warranted neither by the law of God nor men."

- He sought to refute any prior claims that Spain had to the New World, because of Pope Alexander's papal bulls in the fifteenth century. Using scriptures, he argued that the popes' bulls were *ultra vires* (i.e., beyond the powers)—if Christ in the Gospels would not act as a judge in the division of two brothers' inheritance (Matthew 20:20-23), then the pope should not assume to exercise a power that Christ wouldn't.

- He made an attack on what he saw as the pope's lack of impartiality regarding the granting of the bulls to Spain, after all, Pope Borgia was himself Spanish! Hakluyt claimed, "Borgia was beyond all reason carried away with blind affection for his nation."[26]

- He also questioned the whole idea of granting to Spain the New World in its entirety, arguing that for financial reason alone this was beyond them and therefore not something they could effectively attain to. What right then had the pope to legislate against other European countries from benefiting from Spain's underutilization of it? Active occupancy alone was Hakluyt's criteria for ownership not papal donations!

- He finished his discourse arguing, that if the pope had granted land in the New World to Spain on condition of bringing the gospel to the heathen, then such a condition had "been wonderfully neglected" and therefore having "not [been] performed, the donation ought of right to be void."[27]

On the downside in his argument, he had to contend with the fact that the papacy had granted a bull to the Spanish in the New World on the same premise as the papal bull *Laudabiliter,* by which the English Pope Adrian IV gave Ireland to the English in 1155. Hakluyt's response to this is based on his premise that the Papal grant of Ireland to the English was a meaningless one and therefore carried no weight:

> "If the King [of England] had not by his force more than by their gift, helped himself, the Pope's donation had stood him small stead: neither did the Kings of Ireland admit and allow of the Pope's donation. If they had, they would never have rebelled so against the [Catholic] Crown of England."[28]

Hakluyt also reiterated what I mentioned earlier regarding Hayes: by giving the clear warning that they would need to plant a colony very soon, as both the French and Spanish were threatening to override England's claim through the right of discovery by John Cabot in June 1497.

Williams observes that the overall direction in Hakluyt's English colonizing legal discourse was one of seeking to undeniably move away "from its medieval Catholic influences and moorings" into a more secular path towards a "desacralized mercantilist ideology."[29]

—ooo0ooo—

Due to events on the European stage at that time, Queen Elizabeth I was not able to respond to Raleigh's submission in the way that he thought she would. Her purse could only allow for her to deal with the immediate threat of Spain on her own doorstep. Nevertheless, her favor was upon him, and through various expressions of that he became a Member of Parliament; there was also a flow of assorted revenues to him; he received a knighthood and became the governor of Virginia. He was, however, able to put plans in place to send a fleet of ships westward under the command of another veteran of the wars in Ireland, his cousin Richard Grenville.

Grenville arrived off Roanoke Island on the flagship *Tiger* (one of the Queen's own ships, another evidence of her endorsement of the initiative) at the end of June 1585, with five ships, 250 sailors, 140 soldiers and 105 colonists with the intent of establishing a military-style colony there. After a few months, he returned to England leaving—believe it or not—yet another veteran of the Irish wars as its governor, Ralph Lane. Sadly, his attitude was like so many of his day: he saw the conquest of America as something most honorable and that the native population was a savage, wild and barbarous people.

Lane records that the Indians saw themselves as being "miserably oppressed" by the colonists.[30] Little wonder, considering the number of skirmishes, often over food, that the colonists had with them. That led inevitably to them launching a violent preemptive strike on a group of Indians, which they suspected were conspiring against them.

According to Lane, the Indians were just as treacherous and untrustworthy as the wild Irish, and most certainly not to be trusted by the civilized English. Williams makes a comment that "... the Englishmen's God apparently felt little scruple when Englishmen stole Indian corn, quickly eroding any prospects of amity with the neighboring tribes."[30] One should not be amazed that the record of Thomas Harriot, who was appointed by Raleigh as the first English missionary in the New World, discloses that he was unable to bring the savage Indians to either civility or the True Faith! Little wonder, the colony only lasted less than one year!

As I mentioned at the beginning of this chapter the political and spiritual were deeply intertwined in England's will to empire, just as much as Spain and Portugal's monarchies had been under the dictates of the Papacy. I sense that Sir Francis Bacon a contemporary of Raleigh, was not too wrong when he spoke about the motivation of these early English crusades to America: "It cannot be affirmed if we speak ingeniously that it was the propagation of the Christian faith that was the [motive]... of the discovery, entry, and plantation of the New World; but gold and silver, and temporal profit and glory."[31]

Nevertheless, irrespective of that analysis, there was a growing new positivity in the air regarding England's place on the world stage. The Reformation enabled it to gain a new sense of its spiritual, national and material destiny, with American colonization providing an intense expression of that. Empire expansion, increased revenue, standing up against Roman Catholicism and converting the savage, came together as a most convenient and attractive package!

—ooo0ooo—

I quoted in Chapter 3 from Revelations, Ch. 2, *"He who has an ear, let him hear what the Spirit says to the churches."* As I repeatedly read the historical details—some of which would eventually go into these chapters on the Doctrine of Discovery—I have found myself being profoundly saddened by them. In trying to understand why, I kept coming back to what I believe is an identification with a deep sadness in God's heart, for what has been done in His name in North America to the Native Americans. Through embracing the Doctrine of Discovery, we introduced something into the land that has continued to have painful repercussions to this day.

Having mentioned the Puritans several times in this chapter, I now want to look at them in a bit more detail: who they were; their role in England and Ireland and what caused them to leave our shores with a weighty sense of God's calling, to establish a colonial bulkhead in North America. Bear in mind, that any negative perceptions, attitudes, and reactions previously developed between their fellow Englishmen and the Native tribes would have already given Satan a significant foothold in their pending relationships.

References:

1. Robert J. Miller, *"Native America, Discovered and Conquered— Thomas Jefferson, Lewis and Clarke, and Manifest Destiny."* (University of Nebraska Press, 2008), Pg. 25.
2. James Wilson, *"The Earth Shall Weep—A History of Native America."* (Grove Press, New York, 1998), Pg. 64.
3. Robert A. Williams, Jr., *"The American Indian in Western Legal Thought—The Discourse of Conquest."* (Oxford University Press, 1990), Pg. 151.
4. Ibid, Pg. 152.
5. Ibid, pg. 156. Source: *"The Voyages and Colonising Enterprises of Sir Humphrey Gilbert."* 2 Vols. D. B. Quinn ed. 1940. See "Letters Patent to Sir Humphrey Gilbert."
6. Williams, Pg. 163. Source: Edward Hayes, *"Narrative of Sir Humphrey Gilbert's Last Expedition."* (1583?) reprinted in *"The Voyages and Colonising Enterprises of Sir Humphrey Gilbert."* 2 Vols. D. B. Quinn ed. 1940, Pg. 401. Pg. 188.
7. Williams, Pg. 163. Source: Edwards Hayes in 6 above at Pg. 402. Also documented in http://www.canadahistory.com/sections/documents/explorers/gibertnewfoundland1583.htm
8. Ibid.
9. Ibid, Pg. 156.
10. Ibid. Pg. 157. Source: Hayes at 6 above at Pg. 182.
11. Ibid.
12. Wikipedia: http://en.wikipedia.org/wiki/John_Cabot

13. Williams, Pg. 164. Source: Hayes in 6 above, Pg. 386, realizing that "whatsoever is builded upon [an]other foundation shall never obtain happy success nor continuance."
14. Ibid, Pg. 164.
15. P. Millar, *"Errand into the Wilderness."* (1964), Pg. 57.
16. Williams, Pg. 165. Source: Hayes at 4 above, Pg. 386.
17. Ibid, Pg. 386.
18. Ibid, Pg. 165.
19. Ibid. Source: Hayes at 4 above, Pg. 387.
20. Reprinted in *"Documents of American History 6-7."* (H. S. Commager 8th ed. 1968)
21. *"Arthur Barlowe's Discourse of the First Voyage."* (1584-1585), reprinted in *"The Roanoke Voyages 1584-1590."* 2 Vols., Pg. 91 (D. B. Quinn ed. 1955).
22. Ibid, Pg. 45.
23. Ibid.
24. Reprinted in *"The Original Writings and Correspondence of the two Richard Hakluyts."* 2 Vols., (E. G. R. Taylor, ed. 1935), Pg. 211.
25. Ibid, Pg. 241.
26. Ibid, Pg. 302.
27. Ibid.
28. Ibid, Pg. 301.
29. Williams, Pg. 180.
30. Ibid, Pg. 183.
31. Quoted in K. Knorr, *"British Colonial Theories 1570-1850."* (1944), Pg. 31.

Chapter 6

The Puritans

The date is 1620. Before we move on any further, we pause and look at a significant body of people who were to start their migration to America that year—the Puritans.

The name of Oliver Cromwell is still deeply gouged into the psyche of many Irish Catholics and Nationalists, to this day. He was a devout Puritan and had a passionate hatred of the Catholic Church. Before starting the research process for this book, I knew that something did not line up for me regarding his faith and his military campaign in Ireland against the predominantly Catholic population. A place that immediately came to mind was the east coast port of Drogheda. While it is not the remit of this book, it must be noted that what happened there is within the context of centuries of English involvement in Ireland and Scotland, the Reformation, the Plantation of Ulster as they sought to subjugate the "savage" Irish[1] and in the formative years of English colonization in America.

Drogheda

As part of an overall plan to subdue Catholic Ireland on behalf of the English Parliament which in 1649 was under Cromwell's control (see "The Interregnum" below), he tactically chose to attack Drogheda on Ireland's east coast. That would ensure a quick resupply from England of food, armaments, etc., for his troops, before winter arrived. He arrived there on the 3rd of September that year, with a total force of around 12,000 men and eleven heavy 48-pounder, siege artillery pieces. His opposition was a combination of Irish and English Catholics and Protestants led by Arthur Aston. This was an alliance of 3,100 Royalists (people who were still committed to the British monarchy), and an Irish Catholic movement called the Confederate Catholic Association.

Cromwell followed the rules of conventional warfare of the day until he entered the town. At the sight of heaps of his soldiers lying dead at the breaches, all changed. As Cromwell himself put it, "In the heat of the action, I forbade them [his soldiers] to spare any that were in arms in the town... that night they put to the sword about two thousand men."[2]

His soldiers pursued the defenders through the streets and into private properties, sacking churches and defensible positions as they progressed. Some 200 Royalists under Aston had barricaded themselves in Millmount Fort overlooking the southeastern gate, while the rest of the town was being sacked. Wary of trying to storm the fort, which Cromwell described as, "a place very strong, and of difficult access, being exceeding high... and strongly palisaded," Parliamentary Colonel Axtell, "offered to spare the lives of the governor and the 200 men with him if they surrendered on the promise of their lives, which they did." Yet, according to Axtell, about one hour after their surrender, the disarmed men were then taken to a windmill and killed.

Another group of about 80 Royalist soldiers sought refuge in St Peter's church at the northern end of Drogheda. On Cromwell's orders, it was set on fire, resulting in approximately 30 of the defenders being burned to death, with the remainder killed as they fled the flames.

Another concentration of 200 Royalist soldiers was stationed in two other towers, where they 'held out' until they surrendered the following day. All the officers and one in every ten ordinary soldiers were clubbed to death.

Cromwell wrote on 16 September 1649:

> "I believe we put to the sword the whole number of the defenders. I do not think 30 of the whole number escaped with their lives; those that did are in safe custody for Barbados (*mine* – as slaves)." It has never been accurately established how many civilians died in the sacking of Drogheda. Cromwell listed the dead as including, "many inhabitants" of Drogheda, in his

report to Parliament. Hugh Peters, an officer on Cromwell's council of war, gave the total loss of life as 3,552, of whom about 2,800 were soldiers, meaning that between 700-800 civilians were killed. Irish Clerical sources in the 1660s claimed that 4,000 civilians had died and denounced the sacking as "unparalleled savagery and treachery beyond any slaughterhouse."[3]

He defended his actions at Drogheda, as revenge for the massacre of Protestant settlers in Ulster in 1641 (a Catholic rebellion in Portadown in which 100-300 Protestants were killed). In a letter to the Speaker of the House of Commons, he justified it as follows:

"I am persuaded that this is a righteous judgment of God on these barbarous wretches, who have imbrued their hands with so much innocent blood; and that it will tend to prevent the effusion of blood for the future, which are satisfactory grounds for such actions which cannot otherwise but work remorse and regret."[4]

Similar actions took place in Wexford town, where 2000 Irish troops and close to 1,500 civilians were killed, and much of the town was destroyed by fire. Following his conquest of Ireland, lands owned by Catholics were taken from them under the 1652 Act of Settlement and given to his troops in lieu of pay. Over 50,000 Catholic men, women, and children were to be deported by his generals, to Bermuda and Barbados as slaves/indentured servants (debate continues, as to which word best describes them—at various times they could have arrived as either). Some of their descendants remain in Barbados today and are known as the "Redlegs."

As I consider that the Puritans worshipped the same God and read the same Bible that I do, it leaves me with a lot of questions as I read of similar actions taken by them in New England against members of the Pequot Tribe at Fort Mystic.

Before I look at the Puritans in America and the incident at Fort Mystic in more detail, let's look at the wider question.

Who were the Puritans?

They were a grouping of various religious bodies in the 16th and 17th centuries that can be traced back to the Anabaptist[5] movement in Europe that reached England during the reign of Henry VIII (1509-1547). He had broken away from the Catholic Church under the pretext of wanting to reform the Church, though in reality, he wanted to divorce his wife and remarry for the purposes of producing a male heir—something the Catholic Church would not sanction. His son Edward VI, who introduced through Archbishop Cranmer the theology of Luther and Calvin into the Church, only reigned for six years. He was followed by the Catholic Mary Tudor who brought the Church back under the authority of the pope, martyring Cranmer and nearly 270 others in the process.

Following Elizabeth I coming to the throne in 1558, many people who had fled from Mary's persecution returned to England. Among them, were those who rose to places of influence in the Church and who felt that Elizabeth did not go far enough in her reform process. According to most sources I researched, there were two main groups that formed the basis of the Puritan movement and acted as a political pressure group within Parliament throughout Elizabeth I's reign: Separatists and non-Separating. I will adhere to these two classifications, aware that some sources say that the Separatists were known as the Pilgrim Fathers and not Puritans—allocating this name solely to the non-Separating Puritans. Others gave further sub-divisions.

The Puritans sought unsuccessfully to have a Congregational/Presbyterian rather than an Episcopal form of government within the Church of England. They also pressed for changes to the 1559 Book of Common Prayer and opposed in general anything suggestive of Rome: the use of vestments (caps and gowns); kneeling at the sacrament; the use of the Cross during baptisms. Their position regarding the Divine Right of Kings[6] was to bring some of them and especially the Separatists, into direct conflict with the Monarchy, who interpreted this as being close to treason, which led to hundreds leaving the Church of England. The majority, however, choose to remain within it (the non-Separating Puritans), seeking to reform it from within.

This conflict came to a head during James I's reign (1603-1625), as he determined to come against what he saw as extremes of Puritanism within the Church of England. There was no love lost between them, as we see in a letter to his son Charles. In it, he is purported to have written: "Take heed of these Puritans, the very pests of the Church and Commonwealth, whom no deserts can oblige, nor oaths, or promises bind; one that breathes nothing but sedition and calumnies... He is a fanatic spirit; with whom you may find greater ingratitude, more lies, and viler perjuries, than amongst the most infamous thieves."[7] Very different, to how the Puritans saw themselves as "the godly," "the faithful" or "God's elect."[8] However one may view them, history most certainly records that they were "a genuine movement that wielded considerable force within seventeenth-century England and New England" which "sprung from a matrix of religious, social and political events in sixteenth-century Europe."[9]

The Puritan reformers had presented a document to James, called the "Millenary Petition" (so-called because 1000 Puritan Clergy signed it). In it, they expressed their position that the Church of England had, as I have already mentioned, not done enough to rid itself of what they considered to be the errors of the Roman Catholic Church. Aided by William Laud (Bishop of London, later to become Archbishop of Canterbury during his son Charles I's reign), James I aggressively stood against these reformist clerics on issues such as their divisive deviation from the Common Book of Prayer. They did, however, get some concessions, e.g., the "sacrament of penance" was changed to the "remission of sins;" "confirmation" became "the laying on of hands" and in 1611 a new authorized version of the Bible was produced.

The ongoing pressure led to a series of migrations. The first of these comprised of "Separatists" from the town of Scrooby, Nottinghamshire. They had moved to the Netherlands in 1608 with 120 of them returning to England in 1620. On September 16th, much later in the year than desirable, some of them set sail on the Mayflower for America. I will pick their story up again in Chapter 8.

Continued pressure on the Puritans, instigated by people like William Laud, lead to a larger number of them (predominantly non-separatists) leaving for Massachusetts, in what became known as the Great Migration (1630-1640) where they could allow the dictates of their consciences to determine their religious lifestyle unhindered.

In 1625 Charles I came to the throne, having married a zealous Catholic, Henrietta-Marie de Bourbon of France the previous year. She closely allied herself with Laud's intolerance of the Puritans and with them as his closest advisors, Charles pursued the development of policies designed to eliminate the Puritans religious distinctiveness in England. Two already existing institutions were to be adapted by him to that end: The Star Chamber and the Court of High Commissions. These were Courts under his control rather than Parliament and could be used by him to convict and imprison people, who while they had not broken any law passed by Parliament, had invoked his displeasure.

The Interregnum

In England, the ongoing Puritan unrest with both the Crown and Laud paved the way for the English Civil War (1642-1651), during which forces loyal to the Parliament defeated the crown and had both Laud and Charles I executed. His son Charles II was defeated in the Battle of Worcester by Cromwell's forces and went into exile. In his absence, a Republican Commonwealth was established, known as the Interregnum (1649-1660). It was marked by parliamentary and military rule under the Lord Protector Oliver Cromwell. That was to give Puritanism a robust influence within Parliament, with its supporters seeking to impose their worldview on the nation: Christmas, Easter, theatre, gambling, etc., were banned!

It is within this context that the Westminster Assembly (1643-1649) was formed to enable the fundamental restructuring of the Church of England. Two of the main outcomes was the production of the Westminster Confession of Faith and the Westminster Shorter Catechism. During this period, life for Roman Catholics throughout England and Ireland became extremely difficult. Cromwell's 'scorched earth' campaign in the later (1649-1653) was to have devastating effects on its Catholic population, with at least one-third of them either exiled or killed.

Two years after Cromwell's death in 1658, Charles II was restored to the throne. Even though he showed initial signs of allowing the continuance of religious liberty (reformed!), which Cromwell had initiated, it did not last as pressure mounted from loyalists within Anglicanism to have religious conformity restored. Dissent from among many Puritan pastors led to their growing persecution and imprisonment. This along with the death of many of the leaders were key factors in bringing about the demise of Puritanism in England and eventually in New England.

—ooo0ooo—

Before moving on to attempt to tackle the issues surrounding the Puritans in the New World, I want to give a brief overview of some of the core beliefs of the Puritans. They primarily embraced Calvinism[10], which shaped to a large degree their worldview; their strength of character; their commitment to what they believed God was asking of them; how they perceived the rest of society and their response to it. That made them into a people of strong faith with a highly regulated social structure, before they ever reached the shores of America.

Some of the beliefs they embraced[11]

1. Their faith's core principle was that in human affairs God was the ultimate authority—as supremely recorded for them in the Bible. That would require both a corporate and an individual submission to its teachings and the need to pursue the outworking of that in a life of moral purity.

2. Both of these had to be evident if you wanted to enter into full Church membership.

3. The development of strong marriages and family units was greatly encouraged, with illicit sexual behavior equally strongly discouraged: adultery was punishable by death, and you could be flogged for the sin of fornication.

4. Regarding purity, they exercised a strong code of discipline among themselves. Surprisingly for me, dancing and the

consumption of alcohol were apparently allowed (minus sensuality and drunkenness!).

5. At a personal level, studying the Scriptures was emphasized which should result in self-examination, obedience to God and vigilance in their battle against sin and Satan.

6. They greatly admired the teachings of the early church fathers. Because they pre-dated the Roman Catholic Church, their teachings could be used in their fight against it. Such writings would also influence other aspects of their belief system, e.g., Chrysostom spoke out strongly against drama and otherworldly things. That was useful ammunition against what they believed as the social decadence of the day in places like London, famous for its plays and unrefined entertainment.

7. Within the local gathering of Puritans for worship:

    a. They believed that it had to be strictly regulated by what they understood the Bible taught (i.e., the 'regulative principle of worship'). That often meant condemning as idolatry many forms of worship held by other Christian traditions.

    b. Like some of the other Reformed churches on the European continent, Puritan reforms were typified by a simplicity in worship and the exclusion of vestments, images, candles, etc.,

    c. And like the early church fathers, they eliminated (for various theological and practical reasons) the use of musical instruments in their worship services. Outside of church, however, they were quite fond of music and encouraged it in certain ways.

8. Traditional holidays (e.g., Christmas and Easter) were not celebrated, as they believed that these also stood in violation of the 'regulative principle.'

9. Sabbath (Sunday) was obligatory for Christians.

10. Another critical distinction was their approach to church-state relations:

    a. They opposed the Anglican idea of the supremacy of the monarch in the church (Erastianism), and, like other Anabaptists, they argued that the only head of the Church in heaven or earth is Christ (not the Pope or the monarch).

    b. They also believed that secular governors were accountable to God (not through the church, but alongside it) to protect and reward virtue, including 'true religion' and to punish wrongdoers. A policy that is best described as non-interference rather than separation of church and state.

11. The separating Congregationalists believed the Divine Right of Kings was heresy, a belief that became more pronounced during the reign of Charles I of England.

12. Like the Presbyterian Church in Scotland, they had a desire to see education and enlightenment for the masses (so that they could read the Bible for themselves).

Along with promoting lay education, Calvinists wanted to have knowledgeable, educated pastors, who could read the Bible in its original Greek, Hebrew, and Aramaic, as well as ancient and modern church traditions and scholarly works, which were most commonly written in Latin. Most of their divines undertook rigorous studies at the Universities of Oxford or Cambridge before seeking ordination. For this reason, in America, they very quickly established Harvard University.

Family Life

The family unit was at the very center of Puritan society. The home was the place where their religious, social and ethical values were honed. They believed that God, having made man and put the rest of creation under his dominion, wanted the same principles to be applied to the structuring of society: husband over his wife; the parents over their children and masters over any family servants. It should not, therefore, be surprising that the whole family moved to America as a unit. In other attempts at colonization, the tendency had been to send the young and single men first, with the family following later, which was one possible reason why they didn't last.

Their decline
There appear to be several reasons for this, including:

a. Their way of life was extremely demanding which eventually led to them becoming victims of their own religious zeal.

b. Not only had the experience of American living taken the edge off the zeal of the first generation, but it was also not readily embraced with the same fervency by the third. Religious doctrinal pressures such as original sin and predestination and continually having to live with moderation proved to be too hard to sustain. It demanded a rigid way of thinking that was not compatible with their growing society.

c. Alongside this, they became victims of their own success. Economic prosperity and the building of a prosperous society were at the heart of the "puritan work ethic," which led to successful businesses becoming more important than religion.

d. Throughout the 1660s the membership had been declining.

e. By 1700 the leadership had lost control, and the religious experiment was dead.

So, that gives us something of a background to this body of people, the Puritans. Let us now move on to the next chapter and look at them within the context of their move to North America; persecuted and looking for their new promised land, a "city on a hill."

References:

1. Harry Smith, *"Heal Not Lightly."* See Chapter 2, "May Layers, Much Pain" for a broad overview.
2. Source: https://en.wikipedia.org/wiki/Siege_of_Drogheda
3. Ibid.
4. Thomas Carlyle, ed. *"Oliver Cromwell's letter and speeches with elucidations."* William H. Coyler, Pg. 28.
5. Anabaptists. A Protestant movement in the 16th century who believed in adult baptism, seeing it as an external witness to a believer's conscious profession of faith. It was originally seen as a derogatory term, as the word 'Anabaptist' meant "re-baptizer"— some of these believers had been baptized as infants and were baptized again.
   http://christianity.about.com/od/Amish-Religion/a/Anabaptist.htm
6. Divine Right of Kings.
   See—http://en.wikipedia.org/wiki/Divine_right_of_kings
7. Anonymous, *"A Puritane Set Forth in His Lovely Colours."* London; n.p., 1642, Pgs. 2-3.
8. Patrick Collinson, *"The Elizabethan Puritan Movement."* Oxford: Clarendon, 1967, Pgs. 22-28.
9. Kelly M Kapic, *"The Devoted Life: an invitation to the Puritan Classic."* InterVarsity Press, 2004, Pg. 17.
10. Calvinism. The doctrines and teachings of John Calvin or his followers, emphasizing the omnipotence of God, predestination, the sovereignty of God, the supreme authority of the Scriptures, and Salvation by grace alone.
    See also: http://dictionary.reference.com/browse/calvinism & http://www.wordnetweb.princeton.edu/perl/webwn-Calvinism
11. Puritan beliefs. See—
    http://wiki.answers.com/Q/What_were_the_Puritans%27_beliefs

Chapter 7

Our New England: The English Foothold in America

I shared in the Introduction that I am not writing this as a historian or sociologist. It has rather been for me, a journey into God's heart as it relates to my people's history in North America. As I mentioned there, this has not always been an easy journey. I sense that there are foundational issues, which we need to allow God to plant deeply in our hearts, if His purposes for His Church in America and subsequently the United States of America as a nation, are to be embraced. Issues of repentance, unity, healing deep denominational and national wounds regarding Native, Black, Hispanic and White Americans.

I am also aware that a process of ownership, repentance, and healing will also be needed in the United Kingdom regarding these issues. We, after all, were establishing the legal, political and theological precedents, out of which we negatively related to the Native people. This is weighty stuff!

As you read, I again remind you to bear in mind that every negative encounter both sides had with each other, had the potential for Satan to work against God's purposes for them. As the perspective I am coming from is one of healing and reconciliation, I won't dwell so much on the positive encounters, even though I am aware that these were there on both sides. E.g., the original contact the Puritans had with Squanto and Massasoit appear to have been mutually beneficial.

In Chapter 2 we looked at what the Christian scriptures teach us regarding foundations. These are paramount for us to understand as we look at what we build our lives, our cultures and our nations upon. That is also crucial to our understanding of reconciliation issues, especially if we desire to move forward on to a more solid one.

—oooOooo—

First contacts

The first contact between European and Indian societies is believed to have been when Christopher Columbus set foot on American soil on October 12, 1492. Though, there are unverifiable accounts written of the Irish Saint Brendan and the Vikings beating him to it, centuries before! A few years later in 1497, John Cabot became the first European to "discover" Newfoundland. From the outset, it begs the question: "How can you discover a country when others are living there before you do?" As fishermen, fur traders and explorers from Europe began to move up and down the eastern seaboard of America with increasing regularity, it was only a matter of time before they encountered the regions' Native American tribes. That sadly lead to the spread of European diseases, death and ultimately to ongoing violent interactions.

One of the first records of violence between Europeans and Native Americans was in the early 1500s when explorers kidnapped members of the Micmac tribe who lived in the region that is now southeastern Canada/northeastern United States. There was, I suppose, something inevitable regarding conflict, as both sides of this European-American encounter had radically different national and tribal identities and worldviews, which affected them economically, politically, militarily and spiritually. As an ever-increasing number of immigrants came to North America, competition for land and trade were also added to the mix. All of these were to have an ever-increasing threatening effect on the Native Tribes.

—oooOooo—

Setting the scene

Ireland, as I have already mentioned, was in a sense England's oldest colony. Its position right on the edge of Europe also meant that it had not been open to the spiritual, social and political influences of the European Enlightenment. When Catholicism was introduced into Ireland, it was intolerant of the divergent spirituality of Celtic Christianity. This inevitably had to be brought into line and under

Papal authority (see Chapter 3 regarding the *Laudabiliter*). Also, when the Reformation broke forth in Europe in the early 1500s it would soon become a very defining time, not only for Ireland but also for England and its future empire expansion. Before that, without the relevant Papal Bull, the English Catholic Crown could only continue with its oppressive actions in Ireland and its trading along the American coast. Any claim to land there could have resulted in their excommunication.

In 1497, the Catholic Tudor King, Henry VII, appears to have successfully tested this by granting a patent (feudal charter) to John Cabot. That authorized him to sail to lands to the north and west "unknown to all Christians"; lands that belonged to any "heathen and infidel peoples discovered during the voyage... getting unto us the rule, title, and jurisdiction of the same."[1] These words showed that Henry VII, along with his legal advisors, had a working knowledge of the Catholic Churches medieval discourses regarding the ever-evolving Doctrine of Discovery.

Everything was set to change when his son Henry VIII came to the throne. His breaking away from papal authority in 1543, followed by an Act of Parliament the following year, made him Supreme Head of a new Anglican Church. No longer under the threat of excommunication, the whole trajectory of England's colonizing discourse was set in the coming years to change radically, even though after his death, issues at home and among the other European States, were to hinder its progress. For instance, following his death in 1553, Mary Tudor (daughter of his first wife) a devout Catholic, came to the throne and sought to reverse her father's reforms. Her marriage to Philip II, the prince of Spain, assisted that, by putting on hold any thought of England's Empire expansion into the New World.

When Mary died in November 1558, with no heir to follow her, it fell upon her Protestant half-sister Elizabeth (daughter of Henry VIII's second wife), to move things forward again when she assumed the throne. Yet even then, the exploits of Sirs Humphry Gilbert and Walter Raleigh would be under financial constraints, making it difficult for the successful development of the colonies to get firmly established.

One major development was a change in their thinking regarding the Discovery discourse. Robert A. Williams in *"The American Indian in Western Legal Thought."* puts it like this:

> "The genealogy of the legal discourse of the Protestant crusade against the infidels of America traces a process by which the medieval discourses of the Catholic Church were domesticated and combined with other discursive practices appropriated from a number of English and non-English sources. The strange fruit of the seeds planted by this careful Protestant husbandry was a discourse of conquest confirming the election of England as the Christian nation chosen by Providence to pursue a divinely mandated destiny in the New World."[2]

Before getting into that, let's take a wee trip to Scotland!

Following Catholic Mary Queen of Scots' abdication of the Scottish throne in 1557 her son automatically became James VI of Scotland, even though he was only 13 months of age. In 1583, after a season of interim governance by Regents he eventually gained full governmental control. When Queen Elizabeth I of England died in 1603 without an heir, he moved to London and ascended the British throne as James I of England, where, in what became known as the "Union of the Crowns," a single Parliament for Scotland and England was established.

A change of direction was also in the air regarding the ongoing development of England's colonizing process when counter to the liking of Parliament, James I (1566-1625) discontinued his predecessor's Protestant campaign against Catholic Spain. Not only did he enter a peace treaty with Spain, but there was also a definite shift in England's approach to colonizing the New World into one which became primarily based on a trading/profit basis to meet the needs of the Corporations shareholders. In America, the Native Tribes were increasingly looked upon as a barrier to fulfilling this.

Meanwhile back home, although he was initially for freedom of worship for Catholics, that was to change radically. On the evening of November 4, 1605, the Catholic, Guy Fawkes was caught preparing to blow up the second sitting of James's first English Parliament, to kill him, his family, and the members of government; in what became known as the Gunpowder Plot. The following year James was to introduce an extreme measure for controlling all non-conformists English Catholics in what was called the Popish Recusant Act, which required all Catholics to renounce the Pope's authority over that of the King and take an Oath of Allegiance to the Crown.

Puritanism and Plantation

It was also during this period in history, as mentioned in the last chapter, that the Puritans had been gaining power politically and were making demands far beyond anything James was prepared to go, which led to the Separatist Puritans going to the Netherlands and then eventually, as the Pilgrim Fathers, to New England in 1620.

James also initiated what is known as the Plantation of Ulster, predominantly by Scottish Presbyterians, due to their geographical proximity to the north of Ireland, as part of an overall strategy of subjugating the Catholic Irish. They were later to be known as the Ulster-Scots or Scots-Irish, though this is a bit of a misnomer as they also included people from the north England border area. I will pick up this story in more detail in Chapters 10-12.

In 1625 Charles I became King, and he continued with his predecessor's suppression of both the Puritans and other nonconformists in England and Scotland. In 1629, he attempted to neutralize his Puritan opponents in Parliament by dissolving it. Opposition and therefore persecution continued, provoking the mass exodus of over 20,000 Puritans to New England. Some of them returned to England to fight alongside their fellow Puritans and Parliamentarians during the Civil War, which culminated in Charles I's arrest, trial, and execution in 1649.

What followed was a period of Parliamentary rule (the Interregnum) under Cromwell. That meant that the austere Puritan views of the majority within Parliament were imposed, with Irish and English Catholics feeling the full brunt of it. (See Chapter 6)

—oooOooo—

Let's now return to Elizabeth I. Over in Chapter 5 I mentioned the importance of Richard Hakluyt's *"Discourse on Western Planting."* Significantly, it was also during her reign that the legal basis for English Empire expansion would be clarified by two of England's leading theorists of the time—Sir Edward Coke and Alberico Gentili (see Chapter 4). As I mentioned then, they were the "conceptual bridge builders... between the medieval and the modern forms of Western legal thought throughout the Renaissance Discovery era." [3] Let's take a closer look - to a non-legal mind like mine, the next few pages can appear to be rather complex, but here goes at having a try at summarizing it!

Sir Edward Coke

British Lord Chief Justice Coke (1552-1634), while deliberating on a case of land rights between an English man and a Scots man called Robert Calvin (*Calvin's Case*-1608), also gave his reflections on the conquering of an infidel's kingdom by a Christian King.

Calvin was born a few years after the Union of the Crowns and had inherited some land in England, but his rights to it were challenged under feudal law, which stipulated that a person could not own land in two different kingdoms. The Court, however, ruled that following the Union, Calvin was now no longer considered an alien but rather an English subject entitled to the full benefits of the English legal system and therefore as a result, to his land inheritance. The principles, in this case, were eventually to be adopted by courts in the United States, and used to shape a rule of citizenship by birthright—*jus soli* (i.e., the "law of the soil" or having citizenship because you were born within the territory of a sovereign state).[4]

Coke, in his systematic thinking, saw in Calvin's Case something else, that could also have a significant future application. What, therefore, would be the rights and status of "an alien" in English law? Coke put them into two categories: they could either be a friend that is in league with the state or an enemy that is in open war with it. Friends, he considered, could both acquire goods and a house, as necessary requirements to live in the realm. An enemy, on the other hand, could either be *pro tempore* (temporary) or *perpetus* (perpetual). Regarding aliens, which were seen as perpetual enemies, he wrote:

> "But a perpetual enemy (though there be no wars by fire and sword between them) cannot maintain any action or get anything within this realm. All infidels are in law *perpelui inimici*, perpetual enemies (for the law presumes not that they will be converted, that being *remota potentia*, a remote possibility), for between them, as with devils, whose subjects they be, and the Christian, there is perpetual hostility, and can be no peace."[5]

Coke went on to discuss the consequences of a Christian kings' conquest of an infidel kingdom. Regarding this, Williams writes:

> "[He asserted that] the king had absolute prerogative powers in infidel territories that were acquired by conquest." In so doing, he was adopting "without comment, the medieval Catholic Church's Crusading-era discourse on infidel status and rights." He recognized, "[that] this discourse diverged from the ancient Roman law of war, which assumed without distinction that a conquered nation could [only] retain its prior laws until they were changed by the conqueror in the exercise of the prerogatives of conquest. Coke's medievally derived discourse in Calvin's Case denied this privilege to infidel nations conquered by a Christian king: 'the laws of the infidel are abrogated, for that they be… against Christianity… [and] the law of God and of nature, contained in the Decalogue.'"[6] (i.e., *ius naturale*—natural law as interpreted by Europe).

He also held that the king must establish laws among the infidel "and judge their causes according to natural equity."[7] He was purely restating for the benefit of his contemporaries the feudal law of conquest, which denied any *dominium* and legitimacy to the king's infidel enemies. Things were not looking good for the Native American Tribes!

While a later English court would label Coke's position regarding the status of the infidel as the "madness of the crusades," it would at the time be endorsed by the Oxford law professor Gentili (see below). In his discourse related to war—the Law of Nations—Gentili had stipulated that a conquering monarch on assuming rulership over people, "who are alien to humanity and to all religion, these he may most justly compel to change conduct which is contrary to nature."[8]

Williams continues,

> "To Coke and his generation of jurists, medieval Crusading-era legal discourse represented not the 'madness' but the underlying foundation of the recent attempts at conquest of America. All Coke sought to do was restate for his contemporaries the law of feudal conquest, with its Crusading-era distinction denying *dominium* and legitimacy to the king's perpetual infidel enemies... Coke, after all, was there when the English equivalent of the *Requirimiento* was drawn up, the royal charter for the Virginia Company by which the English resumed their war for America."[9]

Indeed, Lord Coke would have a part to play in drawing up the Royal Charter, enabling Sir Walter Raleigh to cross the Atlantic to North America. Part of Raleigh's mandate was to propagate the "Christian religion to such people as yet living in darkness and miserable ignorance of the true knowledge and worship of God and may in time bring the infidels and savages to living civility."

Thanks to Lord Coke, explains Robert Williams, Innocent IV's thirteen-century commentaries on natural law had become the invisible hand that wrote the official royal charter for the first English colony in the New World.

Alberico Gentili

His family fled from Italy to England because of religious persecution, where he became an Oxford civil law professor. His primary focus regarding civil law addressed most significantly the topic of law and war. He was, as a hugely respected Protestant, able to introduce into English legal thinking of the day the work of a Catholic dissenter George Peckham, who in 1583 wrote, *"A True Reporte,"* which was the blending of a discourse on the natural Law of Nations (*ius gentium*) into the existing English colonial theory.

During 1598-99 Gentili wrote, *"De iure belli libri tres."* ("On the Law of War in Three Parts.") In it, while seeking to distance himself from an earlier Renaissance discourse on the Law of Nations produce by the Spanish Catholic Franciscus de Vitoria, he nevertheless came up with similar conclusions concerning the rights of non-Christian people groups—i.e., the European nations could lawfully make war against them, if they violated the European understanding/interpretation of natural law.[10] Like Vitoria, Gentili would also draw from the writings of St. Augustine regarding 'just war' theory.

He clearly supported Coke's position regarding the Law of Nations and both of them accepted and adopted the Catholic Church's Crusading-era discourse on infidel status and rights. What they succeeded to do was to make the Doctrine of Discovery into something that was (accepted as) both English and Protestant!

—oooOooo—

And so, a foothold was established on American soil for the Crown! The English Protestant invasion had begun, and France was making similar moves. With their different political and spiritual allegiances, issues such as the Doctrine of Discovery and the Protestant Reformation would cause them to vigorously oppose each other. Yet, at the same time, they both believed that wars of conquest and dispossession against heathen peoples were justified in the name of

God and Empire. And, neither of them, had any problem when it suited them, in developing alliances with Native Tribes as they fought against each other or other Native Tribes. The war in Europe had now spilled over into North America—something that would be played out for many years to come with negative consequences for the surrounding Native American Tribes!

Willem Theo Oosterveld in Volume 1 of "*The Law of Nations in Early American Foreign Policy*," cites three main theories that were current regarding colonization: conquest, discovery/settlement, and cession. As he discusses these, he also clearly understood that the Doctrine of Discovery was embraced by the Protestant British Crown and legal system.

Regarding discovery and settlement, he writes that it was,

> "... a theory which had much surrender in Catholic countries. This mode of acquisition entailed that land discovered could be considered *res nullius*, [meaning nobody's property and therefore free to be acquired by means of *occupatio* – *mine*][11]... One reason for resorting to claims of discovery is that it was a means to seek equivalence between Spanish and English claims. Under Elizabeth and after, this was done by framing Royal charters in the same way as the Papal bulls justified Spanish claims. One of the attractions of this theory was that it 'justified and explained [according to many] the development of common law institutions abroad better than Coke's theory of conquered lands. The reason being that settlers capable of establishing governments and systems of law had an ambiguous right to occupy the underdeveloped land.' Since the charters were modeled on Papal Bulls, the latter's Roman law language also helped to shape ideas about the law of nations in America."

He finishes that paragraph with these words:

"The obvious problem with the discovery theory was
of course that North America was already inhabited
when the Europeans arrived."[12]

That's a big discussion for another day!!

A key factor
From the perspective of healing our histories, which includes any
reconciliation and repentance issues that arise in the process, what I
am about to write is important!

In Intercessory, Spiritual Warfare and Reconciliation Networks
around the world, which I have had some connections with over many
years, there has been the understanding of the need to examine the
root entry points of Satan's footholds into nations, cities, churches,
lives. I have sought to briefly give a theological understanding of that
position in Chapter 2 - "Legal Footholds." That has not been the role
of historians but nevertheless, subjects like The Doctrine of
Discovery, while being extremely well researched by them, have not
been considered (as far as I know) in the light of this spiritual warfare
framework! The result, as I have observed here in Northern Ireland, is
that we tend to look for political and sociological answers to
something that is primarily a spiritual problem (though both the
politician and sociologist may have a significant part to play in the
healing process). That is surely something the Church needs to
embrace if it is going to critique our histories and the negative roles
they and our national/ethnic groups have played in them. And, where
appropriate, they need to take the lead in owning and repenting of our
wrongs and show the way forward, regarding any repentance/restora-
tive justice issues.

So, while I recognize that the Catholic Church was responsible for the
development of the Doctrine, I do not believe from what I have read
and consequentially written, that it was the Catholic Church that
brought it into what became known as New England. Therefore, it was
not the Catholic Church that laid the dynamics within the Doctrine of
Discovery into the spiritual and political foundations of what was to
become the United States of America. Yes, I recognize that the

93

Catholic King Henry VII granted an original Charter to John Cabot, but it would primarily be a strongly anti-Catholic English Protestant monarchy and Protestant Church that took ownership of it and consolidated it there. We—my tribe—need to take ownership of that and reach out to both Anglo-Americans and Native Americans in humility and repentance.

I know that several of the main Protestant Denominations in the U.S. have groups established to look into the DOD and that some of them have formally approached the Papacy, asking for both an acknowledgment and repentance of it. While I believe this is something that needs to be recognized - regarding the infiltration by the Catholic Spanish Empire into the southern parts of what is now the U.S. - I do not believe that the Protestantization of the Doctrine and its introduction into the original 13 colonies, and hence into the foundations of the United States, is something to be laid at the door of the Vatican. This distinction is something that the Episcopal Church in the United States has recognized and sought to address back in 2009 when a resolution entitled "Repudiate the Doctrine of Discovery" was unanimously passed by the Episcopal House of Bishops. (See Appendix III for its wording) They have certainly recognized that it was a Protestant Doctrine and that it needs to be addressed by Queen Elizabeth II, Supreme Governor of the Church of England.

—ooo0ooo—

Elizabeth I's first Charter

With that overview in mind, let us now backtrack to the 1580s and to Elizabeth I who inherited a political system that was in deep poverty. That required a new class of entrepreneurs to emerge with the vision and energy to enter the fray. They, along with a growing body of men—often the younger sons of merchants—were eager to make their mark on the developing trading systems of Europe into America, through the development of Companies. Alongside them, there was also a group of radical Protestant clergy, with their eyes set on America and an eagerness to counter any activities of the Spanish Catholic Church there.

Closer to home, Elizabeth was aware that she might need to use a military presence in Ireland to thwart any attempts made by Spain to use Catholic Ireland as a back door to attack England. As it turns out, Ireland became a significant Elizabethan training ground for not only developing the means of militarily suppressing its people but also in the development of a Protestant discourse of conquest, both of which would soon be exported to America. Conveniently, the Doctrine of Discovery was at hand.

So, in March 1584 Elizabeth I granted to Sir Walter Raleigh a Royal Charter, with the explicit aim of establishing a colony in North America. Along with some of his friends, he sponsored an exploratory voyage led by Arthur Barlowe and Philip Amadas. A second expedition followed, conducted by Sir Richard Grenville, who, along with 100 householders, landed at Roanoke in June 1585. It was later to be named **Virginia in honor of the "Virgin Queen"** Elizabeth! That was 22 years before the founding of Jamestown and 37 years before the Puritans set sail for Massachusetts.

All appeared to go well until the disappearance of a silver cup led to an expeditionary force going to the nearby Indian village of Roanoke to try and retrieve it. Even though the natives denied taking it, the English burned their village to the ground and destroyed their corn supply. That, along with other incidents, led to a rapid deterioration of relationships. One of their members, Thomas Harriot, recorded: **"Some of our company towards the end of the year showed themselves too fierce in slaying some of the people in some towns upon causes that on our part might easily have been borne withal."**[13] Raleigh arrived later, having taken a detour to destroy the Spanish Catholic colony of St. Augustine in the Caribbean.

Due to the ill-prepared nature of the whole venture, it became unsustainable, leading inevitably to many of them returning to England! Drake was to leave fifteen of his men there, who were never to be heard of again! Two subsequent trips equally ended in disaster, with the later also finding no members of the former colony alive!

In 1602, a survivor of the Roanoke adventure, Bartholomew Gosnold, set sail for the northern fishing banks. There the coastal natives were found to be amiable and willing to trade, yet once again peace was short lived when two of the crew were inexplicably attacked. As Vaughan comments "The cause of the trouble is now obscure and perhaps was obscure even to the participants. Possibly a gesture was misinterpreted, or a thoughtless act magnified out of its true proportions..."[14] Whether or not that paved the way for an incident the following year is unknown, but the local Nauset Tribe having welcomed and traded with two English ships under the command of Martin Pring, were attacked by two large mastiff dogs. Why that happened is also uncertain, but clearly, a cycle of suspicion and fear was being set in motion. "Seeds had been sown for conflict as well as for commerce."[15]

Three years later a similar scenario was repeated in the same area, as Captain George Weymouth also sought to establish trading relationships with the local tribe. This time, even though they received a welcome from the native people, the English response was one of suspicion, and on fearing an ambush, they preemptively took "some of them, before they should suspect we had discovered their plot."[16] Two of them, Chief Tahanedo and Skidowares, were subsequently taken to England, returning to America in 1606 and 1607 respectively. Weymouth's crew justified it, as being for the "publique good, and a true zeale of promulgating God's holy Church."[17] Thankfully, they did not mistreat the Indians, and in the process, each learned something of each other's language! Nevertheless, it once again added to the Indians perceptions of the English, with each negative interaction giving Satan another foothold through which he could thwart the purposes of God among them.

—oooOooo—

James I's Royal Charters

In 1606, James I was to grant two identical Royal Charters: one to The Virginia Company of London (the London Company) and the other to The Virginia Company of Plymouth (the Plymouth Company, later to become the Massachusetts Bay Colony in 1628. Each of these privately funded ventures was hoping to not only claim land for

96

England but also to make a profit through trading between the colonies and London.

The Plymouth Company was designated land north of the 38th parallel while the London Company was allotted land south of the 41st parallel which created something of an overlap. They overcame that by agreeing not to establish colonies within that area. The Powhatan Indian Confederacy[18] were living on land apportioned to both Companies.

When the Royal Charters for Virginia were issued, the Companies were not only given "license to make habitation, plantation and to deduce a colony of sundry of our people into that part of America... not now actually possessed by any Christian Prince or people."[19] They also communicated something of the Crown's understanding regarding the religious goals of the Virginia Company:

> "We, greatly commending, and graciously accepting of, their Desires for the Furtherance of so noble a Work, which may, by the Providence of Almighty God, hereafter tend to the Glory of his Divine Majesty, in propagating of Christian Religion to such People, as yet live in Darkness and miserable Ignorance of the true Knowledge and Worship of God, and may in time bring the Infidels and Savages, living in those Parts, to human Civility, and to a settled and quiet Government; Do, by these Letters Patents, graciously accept of, and agree to, their humble and well-intended Desires."[20]

There is two parallel, yet at times intertwined histories developing at this point, so I will over the next two chapters look at their developments separately. Starting with the growth of the London Company before moving on to look at the Plymouth Company.

References:

1. Reprinted in *"Documents of American History."* 5-6 (H. S. Commager 8th ed, 1968.)

2. Robert A. Williams Jnr, *"The American Indian in Western Legal Thought – The Discourses of Conquest."* (Oxford University Press, 1990), Pg. 122.
3. Williams, Pg. 194.
4. Source: http://en.wikipedia.org/wiki/Calvin's_Case
5. Williams, Pg. 200. Source: note 38, Pg. 223.
6. Ibid. Pg. 200. Source note 40. Pg. 223.
7. Ibid. Pg. 200. Source note 39. Pg. 223.
8. Ibid. Pg. 200. Source note 42. Pg. 223. On Gentili's life and career, see C. Phillipson, "Introduction," in A. Gentili, De jure belli libri tres 9a-15a (J. Rolfe trans. 1964). Also G. van der Molen, *"Alberico Gentili and the Development of International Law."* 1-63 (1968). Pg. 341.
9. Ibid. Pg. 200.
10. Ibid. Pg. 195. Source as from Note 8 above.
11. Source: https://en.wikipedia.org/wiki/Res_nullius. Res nullius (lit: nobody's property) is a Latin term derived from Roman law whereby **res** (an object in the legal sense, anything that can be owned, even a slave, but not a subject in law such as a citizen) is not yet the object of rights of any specific subject. Such items are considered ownerless property and are free to be acquired by means of occupatio.
12. Willem Theo Oosterveld, *"The Law of Nations in Early American Foreign Policy."* Vol. 1. Pg. 53.
13. Debra Meyers, Mélanie Perreault, *"Colonial Chesapeake: New Perspectives."* by (Lexington Books, 2006), Pg. 26.
14. Alden T. Vaughan, *"New England Frontier: Puritans and Indians. 1620-1675."* Revised ed. (New York: Norton, 1979), Pg. 7.
15. Ibid. Pg. 7. Reference is taken from *"Documents Relating to Gosnold's Voyage, A.D. 1602."* in Mass. Hist. Soc. Coll., 3 ser. VIII (1843), Pgs. 80-81.
16. Ibid, Pg. 9.
17. Ibid, Pg. 9.
18. The Powhatan Confederacy was a significant Tribal grouping in the region, also known as the Algonquians, as they spoke an eastern Algonquian language known as Powhatan. It is thought that they had been driven north to Virginia by the Spanish, where under their chief Wahunsonacock (also known as Powhatan, just

to confuse things!) they were, through a mixture of coercion and subjugation, to be molded together with five other Virginia tribes to form the Powhatan empire. It was comprised of some 30 different people groups (population estimates: 14,000-21,000) spread over 200 settlements. By the time the earliest of English colonies were being established under the Plymouth and London Company's, Wahunsonacock's younger brother Opechancanough was their much-feared charismatic, warrior leader. He would soon prove to be a "thorn in the flesh" to both!

19. Williams, Pg. 201. (Source: "The First Charter of Virginia." in *"Documents of American History."* At Pgs. 8-10, (H. S. Commager 8th ed, 1968.)
20. Ibid. Pg. 201. Same Source as above, Pg. 8.

Chapter 8

Our New England: The London Company

The Jamestown venture

In 1607, despite a precarious beginning and physical hardship, the London Company established itself in Jamestown under the first Presidency of Edward Wingfield, who following a period of rebellion was deposed and returned home. Capt. John Smith, who was also not liked by others, took on the leadership role in September 1608. He too had to leave for England just over a year later because of a mysterious leg injury he received that involved an explosion! Incidentally, he is the person who named the region New England, and he was also the first to explore and map the Chesapeake Bay area!

In December of that year, while Smith was searching for food, he was captured by Powhatan's (see Chapter 7, Note 18) brother Opechancanough. It is believed that he gained his freedom through the actions of Powhatan's daughter, Pocahontas and that she was also instrumental in providing much-needed food for the colony, though some historical accounts differ regarding her role!

During the winter of 1609-10, it is thought that only 60 colonists survived (some sources say as many as one quarter) what became known as the "Starving Time." That was due, in part, to the poor leadership of Smith's successor George Percy who was sick, and because of their overall ill-preparedness to face the harshness of winter there. The day was saved by the arrival of the new Governor, Sir Thomas Gates with fresh supplies.

Conflict stirs in North America

One of Smith's close associates, Thomas Hunt (who had command of the second ship in the expedition) was to develop an aggressive stance towards the native Patuxet and Nauset tribes (members of another local Confederacy—the Wampanoag[1]). It is known that he captured more than twenty of them while under the guise of trading with them and sold them into slavery in Spain. That included the Patuxet Indian called Squanto,[2] who somehow was saved by local Spanish Friars and was eventually able to make his way to London where he learned English.

One of Hunt's companions left us a record of the native response to his dealing with them: "[they] contracted such an hatred against our whole nation as they immediately studied how to be revenged."[3] Sir Ferdinando Gorges called Hunt, "a worthless fellow of our nation" and Vaughan summed it up, when he wrote: "by the time the first Puritans arrived in New England some tribes had particular reasons to question the friendliness and integrity of Europeans. It is not hard to imagine the impact of Hunt's kidnapping excursion on the wronged [Wampanoag] tribe in particular and on the coastal tribes in general."[4]

Interestingly, John Smith returned to the colony at Plymouth in 1619 with Squanto on board. He had somehow been connected to Smith's expedition which enabled him to come home, where he was to settle among the Pilgrims and assisted them the following year to survive the approaching winter. One can only have a guess at the devastation he must have personally experienced when he found that in his absence an epidemic (formerly thought to be smallpox, though recent analysis concludes that it was the lesser known leptospirosis) had wiped out approximately 90% of the Native population along the Massachusetts coast. That also included the Patuxet community of around 2000 Wampanoag Indians, who lived on what is now Plymouth Bay. They were allied by kinship and politically to other Wampanoag communities that lay between the eastern shore of Narragansett Bay and Cape Cod as well as the Islands of Nantucket and Martha's Vineyard. The colonists, on the other hand, saw this as a providential sign—God had cleared the way for them!

—ooo0ooo—

Powhatan and the English were trying to develop a way of accommodating each other. Powhatan saw them and their new and powerful weapons as potential allies in their struggle against other local tribes, with the English equally seeing Powhatan as a useful ally as they sought to extend their Empire.

Nevertheless, their juxtaposed understandings of each other's cultures became quite apparent in an attempt at formalizing their relationship by making a treaty. Christopher Newport, who had captained one of the earlier ships, had returned with instructions from London to crown Powhatan; build him an English house and provide him with European furniture and clothing. It would appear that they wanted to bestow on Powhatan an official position as one of their "under" lords; part of a plan to encourage an increase in English migration. Most certainly, not what Powhatan would have had in mind!

Wesley Craven in his book, *"The Southern Colonies in the Seventeenth Century, 1607-1689."* writes,

> "By accepting the crown Powhatan might be understood to have conceded the English title, a point of considerable legal importance to the Europeans, while in the offer of it the English gave due recognition, or so presumably it was felt, to the Indians' right in the land."[5] That was nothing other than England seeking to exercise its understanding of the Doctrine of Discovery/Crusading-era-derived legal discourse which denied the infidel any *dominium.*

> As it turned out, Powhatan was not to be taken in by any of it. Smith went upriver to the chief's village with an invitation to come to Jamestown for a coronation ceremony to be performed by Newport, the king's agent. Powhatan's reported response was, "If your king has sent me presents, I also am a king, and this is my land. Eight days I will stay to receive him [Newport], your father is to come to me, not I to him, nor yet to your fort, neither will I bite at such a bait."[6]

Yet back home in England, the Company reported that the "emperor" of Virginia had accepted "voluntarily a crown and a sceptre, with full acknowledgment of duty and submission" and that he "hath licensed us to negotiate among them, and to possess their country with them."[7]

On the ground in Virginia however, the colonists continued to be dependent on the Indians to make up their shortfall of food. That led Smith to acknowledge that the Virginian Indians were living in settled villages, surrounded by agricultural land. He also must have respected Powhatan's skills as a leader to be able to write regarding the tribe: "such government as that their magistrates for good commanding, and their people for due obedience and obeying, excel many places that would be accounted very civil."[8] Such a report, needless to say, didn't go down to well back home, where the Virginia Company's (London Company) shareholders were looking to benefit from the venture. For this to happen a radical restructuring was required: a second charter was drawn up; more funds were released; the Company grew to incorporate 50 London Companies and 650 wealthy individuals. A new plan was also devised to see 1,500 men and women immigrated to Virginia in the coming year.

When Sir Thomas Gates took up his appointment in 1610 as the colony's new governor, he had left England with clear instructions for dealing with the savages if they did not fall in line with their advertised role of being dependents of the Crown. He was also authorized to capture the spiritual leaders of the Indians, as they stood in the way of Christianizing the Indians, which was seen as one of the ultimate goals of the developing colony! The position of the Company on this was quite clear—"in case of necessity or convenience, we pronounce it not cruelty nor breach of charity to deal more sharply with them and to proceed even to death with these murderers of souls and sacrificers of God's image to the Devil..."[9]

Such an analysis for converting the Indian to Christianity and English civility was no different than that used by Pope Innocent or the Spanish Dominican Franciscus de Vitoria when they determined that idolatrous religious practice was a breach of medieval Christian natural law and therefore if necessary, punishable by war.

Some of the "notables" of the day were called upon to add their weight to the campaign. For instance, Robert Johnson, the director of the East India Company (a man of considerable means and connections, with invested interested in the Jamestown venture), made a speech entitled "*Nova Britannia*," which was subsequently published and became a significant factor in attracting settlers. In his speech, he said that England's "just conquest by the sword" could be defended as an honorable effort "to subdue the tyranny of the roaring lion, that devours those poor souls in their ignorance and leads them to hell for want of light." Any Indians who "obstinately refused to unite themselves unto us" are to be declared "recusant" and "shall be dealt with as enemies of the commonwealth of their country."[10] Note the wording, which implies that "their" country is now really "our" country. Undoubtedly, his influential father-in-law, Sir Thomas Smythe (treasurer and head of the Virginia Company) fully supported him, as his policy regarding the Native tribes was one of "rooting them out."

Of interest is Robert Gray, a popular Puritan preacher at the time. He preached a sermon called *"A Good Speed to Virginia,"* in which he sought to use biblical exegesis to parallel the English war against the heathen in America with Joshua's entrance into the biblical Promised Land. Joshua's children, the elect English, were to "destroy those idolaters and possess their lands." He also drew support from St. Augustine, arguing "That a Christian king may lawfully make war upon a barbarous and savage people, and such as live under no lawful or warrantable government, and may make a conquest of them, so that the way be undertaken to this end, to reclaim and reduce those savages from their barbarous kinds of life and from their brutish manners to humanity, piety, and honesty."[11]

He was also able to justify, with the use of the Bible, very practical reasons why they should have a right to be in America. If God has given the earth to the children of men, then man can declare, "The earth is mine, God has given it to me and my posterity." However, if "the greatest part of it [is] possessed by wild beasts and unreasonable creatures, or by brutish savages, which by reason of their godless ignorance and blasphemous idolatry are worse than those beasts." then man committed a sin whenever he permitted the earth to remain in "the hands of beasts and brutish savages, which have no interest in it, because they participate rather of the nature of beasts than men."[12]

That is not so dissimilar to the work of Gentili regarding war being just when waged against "brutish" men who had: practiced "abominable lewdness" and committed crimes contrary to human nature. "For a truth those seem to be dangerous to all men who wearing the human form, live the life of the most brutal beasts."[13]

In the closing argument in his sermon Gray appears to be appealing directly to *ius gentium* (the Law of Nations) and *Terra Nullius* when he says:

> "Some affirm, and it is likely to be true, that these savages have no particular propriety in any part or parcel of that country, but only a general residency there, as wild beasts in the forest; for they range and wander up and down the country without any law or government, being only led by their own lusts and sensuality. There is not *meum* and *tuum* [mine and thine] amongst them. So that if the whole land should be taken from them, there is not a man that can complain of any particular wrong done unto him."[14]

As we have already seen, this ran contrary to the picture that John Smith had painted regarding life in the Virginian Indian villages. It was nevertheless making the possibility of conflict more certain as the Indians were clearly not acknowledging any superiority regarding English civilization or its religion and the Virginia Company's actions and words left no room for Indian intransigence.

Indeed, the Virginia Company's discourse of conquest meant that both cultures were on a collision course to war. As Williams so succinctly puts it: "[Their] discourse drew its energizing and legitimating power from the West's ancient mandate to exterminate the radical difference presented to its will to empire by normatively divergent non-Christian peoples and their opposed vision of truth."[15]

Consolidation
And so, the Virginia Company's mandate to establish a colony was consolidating. The Indians became on-lookers as the number of well-provisioned and well-armed people continued to arrive from England:

- In May 1609, Governor Gates' fleet of ships with 800 men, women, and children on board set sail from London

- More ships, carrying 150 passengers, arrived in April 1610

- Another 300 people came in March 1611, including Sir Thomas Dale who had been appointed as Knight Marshal of the colony. He concluded that if 2000 men were released from jail in England and sent over to him, he could without much difficulty either clear Virginia of Powhatan's people or else bring them quickly under subjection

- In 1616 and 1618 new incentives of increased acreage per grant was developed, to encourage the flow of settlers from England

- Between the spring of 1619 and the summer of 1620, a further 1,261 people migrated to Virginia, with more than two-thirds having their passage paid for by the company, now under the assertive leadership of Sir Edwin Sandys

- Regardless of such growth, it was recorded that many people also returned home disappointed, having spent only a few years there

- By December 1621, the colony's population was thought to stand at around 1,640.[16]

Each ship arriving with new colonists had two conflicting outcomes: they became part of a growing trade between the colonists, the Indians and those seeking benefits from the trade back in England; it was also producing an inevitable tension for the Indians, as an increasing number of armed usurpers contended for their tribal lands.

Confrontation

Following Powhatan's death in 1618, ten years of relative peace were abruptly ended when his militant brother, Opechancanough, became the head of the Powhatan Confederacy. He was to maintain what had been his confrontational posture, complaining to the English authorities over anything the colonists did against them.

In July the following year, a situation arose which demanded the full attention of the newly arrived Governor of the colony, George Yeardley. Opechancanough made a complaint to the colony's General Assembly that Captain Martin had acted inappropriately while trading for much-needed corn. He had sent out a small boat (shallop) to trade for corn when they met a canoe coming out of a creek where theirs could not go. When the Indians had refused to sell them any of their corn, "those of the shallop entered the canoe with their arms and took it by force, measuring out the corn with a basket... and... giving them satisfaction in copper beads and other trucking stuff."[17]

Along with the other members of the colony's legislature, Yeardley was to take Opechancanough's demands for justice very seriously. He was conscious that "such outrages as this might breed danger and loss of life to others of the colony which should have leave to trade in the bay hereafter, and for prevention of the like violences against the Indians." They passed several laws to enable the regulation of trade, e.g. who could visit Indian towns and when, etc., Guidelines were also drawn up for those seeking to trade by boat, so that no licensed trader would "force or wrong the Indians."[18] "The sale of guns, shot, powder, and any other arms to an Indian savage was [also] declared a treasonous, capital offense 'without all redemption.'"[19]

—ooo0ooo—

In the period between 1620 and 1621, another issue was brewing that was to have far-reaching consequences. Opechancanough continued to maintain his unfriendly stance, despite Yeardley's ongoing attempts at coaxing him. In a desperate effort to placate the emperor, he appears to have agreed that all future grants for land beyond the existing English settlement and within the emperor's Confederacy, had to meet Opechancanough's approval.

While this could have been seen as a prudent action to ensure future claims by the English within Indians lands, it was certainly not interpreted as such back in England, as the following case shows!

107

Barkham's Case

A Mr. Barkham had appeared before the Virginia Company to seek for the final approval of a grant for a piece of land north of the Jamestown settlement, "upon condition that he [Barkham] compounded for the same with Opachankana (i.e., Opechancanough) and procured a confirmation thereof from the company."[20] Even though Opechancanough had granted Barkham the piece of land, the whole dynamic of needing consent from an Indian Chief created quite a stir!

In what was to become known as *Barkham's Case*, the Virginia Company exercised its judicial powers invested in it by the Crown, as it deliberated over the dilemma. It was the first legal case under English colonial law to address the issue of Indian rights and status in America.

The Company was disturbed at Yeardley making the grant to Barkham conditional on the permission of a savage. It raised several issues, but in particular it conflicted with a ruling which Lord Coke had established in *Calvin's Case*: that the king had exclusive powers given to him in infidel lands, that simply by right of conquest the infidel's laws were immediately repealed, as they were in violation of the laws of God and nature. In keeping with that, the Virginia Company should have been exercising in America the authority invested in them through the King's charter, and the ruling determined by *Calvin's Case*, not Opechancanough.

Much to its ongoing vexation, the Company had continually failed to bring the Indians in Virginia under its control, and it was now clear that because of the precedent established in *Barkham's Case* that the Company needed to make some revision in its relationship with Opechancanough. There could be no room for an effective, hostile and unsubdued military foe to assert himself against the Virginia Company's sovereign right to be there.

While it may have been initially acceptable to acknowledge the "savages" occupancy of the land until the colony had sufficiently built up its military presence, nevertheless in English colonizing legal

108

theory, Opechancanough could no longer be allowed to continue to do so. Sovereignty, by its very definition, was, after all, a power that could only be recognized in people who were civilized and had laws that conformed with those of God and nature.

The Virginia Company's verdict?

1. The Court considered that Yeardley had acted beyond the remit of his authority over the granting of lands, having to, first, consult Opechancanough regarding them. They also ruled that Yeardley's decision was not considered as "absolute."

2. The court went on to state that "this grant of Barkham's was held to be very dishonorable and prejudicial to the Company... whereby a sovereignty in that heathen infidel was acknowledged, and the Company's title [acquired by Royal Charter] thereby much infringed."[21]

3. It also stipulated that the Indians had to be in "effective" possession of their lands. Otherwise, any claim to it would not be recognized.

4. From an English perspective, the accepted sovereign, according to English legal colonizing theory, was the King, by virtue of his subjects having discovered and lain claim to it in his name. All prior claims to the land by the non-Christian "heathen infidels" were considered invalid, and henceforth no English colonist could enter into an agreement with them to obtain a title to territory within Virginia's chartered territory.

Yeardley's concession with Opechancanough was seen as not only "prejudicial to the Company" and an acceptance of a "competing sovereignty" but also in practical terms it would have meant that the surrounding Indian tribes could ultimately have controlled the colony's rate of demographic and financial development. That necessitated bringing Opechancanough under the Virginia Company's control, if needs be, through conquest. The Court's ruling on *Barkham's Case*, July 7, 1622, provided the necessary legal permission.

The Virginia "Massacre" of 1622

Realizing that he was on a collision course with the English crown over sovereignty issues, Opechancanough made the first move. Word reached London on March 22nd that Opechancanough, with a confederacy of Tidewater tribes, had made a planned attack on many of the scattered English settlements. Some of these were over 60 plus miles out from Jamestown. It left 350 of their 1,240 colonists dead.

Though not an eye-witness, having not been there since 1609, Captain John Smith recorded in his "History of Virginia." that the Indians "came unarmed into our houses with deer, turkeys, fish, fruits, and other provisions to sell us."[22] They then suddenly grabbed hold of any tools or weapons at hand and killed the English settlers who were there—men, women, and children. Opechancanough went on to coordinate further surprise attacks, which led to many smaller settlements along the James River being destroyed and abandoned.

Three other records give us insight into the way the colonists interpreted the situation. One is from some of the colonists, who on writing home, admitted that the cause of the Indian attack was "our own perfidious dealing with them." Even the Virginia Company had to acknowledge that fear of dispossession had inspired the Indians action.

The second is from Edward Waterhouse, a Calvinist Lawyer who authored the Company's account of the atrocities perpetrated by the Indians. He saw that the "greatest cause" of the massacre was a misconception among the colonists who believed in the "speedy winning [of] the savages to civility and religion by kind usage and fair conversing among them"[23] and also that the devil had a prominent role to play:

> "[T]he true cause of this surprise was most by the instigation of the Devil (enemy to their salvation) and the daily fear that possessed them, that in time we by our growing continually upon them, would dispossess them of this country, as they had been formerly of the West Indies by the Spaniard."[24]

Waterhouse believed that such fears were unjustified, as was the belief of the colonists that the Indians would be converted through their good works. John Calvin, he reminded them, had taught that faith, not works, was all that was necessary for conversion and that God, "in His good time, and by such means as we think most unlikely"[25] would procure their conversion. Counter to the Royal mandate to plant the seed of faith among the heathen, Waterhouse absolved the Company of such a responsibility, freeing them to make war on the "wicked infidels:"

> "[O]ur hands which before were tied with gentleness and fair usage, are now set at liberty by the treacherous violence of the savages, not untying the knot, but cutting it: So that we... may now by right of war, and law of nations, invade the country and destroy them who sought to destroy us."[26]

On the strength of Waterhouse's analysis, a new code of practice was drawn up, which empowered the governor in Jamestown to not only stop all trade with the savages but also to set "upon the Indians in all places."[27]

A Discourse of Conquest
The Puritan preacher, Samuel Purchas, gives us the third insight. In 1625, he published "*A Discourse on Virginia.*" in which he illustrates a more aggressive approach to their dealings with the Indians.

In it, he reasons that Christians, "such as have the Grace of the spirit of Christ... have and hold the world" by divine appointment. The "Heathens [on the other hand] are not capable" of this. They "range rather than inhabite" their "unmanned wild country" and they therefore "have only a natural right [to be there], by the relics of the Law of Nature left in man." He goes on to proclaim that the Indians' violent actions towards them meant that even these natural rights should be "confiscated" by the English through "just invasion and conquest." Their actions against the English had lost them "their own natural and given us another natural right... so that England may both by Law of Nature and Nations challenge Virginia for her own peculiar property."[28]

English retribution against the Virginia Indians was both quick and pervasive as they offered an award for Opechancanough's capture, destroyed villages and burned their crops. Historian Nancy Lurie records that "The tribes were scattered, some far beyond the traditional boundaries of their land, and several of the small groups simply ceased to exist as definable entities."[29]

Opechancanough made another attempted at an uprising in 1644, which resulted in the deaths of approximately 500 English inhabitants. A successful counter-attack, led to Opechancanough's eventual arrest in 1646, only for him to be fatally shot in the back by a soldier before he was deported to England for trial.

His successor, Necotowance was to sign a treaty, which ceded most of the Powhatan Confederacy's remaining lands to the English by right of conquest, with an area north of the River York, being designated as Indian territory from the "King's Majesty of England." This land was later to be reduced in size through a series of adjustments imposed on them by England.

Conclusion

What we have looked at here, covers approximately 40 years. It is a period when England's thinking on colonizing discourse regarding their relationship with the Indians, the acquisition of their lands, etc., was emerging. At no point, did they see themselves playing the inferior role, the Indians were always seen as: "extras;" trading partners; converts and potential allies in their will to empire and in the bigger story taking place in the background, Protestant England's ongoing rivalry with Papist Spain.

When the Indians were to eventually reject their supplementary status and rise in resistance to the growing English need for more of their land, the prevalent belief systems regarding English feudal law and discovery discourse proved extremely useful. It empowered and legitimized England's war against the Virginia tribes and any sovereignty they may have thought they possessed.

These themes would continue to provide a firm and self-confident foundation for England as it pursued the development of its empire in the New World, right up to the outbreak of the American War of Independence. They would continue to use them as English-Americans following Independence, with their devolved mandate to subjugate the Indian's wild country further West.

From a theological perspective, the actions of the English in Virginia not only gave them a foothold in North America using the Doctrine of Discovery but also, as I have already contended, it significantly gave Satan a foothold into what was to become the United States of America. Their actions became a tool in Satan's hands to keep the Native people from experiencing a positive encounter with Christianity. If that sounds a bit extreme to you, I again point you in the direction of Chapter 2.

Let us now look at how the second of the colonies established under the Virginia Company Charter faired—the Plymouth Company.

References:
1. The Wampanoag Indians lived in what is now southeastern Massachusetts and Rhode Island, Martha's Vineyard and Nantucket in the early part of the 17th century. The name means "easterners" or "People of the Dawn," and at one point their population was approximately 12,000, which could be readily sustained due to the richness of the soil on which they could cultivate corn, beans, and squash. Prior to the arrival of the Pilgrims in 1620, their population had declined dramatically through diseases contracted from traders and fishermen who visited their shores. Among their more famous chiefs were Squanto, Samoset, Metacomet, and Massasoit. They spoke a language called Massachusett or Natick, which had been extinct since the 1800s and is now experiencing something of a revival, based on existing texts. For further information see: http://www.indians.org/articles/wampanoag-indians.html

http://en.wikipaedia.org/wiki/Wampanoag_people

2. Squanto, also known as Tisquantum. He ended up with some Spanish friars, who eventually allowed him to attempt to go home. However, he ended up in London where he learned English, returning to New England in 1619 on board one of John Smith's ships

3. Vaughan, Pg. 16. Source: William Bradford, *"History of Plymouth Plantation I."* Pgs. 228-229; Ferdinando Georges, *"A Brief Relation of the Discovery and Plantation of New England."* in Mass. Hist. Soc. Coll., 2 ser. IX (1823), Pg. 6.

4. Ibid. Pg. 59.

5. Craven, *"The Southern Colonies in the Seventeenth Century 1607-1689."* (Louisiana State University Press, 1949), Pg. 80.

6. P. L. Barbour, *"The Jamestown Voyages Under the First Charter 1606-1609."* (1969), *"Captain John Smith's Summary: A Map of Virginia."* Pg. 413.

7. Williams, Pg. 208. Quoting from H. C. Porter, *"The Inconstant Savage."* 1979, Pg. 296.

8. Same as 27 above. Pg. 369.

9. Williams, Pg. 209. Source: See *"Instructions from the Virginia Council in London Advocating Christian Conversion of the Indians, tributary Status for Powhatan and Agreement with His Enemies."* In Early American Indian Documents: Treaties and Laws, 1607-1789, Vol. 4: Virginia Treaties, 1607-1722." 6-7 (W. S. Robinson ed., Alden T. Vaughan gen. ed. 1983).

10. H. C. Porter, *"The Inconstant Savage."* Duckworth Pub (1979), Pg. 354.

11. Ibid. Pg. 354.

12. Ibid. Pg. 356.

13. C. Phillipson, *"A. Gentili, De iure belli libri tres."* (J. Rolfe trans. 1964), Pg. 41.

14. H. C. Porter, Source: as 31 above, Pg. 357.

15. Williams, Pg. 212.

16. Statistics deduced from Williams, Pgs. 212-213.

17. Ibid. Pg. 213. Source: *"The Records of the Virginia Company of London."* Vol. 3: *"A Justification for Planting Virginia."* (S. M. Kingsbury ed. 1933), Pg. 157.

18. Ibid. Pg. 214. Source: same as 38 above, Pgs. 172-173.

19. Ibid. Pg. 214. Source: same as 38 above, Pgs. 170-171.

20. Ibid. Pg. 214. Primary source: *"Denial by the Virginia Company in London of the Sovereign Rights of the Indians in the Land."* In Vol. 4 of *"Early American Indian Documents."* Pg. 28. (W. S. Robinson ed., Alden T. Vaughan gen. ed. 1983)
21. Ibid. Pgs. 215-216. Primary source: same as 30 above. Pgs. 6-8.
22. Source: http://en.wikipedia.org/wiki/Indian_massacre_of_1622
23. Williams, Pg. 217. Source: 38 above, Pg. 553.
24. Ibid. Source: 17 above, Pg. 556.
25. Ibid. Source: 17 above, Pgs. 553-554.
26. Ibid. Source: 17 above, Pg. 556.
27. Porter, Source as 31 above. Pg. 468.
28. Williams, Pgs. 218-219. Source: S. Purchas, *"Hakluytus Posthumus or Purchas His Pilgrimes."* (James MacLehose and Sons, 1906), Pgs. 219-225.
29. Ibid. Pg. 218. Source: Essay by N. Lurie, *"Indian Cultural Adjustment to European Civilization."* in *"Seventeenth-Century America."* (J. Smith ed. Univ. of North Carolina Press, 1959), Pg. 50.

Chapter 9

Our New England: The Plymouth Company

Despite previous negative contact with the local tribes in the area made by Captains Bartholomew Gosnold, Martin Pring, and George Waymouth, things initially looked much more promising for the Plymouth Company than it had been for its London sister. Overseeing the development of it from England was Sir Ferdinando Gorges (he had the Indian called Skidowares, who had been kidnapped by Waymouth, living with him for two years) and Chief Justice Popham whose nephew George Popham was given the overall leadership of the expedition in 1607.

Skidowares went with them as a go-between and interpreter and introduced Popham and Captain Raleigh Gilbert to Tahanedo, the local Native chief of the Abenakis Confederacy. They were part of the Algonquian linguistic group of tribes in the Maine, New England area. Not surprisingly, many of the tribe's members were suspicious of the English and soon after, when Skidowares left to rejoin his people, relationships started going downhill.

Immediately on disembarking at the mouth of the Kennebec (Sagadahoc) River the 120 colonists quickly got to work constructing Fort St. George and make the necessary preparations for the pending winter. Due to competition and the lack of consideration from the French and other European based fishermen, trading relationship with the local Indians suffered. Pioneering trips by other English interests only served to further antagonize the Indians, when attempts were made at kidnapping some of them. By the Spring of 1608, these had knock-on effects on the colony as essential local supplies were scarce. On top of that, a series of other unforeseen events led to the eventual demise of the colony: George Popham died, as did his main promoter Chief Justice Popham; Raleigh Gilbert took up the leadership but with the death of his brother in England he had to return home. With the loss of the colony's leadership, things on the ground began to deteriorate: they no longer treated "the natives of the area with justice and goodwill"[1] causing an increase in hostilities with them. The result? They lost heart and returned to England!

While attending a course about Manifest Destiny in Queen's University, Belfast, our lecturer told us that any colonization in America that had profit-making as its sole aim was doomed to fail unless a viable community of men and women was established as part of that venture. That was certainly the opinion of Sir Edwin Sandy, Treasurer of the Virginia Company of London who stated in 1620 that a "... plantation can never flourish till families be planted and the respect of wives and children fix the people on the soil."[3]

The Pilgrim Fathers

With that in mind, the first serious attempt at establishing a colony in North America was made by the Pilgrim Fathers, having been granted a charter by the London Virginia Company. Their whole expedition was financed by the Merchant Adventurers, who viewed the venture, solely to one end - profit!

It was only in 1620, with their arrival, that the Virginia Company of Plymouth was able to reestablish its Royal Charter[2] under the umbrella of a newly formed and more successful Plymouth Council for New England, led by Sir Ferdinando Gorges. It was established with the purpose of being able to found further colonial settlements, leading in 1629 to the formation of the Massachusetts Bay Colony.

The 102 passengers included 35 radical Separatists who had fled for safety to the Netherlands; non-Separatists who were hired to protect the interests of the Company and some family groups. They crossed the Atlantic on the Mayflower, which was manned by approximately 50 officers and crew. Due to unfavorable weather conditions they were forced to drop anchor much further north of their designated destination (the mouth of the Hudson River), off the tip of Cape Cod on November 11th, 1620—now called Provincetown. When some of the passengers queried their right to land there, because they did not have any legal authority to do so, they overcame their predicament by drafting and ratifying the Mayflower Compact which was signed by all the males onboard ship. It was a means of obtaining "a temporary, legally-binding form of self-government until such time as the Company could get formal permission from the Council of New England."[5]

When they found that the soil was poor and that there was an inadequate water supply, they moved on, to eventually drop anchor on the December 17th at Plymouth Harbor (the location of Patuxet, a former Indian settlement, and Plymouth Rock). After several days of surveying the area, they began under the governance of John Carver[4] to establish the Plymouth Colony (not to be confused with the Plymouth Company which sanctioned the formation of the Colony) in Massachusetts Bay. They were to find that the coastal area had been "providentially" stripped of Native American habitation because of the disastrous effects of European diseases on them. From their perspective, God had been preparing the way for them!

However, the harsh winter conditions were to have a devastating effect on the colonist's food supply. Which led to some of them taking a quantity of corn from an Indian winter storage area they had found, along with craft-ware from some wigwams—very close to the place where the Thomas Hunt (see the last Chapter) kidnappings took place a few years earlier. That provoked an attack on them by the Indians from the Nauset tribe (closely related in language and culture to the Wampanoag). Thankfully, the natives desire for some of the utilities the colonists had, along with the military aid they could provide through becoming allies with them against their enemies, won the day! The Nauset turned out to become the colonists greatest ally!

The overall analysis of this venture was that they were in no way prepared to face the cold winter; they were also inadequately supplied with the right types and amounts of foods to stave off conditions such as scurvy and starvation—all of which collectively led to over half of the passengers dying. Under such circumstances, the ship returned to England in 1621 with an empty hold. That didn't go down too well with Thomas Weston, their London investor, and led to a dispute between himself and the new governor, William Bradford; the successor to Carver, who died earlier that year. Weston blamed the selfishness of the Pilgrims while Bradford placed it squarely on

Weston, not only for the ill-preparedness of the trip but also for the unnecessary deaths. Bradford also defended Carver, saying that he "had worked himself to death that spring and [that] the loss of him and other industrious men's lives cannot be valued at any price."[6] He was to hold the office of Governor, with distinction, for thirty-three years.[7]

On board was another notable—Myles Standish (1584-1656). He was an English military officer who was hired by the Pilgrims as their military adviser. Standish also held important defense, administrative, and governing roles for the Plymouth Colony until his death. Unfortunately, he is perhaps best known for his pre-emptive and at time brutal strikes against the Indians—in particular, the Wessagusset massacre in April 1623 which did nothing to enhance Indian/Pilgrim relations! There is no evidence that he joined their church.[8]

Other newly founded colonies under the banner of the Plymouth Company were: New Hampshire (1629), Connecticut (1633), Maine (1635), Rhode Island (1636), and New Haven (1638). Each of them having to develop their own relationships with the local tribes: Wampanoag, Nipmuck, Narragansett, Mohegan, and Pequot.

—oooOooo—

The Massachusetts Bay Colony

In 1629, the increasing pressure put upon the Puritans in England by Charles I came to a head, as he sought to suppress their increased influence in Parliament, leading to him dissolving it in March of that year. Motivated by the political changes going on around them, a group of wealthy Puritan leaders managed to obtain a Royal Charter to establish a colony at Massachusetts Bay in America.

Interestingly, Charles I, with the understanding that this was primarily a business venture, granted the new charter to them, apparently unaware that it would facilitate a massive Puritan migration. Because a clause regarding its annual stockholder's meeting venue had been excluded, it also meant that the Board of Governors—all committed Puritans—became the first Board not to meet in England. That made it easier for the colony to maintain a strict Puritan identity without direct interference from the King or the Anglican Church until its Charter was revoked in 1684 by Charles II on the grounds of colonial noncompliance over various trade, duty, and navigation laws.

An advance party of some 300 colonists set sail. Others, along with John Winthrop, their elected leader, stayed on in England to recruit enough skilled people to ensure the development of a robust colony. Winthrop set sail on April 8, 1630, aboard the Arbella, arriving at Salem, Massachusetts on June 12th. It is understood that he delivered His infamous "City on a Hill" sermon, not long before they landed. Part of which reads:

> "We must delight in each other; make others' conditions our own; rejoice together, mourn together, labor and suffer together, always having before our eyes our commission and community in the work, as members of the same body. So, shall we keep the unity of the spirit in the bond of peace. The Lord will be our God, and delight to dwell among us, as His own people, and will command a blessing upon us in all our ways, so that we shall see much more of His wisdom, power, goodness, and truth than formerly we have been acquainted with. We shall find that the God of Israel is among us, when ten of us shall be able to resist a thousand of our enemies; when He shall make us a praise and glory that men shall say of succeeding plantations, 'may the Lord make it like that of New England.' For we must consider that we shall be as a city upon a hill. The eyes of all people are upon us. So that if we shall deal falsely with our God in this work we have undertaken, and so cause Him to withdraw His present help from us, we shall be made a story and a by-word through the world. We shall open the mouths of enemies to speak evil of the ways of God, and all professors for God's sake. We shall shame the faces of many of God's worthy servants and cause their prayers to be turned into curses upon us till we be consumed out of the good land whither we are going."[9]

His sermon also showed something of his belief that the Church of England had violated its covenant relationship with God, through their acceptance of what he saw as Catholic rituals. In going to America, they were expressing that they were entering a new covenanted relationship with God and establishing a purified expression of Christianity there, serving as an example of what God wanted back in England. He did not seem to think that any future wrongdoings against the Native people had any bearing on dealing "falsely with our God in this work we have undertaken."

Due to their careful planning, the Massachusetts Bay Colony was solidly established, leading to a steady flow of Puritans coming from England over the following ten years of the "Great Migration."

—oooOooo—

I now want to take a more detailed look at how the colonies developed their land purchasing policies.

Over-riding all that I am going to share here is the fact that each colonial government, through their charters, operated on the assumption that they held the legal authority over both the white colonists and the Indians. It would seem in those early days of colonialism that this was mostly accepted by the tribal leadership, who at times were even required to appear before the Court to address issues relating to tribal members who had violated English law.

Also, contrary to the myth that the Puritan settlers either stole the land of the Indians or bought it from them for mere trinkets, the Indians were often willing to sell the land to them. While they did not have the same measuring scale regarding its value, there is no evidence that the Indians felt in any way "short-changed" in the process. There was, in fact, much that was spare and up for sale following the leptospirosis epidemic in late 1633 into the spring of '34 (the worst since an earlier one in 1616-1617), which killed thousands of New England's native population.

It would also seem that both parties had quite a similar understanding of land tenure, with the Indian sachem having general authority over

121

the lands held by his subjects (not unlike a European monarch), while a tribesman could hold property in keeping with the rights and customs of the tribe. Like the Colonial authorities, they also oversaw the purchase of lands which often took the form of much sought after white man's goods: metal knives, agricultural implements, cloth, jewelry, clothing, and etc.

Of further interest is the fact that even though the colonists bought the lands, they allowed the Natives to have, other than the right to inhabit them, full access for purposes of hunting and fishing. There appears to be some level of agreement here, with the settlers farming it and also trading with the Indians such things as the highly sought after, beaver pelts.

The patent, purchase, and possession
Alongside this, Alden T Vaughan lays out what he calls "three separate theoretical justifications for occupying the soil of New England: they were 'patent, purchase, and possession.'" We shall see, as I unpack these, that the colonists had a clear understanding of much that is integral to the Doctrine of Discovery:[10]

> "[A **patent**] is simply the right derived from discovery. According to prevailing European concepts, a Christian monarch had full authority over lands discovered in his name, so long as the inhabitants were not themselves Christian. A patent [is similar to what the Popes called a 'bull' – *mine*] issued by a Christian king to any individual or corporation, such as 'the Governor and Company of the Massachusetts Bay in New England,' permitted the grantees to act on his behalf... The Puritan, therefore, had every right... simply to dispossess the heathen natives."[11]

That was certainly how John Winthrop saw it, even before he set foot in New England:

> "As for the Natives of New England, they inclose noe Land, neither have any settled habytation, nor any

Cattle to improve the Land by, and soe have noe other than a Naturall Right (Natural Law – *mine*) to those Countries, soe as if we leave them sufficient for their use, we may lawfully take the rest, there being more than enough for them and us."[12]

What Winthrop was articulating was *vacuum domicilium*; another aspect of The Doctrine of Discovery that allowed the Puritans to occupy any land that was either desolate or had at one time been inhabited. Should any native come to them later, claiming prior ownership it, he would have been recompensed (**purchase**). The Algonquian Indians seemed to have no difficulty with this, and on occasions like the one in which their coastal lands were stripped of them, following the 1616-17 plague, they were only all too happy to let go of it and receive payment for what to them was now wilderness. As Vaughan points out, there is no evidence that *vacuum domicilium* was formally used by the Puritans to forcibly remove the natives off the land, as they made their first footholds in New England (**possession**)—disease, having done that job for them! Nevertheless, they did exercise it as their right to be on New England soil, before they were given any formal consent from the local Indian chiefs.

It is evident in all that I have shared that the Puritans didn't fully exercise what they saw as their "patent rights." They recognized that the Indians had "natural law right" to be the proprietors of the land while holding firmly to their belief that they had nevertheless the full political jurisdiction regarding it - they were in charge!

An alliance formed with the Wampanoag tribe

Just months before his death, John Carver was able to establish a peace treaty with Chief Massasoit of the Wampanoag[see Reference 22, Ch. 7] tribe (March 1621). It turned out to be a very successful treaty, and even though it was a bit shaky at times, it lasted for more than fifty years.[13]

Under its terms, Massasoit promised that his people would not harm the English and that, if they did, he would hand the offenders over to them for punishment, even though there was no reciprocal obligation to do likewise on the part of the settlers. Carver and Massasoit, with

Squanto as an interpreter, agreed to aid the other in the event "any did unjustly war against him." The wording of the treaty ended with a declaration that King James would esteem Massasoit "as his friend and ally."

However, the Puritans appear to have interpreted the treaty as subjecting Massasoit to the King of England, even though there was nothing in its text to confirm that view from Massasoit's perspective.[14] Again, we see a repeating of the pattern in Indian/English affairs—the Indians saw things as reciprocal actions between two equals while the English saw themselves as the superior party with the Indian being subservient to them.

In July of that year, the Puritans also entered a trading compact with Massasoit, who agreed to trade exclusively with them, which meant that their frequent trading with the French came to an end. That along with the cumulative effect of ongoing land acquisition (voluntary sales or otherwise) invariably led to an increase in English domination, both politically and culturally over the Native Americans. That undoubtedly was to add to what would inevitably become a cycle of increased native insecurity, resistance, and conflict.

Trading with the Indians was however to have another negative knock-on effect for both groups. While both sides were eager to trade, the result ultimately led to the destruction of native society. Not only did the desire for western goods: firearms, metal tools, etc., produce rivalry among tribes, it also shifted them away from self-sufficiency in hunting and agriculture to dependence on the colonies. Those tribal rivalries would also be used by the European nations to divide and conquer the indigenous peoples.

The Puritans were also in an increasingly compromising environment. There was accountability to the Company back home who were looking for profits; they had to work alongside other colonists who did not hold to their often hypocritical spiritual/cultural values, and there was also the development of political/trading alliances with the local Indian tribes. Undergirding all of this was the European worldview of the Doctrine of Discovery which they politically and spiritually embraced, even though it conflicted with the Gospel they sought to live by. All of this invariably meant that they led a lifestyle that was counter to living amicably with their Indian neighbors and importantly it was also counter to how God would have expected them to live.

In all fairness, I don't think that they were fully aware of these dynamics. Again, that did not lessen the spiritual dynamics and outcomes! From my perspective, the actions of the English among the Native population went into the corporate data bank of negative experiences they had with my cultural ancestors. And again, I can but ask myself: what was going on in the "heavenly realms?" What footholds of Satan were being consolidated in the foundations of what would eventually become the United States of America and its Indian policies? It certainly wasn't looking good for them!

—ooo0ooo—

Puritan perspectives

I am indebted for most of the information below regarding evangelism among the Native Americans and on what became known as Praying Towns, to the research done by Alden Vaughan[15]

I have already noted that the conversion of Native Americans was considered a major part of the reasoning for the English—and especially the Puritans—in establishing the colonies in New England. King Charles in 1628 had stated that conversion was "the principall Ende of this plantacion." Governor Winthrop included it as one of his Particular Considerations: "It is a scandale to our Religion that we shewe not as much zeale in seekinge the conversion of the heathen, as the Papists doe." Though he was perhaps more aware that their primary focus in going to America was to do with establishing "a haven for his kind of English dissenters than with bringing the gospel to the red man."[16] That is borne out by the fact that in the first twenty years of Puritan settlement the number of converts was negligible. Undoubtedly other factors were also built in here: the genuine struggle they faced to establish the first settlements, and a reluctance among the natives to embrace the white man's religion.

One must also bear in mind that as Puritans, their evangelism was not just about getting people baptized or avoiding the accommodation of any form of syncretism with native religion, as Anglicans and Roman Catholics were being accused of. They were looking for "real conversion experiences" as they perceived them, not just "symbolic allegiance or regular attendance at services, but full church membership." Without this, no one, white or native, could become a communicant member of his or her congregation![17]

Herein lay a problem, as such a "conversion experience" required:

- An in-depth knowledge of the Bible (which at that time was only in English) and its complex theology
- A deep understanding of the Puritan creed
- The passing of a rigorous testing of the above, before the congregational elders
- Them, to exhibit a lifestyle in keeping with all of this
- Them, to no longer rely on the direction and protection of their tribes' sachem. Indeed, if their sachem did not embrace Christianity, the Indian converts were taught that they were agents of Satan and had to be shunned.

That was made more difficult if English and Algonquian were not understood or spoken by all concerned to enable meaningful communication!

Vaughan summed it up as follows: "Religious conversion must be preceded, or at least accompanied by social conversion... the native, in short, must live like the Puritan's image of a true Christian..."[18] "As a result, Puritanism presented a rigorous intellectual and moral challenge to the potential convert and demanded that they change their ancient patterns of life. That relatively few Indians were able to make so drastic an adjustment should not evoke surprise."[19]

Also, seen from an Indian perspective, the conversion would require a massive shift not only at the level of their personal morality but also in their continuing relationships within their tribe and how it organized itself politically and economically as well as spiritually.[20]

126

That was a tough call, one that many converts were not able to meet or sustain!

And for many of the tribes such as the Wampanoag, Narragansett, Niantic, and Mohegan, they kept themselves at arm's length from the growing English communities. That was encouraged by their spiritual leaders, who saw any attempts at Christianization as a threat to their power and authority.

Added to all of this was the frustratingly high mortality rate among those they sought to convert and civilize, due ironically to the fact that these Indians were in closer contact with white men and their diseases.

Praying Towns – the answer?

John Eliot,[21] known as the Apostle to the Indians, came up with a solution to this last point: the development of what became known as Praying Towns. They were to be "remote from the English, where [the Indians] must have the word constantly taught, and government constantly exercised, meanes of good subsistence provided, [and] encouragements for the industrious." He concluded however that there was one major drawback to this: "I feare it will be too chargeable."[22] (i.e., taxing, demanding.)

By 1651 the first praying town at Natick, Massachusetts was established on land purchased some eighteen miles from Boston, on the Charles River. That was made all the easier with Waban, who came from there and is thought to be the first Native American convert to Christianity, endorsing it. Later that year Governor Endicott along with the Rev. Wilson visited Natick to find that a thriving village was already fully operational.[23] It is clear from written records that Eliot had thought through what sort of government this community was to be built upon—it was to be a model community that would firmly establish a pattern of what was to follow. They had to make "the Word of God theire only magna charta." to which they had to "fly... for every Law, Rule, Direction, Form, or whatever we do."[24] A major difficulty was, however, to still be faced. There was no church!

For the Puritans, Church was not just a building. It required a minimum of eight to ten truly regenerated Christians, who had entered into a covenanted commitment to God and each other. So, the following year (1652), Eliot submitted a written account he had made of Native conversions to a body of prominent Puritan clergymen, who in turn met each of them to listen to their story of spiritual awakening. In most instances, the Indian converts accentuated their former sinfulness, their joy in knowing Christ and the persecution they had received from their friends, powwows, and sachems. One can only imagine what Eliot and those Indians must have felt when they were informed that they had failed the test. It was considered that more time was required; a longer apprenticeship needed.[25] For some it would take another eight years before they were to pass the rigorous process and for a recognized congregation to be formed.

Meanwhile, this barred them from participating in Holy Communion! It was also during this period (1658), again under Eliot's oversight, that the first draft of a Bible in the Native language was completed. That would have been a tremendous asset for the few Indians who were bilingual.

On Martha's Vineyard and Nantucket Island, which were bought in 1641 by Thomas Mayhew, Sr, his son Thomas Mayhew, Jr.—a Congregational Minister—was also experiencing success, though being on an Island the results of his work tended to be overshadowed by what Eliot was attaining. Out of a population of 1500 Natives on Martha's Vineyard in 1652, 283 of them had made a confession of Christian faith. He was never to see the continuing development of his work, as in the winter of 1657 he was declared missing on a voyage back to England which left his father Thomas Mayhew Snr., to continue with it. The following year, he was able to report that on Martha's Vineyard there were fifty full communicants, with most of the rest of the Indians being nominally Christian. While on Nantucket, he could claim to have one church of thirty communicants, three Praying Towns, and four native preachers.[26]

Moving beyond this was fraught with difficulties, especially regarding any thoughts of integrating the Native and white congregations. As very few of the Puritans spoke the Native language with any degree of fluency, it was left to trained Natives to teach their fellow Indians their theology. That meant however that what was perceived as negative differences in their customs went unchecked. For example, because of a different work ethic, many did not see the need to increase productivity; neither did they have a desire to improve their lifestyle or develop their educational standards.

Meanwhile back in England, with the restoration of the monarchy (May 1660), Charles II came to the throne. Because the Puritans had executed his father, he was to end the previously formed Puritan Society for the Propagation of the Gospel in New England. With the aid of the Earl of Clarendon and the purging from their ranks of any ardent anti-Royalists, a new Charter was drawn up in February 1662 known as the "Company for Propagacion of the Gospell in New England and the parts adjacent in America." It was commonly known as the New England Company.[27]

The Bay Colony was to continue to take the lead in the development of the Praying Towns. By 1665 six more had been established and Eliot was actively advocating the establishment of "Schools for the instruction of the [Indian] youth in reading, that they may be able to read the scriptures at least."[28] Over the following five years a further six Towns were built, all roughly modeled after the first one in Natick.

In 1674, Major General Daniel Gookin[29] also recorded the success of another one of these pioneer missionaries—Richard Bourne. In his work among the Nauset tribe of Cape Cod, eight praying towns were formed with a population of 497 Indians. But overall, work among the other Native tribes in New England was discouraging.

Opposition

In the Plymouth colony, it was felt that they would have made more progress in converting the Indians had it not been for resistance from the sachems: Massasoit (Wampanoag), Uncas (Mohegan) and Canonicus (Narragansett). While they may have been friendly towards the Puritans, they continued to resisted any evangelistic endeavors made among them. That should not be surprising, as they like the other influential Native leaders in New England were going to be protective, not only of their authority but also of what they saw as the subversion of their spiritual beliefs, customs, tribal cohesion, and loyalty, etc.[30]

Opposition was also apparent among the colonists who did not trust the Indian enough to integrate them fully into colonial society. That was seen especially during times of heightened tension when they feared that Native tribal loyalty would win out over loyalty to them. As a result, they wouldn't even trust Indians when they warned the colonial authorities of imminent attacks. Such was the English distrust of them during King Philips War (1675-76) that the General Council in Boston removed the Praying Indians to Deer Island in Boston Harbor:

> "By December of that year, there were over 500 Christian Indians confined to the island. 'The enmity, jealousy, and clamors of some people against them put the magistracy upon a kind of necessity to send them all to the Island...' where they '... lived chiefly upon clams and shell-fish, that they digged out of the sand, at low water; the Island was bleak and cold, their wigwams poor and mean, their clothes few and thin; some little corn they had of their own, which the Council ordered to be fetched from their plantations, and conveyed to them by little and little...'"[31]

Following the War, the released Indians were to find themselves in a vastly different world, like strangers in a foreign land.

—ooo0ooo—

A few personal thoughts

1. To transform the native culture of New England into European-defined Christianity and civilization was no mean task. Nor, dare I say it, should this have been what it was all about. I know one could argue that this is the way it was; that the Puritans were acting out of all sincerity and that they didn't have the benefit of modern cross-cultural missions training, etc. But nevertheless, it

was not the way of the Spirit of Christ—any errors made in these early foundational days, consciously or otherwise, were there to give Satan the necessary tools he was looking for, to hinder the spread of the gospel among the Native tribes. On the positive side, there is no doubting that many of the Indians who embrace the Europeanized Christian message of the Puritans became genuine followers of Christ.

2. Very early on in the New Testament the Church realized that a very culturally different Gentile coming to faith did not have to become Jewish as part of that process. The Gentile church did not have the Bible as we now know it (which at that time was only the Hebraic Old Testament), yet they could grow in their faith and enter fully into the life of the local Christian community, even in critical leadership roles. Granted they did have apostolic figures moving among them to instruct them, helping them to contextualize it and who knew the common language of the Roman Empire, which was Greek. This is the sort of model the Puritans should have been seeking to emulate.

3. While we should anticipate that certain changes in lifestyle are both inevitable and necessary when one becomes a follower of Creator's son, I believe that many of these changes will progressively appear as we live out a lifestyle of an increasingly intimate relationship with God. It is doubtful if any of us will complete that process during our own lifetime! Grace is needed!

4. I grew up in Northern Ireland in a Church which theologically had aspects not too far removed from Puritan theology. Some of it I would no longer accept as either biblical or as very grace-filled, tending to be more on the side of legalistic. Our culture's attitudes toward the Roman Catholic community in Ireland were, to say the least, sectarian and deplorable! And sadly, for many, that is still the case! When God poured out His Spirit during the 1970s to the 90s, in what became known as the Charismatic Renewal, many Catholics and Protestants had a deep and profound life-changing encounter with God. They were theologically poles apart, yet there was no doubt about one thing, they were brothers and sisters in Christ, and God was dealing with deeply ingrained cultural and

theological attitudes! They knelt as equals before the Cross! How different things may have been if the Puritans had treated the new Native American converts as co-equal brothers and sisters in Christ and sought with the Indians to develop and cultivate culturally appropriate expressions of faith and church for them.

With that in mind, we will look in the next chapter at the outbreak of conflict between the colonists and the native tribes as white expansion continued with its inevitable push west.

References:

1. Alden T. Vaughan, *"New England Frontier: Puritans and Indians, 1620-1675."* Third Edition, University of Oklahoma Press, 1965. Pg. 14.
2. Source: https://en.wikipaedia.org/wiki/Virginia_Company
3. Source: http://www.nps.gov/jame/historyculture/the-indispensible-role-of-women-at-jamestown.htm
4. John Carver (c. 1576-April 1621). He was a wealthy English merchant and a member of the Separatist Puritan movement which moved from England to Holland during the reign of James I to avoid religious persecution. Along with other Separatists, he took the decision in 1620 to make the journey on board the Mayflower to the New World, where he was appointed their first governor, albeit short-lived, due to his untimely death four months later. For further information see, https://en.wikipedia.org/wiki/John_Carver_(Plymouth_Colony_governor)
5. Source: http://mayflowerhistory.com/mayflower-compact/
6. William Bradford, *"History of Plymouth Plantation by William Bradford, the second Governor of Plymouth."* (Boston. 1856 Not in copyright). Pg. 306.
7. Jacob Bailey Moore, *"Memoirs of American Governors."* (N. Y. Gates & Stedman, 136 Nassau St. 1846) Vol. 1. Pg. 46.
8. Source: https://en.m.wikipedia.org/wiki/Myles_Standish
9. The wording of the original text of the "City on a Hill" sermon: http://www.digitalhistory.uh.edu/disp_textbook.cfm?smtID=3&psid=3918

10. Vaughan, Pg. 109. Referencing: David Pulsifer, ed., *"Acts of the Commissioners of the United Colonies of New England."* (2 vols. [Ply. Col. Rec., IX-X], Boston, 1859), I, 112, II, 13; Winthrop, Journal, II. Pg. 331.

11. Ibid. Pgs. 110-111.

12. Heinsohn, Robert Jennings. Sail 1620, *"Pilgrims and Wampanoag: The Prudence of Bradford and Massasoit."*

13. William Bradford. Pgs. 107-109.

14. Massasoit. Vaughan, Pgs. 70-82, including a synopsis of the treaty articles.

15. Ibid. Pgs. 235-308.

16. Ibid. Pgs. 235-236.

17. Ibid. Pg. 237.

18. Ibid. Pgs. 237-238.

19. Ibid. Pg. 238.

20. Ibid. Pg. 259.

21. John Eliot, also known as the "Apostle to the Indians," embraced Puritanism while at Jesus College, Cambridge. He emigrated in 1631, to settle for the rest of his life in Roxbury, Massachusetts. Vaughan describes him in these terms: "No man in New England was so universally appreciated and loved... He seems to have won a devoted following largely from a single-hearted dedication to duty and service, coupled with a becoming modesty and sweetness. He was generous, thoughtful of others, forgiving." He learned the native language, and by 1646 he was even confident enough with his grasp of the Algonquian language to discuss theological issues with the local tribes.

22. Ibid. Pgs. 262-263.

23. Ibid. Pgs. 264-265.

24. Ibid. Pg. 265.

25. Ibid. Pg. 267.

26. Ibid. Pgs. 296-297.

27. Ibid. Pgs. 274-275.

28. Ibid. Pg. 286.

29. Major-General Daniel Gookin. It is thought that he came from Cork, in the south of Ireland, where he spent his childhood. From there he went to England to be educated, before migrating with his parents to Virginia, Massachusetts. Through his writings, he has given us a lot of insights into the region. He was certainly

under the impression that the missionary program of the Puritans was quite successful, albeit amid setbacks: some of the Indians who showed real leadership qualities died prematurely (often due to European diseases); others lost their early enthusiasm; there was ongoing hostility between them and their fellow natives and funding from England was constantly in short measure.

In 1674, he estimated that close to eleven hundred Christian Indians lived in the fourteen Praying Towns of the Bay Colony, although there were only two recognized congregations-Natick and Punkapog.

30. Ibid. Pg. 305.
31. From records of the Massachusetts Bay in New England 1628-86. Vol. 5, Pgs. 57, 64, 84, 86. Boston.

Chapter 10

Continued Expansion—Growing Conflict

Expansion with conflict

In 1628, the owners of the Massachusetts Bay Company founded the Massachusetts Bay Colony, which included the absorption of the unsuccessful Dorchester Company. That was to become a well-established venture, with approximately 20,000 people migrating to it from England during the 1630s. They, along with the other colonies, were seeking to keep conflict with the local Native population to a minimum by developing a centrally controlled, highly regulated, land distribution system.

During this decade, with the population expanding, the Puritans started to seek out more land in the interior, especially up the Connecticut Valley, to develop further settlements. That was, however, to bring them into an ever-increasing negative contact with the powerful and hostile Pequot who had settled there a few years earlier, having ousted the River Indians in 1622-23. The Puritans answer to this was to seek out allies among some of the other tribes, who had no love for the Pequot either.

This was undoubtedly a time of great uncertainty for all the Native tribes of the region: the Pequot, Narragansett, Mohawk, Western Niantic, and Mohegan. There had been another devastating outbreak of leptospirosis (it is thought that the Pequot population dropped from 30,000 to approx. 3,000) and with the Dutch and English vying for dominance in trade, that only added to the increased conflict with and among the Indians allied to them. Uncertainty was also in the air as the tribes sought to develop working relationships with the Europeans, which invariably lead to misconceptions and miscommunications at various levels between the different tribes and the white settlers. It was an uneasy mix which inevitably led to what became known as the Pequot War (1636-37).

In this chapter, we shall see how some of these tribes were to relate to the colonies, as either ally or enemy and sometimes as both. It was an incredibly turbulent period in New England's formative history, one that progressively drew in all the above tribes, other minor ones and all the English colonies. It would lead to the establishment of precedents in how the English and eventually how Euro-Americans would relate to the Native American in their midst, as they constantly pushed west in their quest for more land.

The Pequot War and its background

The Pequot War was the first significant local war with the Indians which threw up several issues for me regarding the actions of the Puritans in their behavior; political subterfuge and genocide.

It was around this time that the Dutch,[1] as they expanded their fur trade, also moved up into the Connecticut Valley, where they made a treaty with the Pequot who sold them a plot of land close to present day Hartford, where they erected a trading post, The House of Good Hope. Not to be outdone, the Plymouth colony drew up a deed for land further up the valley, to intercept the lucrative trade coming down the river, before it reached the Dutch. Though they had no official Charter, they claimed prior rights to it on the basis that they had bought it earlier from a former Pequot sachem, who had since been expelled from the tribe.

Before the Dutch could hit back, a Puritan business venture established the fortified Saybrook Company at the mouth of the Connecticut River, with John Winthrop Jnr., son of the Massachusetts Bay Colony's Governor appointed as its Governor. Over and above the land sale to the Dutch, the Pequot, along with their tributary tribe the Western Niantic, saw the southern stretches of the valley and what is now southeastern Connecticut as their territory.

Why it happened one is not sure, but in early 1634, counter to an agreement not to interfere with the Dutch trade on the river, members of either the Pequot or Western Niantic murdered some Narragansett Indians on their way to trade at the House of Good Hope. The Dutch retaliated and captured Tatobem the Pequot sachem, and even though a ransom for his release had been paid, he was murdered. After Tatobem's death, Sassacus became the Pequot's Grand Sachem and responded by attacking Good Hope. Tension only increased as the Narragansett prepared for war.

Attempts were made at negotiating peace between the Pequot and the Massachusetts Bay Colony. The Pequot wanted the English to be arbitrators of peace with the Narragansett and to re-establish trading with them. When the Colony demanded payment of a very high tribute and that the killers of a man called John Stone were to be handed over, that was unacceptable to them.

The John Stone Affair

John Stone, known as "a smuggler, privateer, and slaver,"[2] had been continuously in legal trouble with both Plymouth and Massachusetts Bay authorities[3] and was eventually banished from these Colonies. Having left them, he sailed up the Connecticut River where he kidnapped some Indians and held them to ransom. However, he and his crew were slack in keeping watch, resulting in some Indians coming on board, killing him and his crew members.

I have read several theories surrounding this, though most seem to agree that it was the Pequot, who on thinking that Stone was Dutch, murdered him in revenge for the death of Tatobem. Whoever it was, it only served to increase the Puritans distrust of Sassacus and the Pequot. Some sources went as far as saying that the Puritan-Pequot conflict began because of Stone's death. That seems rather strange to me, considering the Pequot's, if they were the culprits, had, albeit inadvertently, done the Puritans a favor. The Puritans had certainly no regard for Stone that would have merited any actions against the Pequot! Indeed, Roger Clapp in his memoir states, "Thus God destroyed him and delivered us at that time also."[4]

Francis Jennings writes,

> "Stone, dead, became more cherished and more useful than Stone, alive, had ever been. When substantial considerations of plunder and dominion induced the

Bay magistrates to conquer the Pequot, they felt obliged to mask their real motives with a semblance of righteous retribution. The time-honored tradition in such circumstances is to wave a bloodied shirt. For the Bay's purposes, Stone's shirt would serve nicely."[5]

In June 1636 following a dispute with Sassacus, Uncas left the Pequot and formed a tribe called the Mohegan's. Jonathan Brewster, a trader from Plymouth, reported that Uncas had said to him, "the Pequots have some mistrust that the English will shortly come against them... and therefore out of desperate madness do threaten shortly to set both upon Indians and English jointly."[6] Stephen Katz, writing in *"The Pequot War Reconsidered,"* believes that Uncas made up the report because of animosities he held towards the Pequot. Whether this was true or not, the colonists took it seriously, mindful of the 1622 uprising in Virginia and because of their small numbers.

So, in early July, the Massachusetts Bay colony reiterated its demands to the Pequot's, regarding the surrender of Stone's murderers. Along with responding to other issues between them, they warned the Pequot's that they would not only nullify their treaty with them but also "revenge the blood of our countryman as occasion shall serve."[7]

John Oldham (1592-1636)

Another person of interest is John Oldham. He was a captain, trader and Indian merchant and appears to be something of a contentious character. At one point, having been found guilty of disturbing the peace, he was banished from Plymouth. Later, in July 1636, tensions further heightened when he, along with five crew members were murdered off Block Island while on a trading voyage - presumably by its inhabitants. According to the notes at the end of *"Major Mason's Brief History of the Pequot War"* the "Evidence suggests that Oldham was killed by members of the Narragansett, two of who were serving among his crew, and not by their rivals the Pequots."[8] While others suggest that it could have been their allies, the Eastern Niantic!

However, one tries to analyze it today, the reality is that on the 25th August 1636, Captains John Endecott, John Underhill, William

Turner, and ninety men were mobilized and sent to Block Island to find the killers of Oldham and then go after the murderers of Stone.

Their commission, according to Winthrop was "to put to death the men of Block Island, but to spare the women and children, and to bring them away, and to take possession of the island; and from thence to go to the Pequot's to demand the murderers of Captain Stone and other English, and one thousand fathom of wampum for damages etc., and some of their children for hostages, which if they should refuse, they were to obtain it by force."[9] Henry Vane, the Governor of Massachusetts, put it more succinctly when he gave the command to "massacre all of the Native men on the island."[10] Finding that most of the Islanders had left before their arrival, Endecott spent the following few days in pursuit: killing fourteen of them, destroying their wigwams, crops, and canoes before moving on towards Fort Saybrook to pursue the Pequots.[11] He had an unfruitful meeting with an envoy of the Pequots at their village at the mouth of the Thames River. A break down in the proceedings, led to an eruption of violence, with Endecott's troops looting and causing destruction in the village. Clearly, the English policy of leniency was now changing into one of aggression.

Not surprisingly, throughout that winter and into 1637, the Pequot made a series of attacks on settlers in Connecticut at Fort Saybrook and Wethersfield and they also made attempts to form an alliance with the Narragansett against the English. The Massachusetts colony was, however, able to persuade the Narragansett to align themselves with the colonies to help them avenge the death of Oldham. That was made possible, no doubt, by the Narragansett former hatred of the Pequot and their respect for the superior arms of the English! It also wasn't difficult for the Mohegan's to be brought onside against Sassacus.

Following the killing of 7-9 people by the Pequot, in retaliation for the confiscation of some of their land, the response of the Plymouth, Massachusetts and Connecticut colonies was to collectively commit themselves along with their allies to fight the Pequot. War was declared!

Fort Mystic massacre—26 May 1637

Rather than execute a full-frontal attack on the main Pequot village, John Mason (a Puritan) suggested an alternative flanking attack on another Pequot habitation, Fort Mystic. As this would have been contrary to the plans initially decided upon, Mason sought the council of their Chaplain, asking him to "commend our Condition to the Lord... to direct how and in what manner we should demean ourselves in that Respect." Having sought the mind of God overnight, he pronounced that He approved of using a flanking move.[12]

In the evening of that day, under the leadership of Underhill and Mason, they led their troops and their native allies (comprising of 70 Mohegan and 200 Narragansett and Eastern Niantic warriors) through Narragansett territory towards the palisaded Fort Mystic. While the Pequot slept, they prepared for a surprise attack by surrounding the Fort and forming two concentric rings with the English on the inner one and their native allies on the outer. Striking at dawn with a volley of shots, Underhill and his men entered the Fort through the southwest entrance and Mason did likewise on the northeast. Numbers vary slightly regarding the account of what happened next but having set fire to the Pequot's accommodation, approximately 600-700 men, women, and children were to die over the next hour either within the Fort or as they tried to escape. The English lost two of their men, with a number being injured.

Regarding the attack on Fort Mystic, here are Mason's recorded words:

> "We must burn them; and immediately... brought out a Fire Brand, and putting it into the Matts with which they were covered, set the Wigwams on Fire... the Indians ran as men most dreadfully Amazed. And indeed such a dreadful Terror did the ALMIGHTY let fall upon their Spirits, that they would fly from us and run into the very Flames, where many of them perished... And thus in little more than one Hour's space was their impregnable Fort with themselves utterly Destroyed, to the Number of Six or Seven

Hundred... There were only Seven taken Captive & about Seven escaped... Thus was God seen in the Mount, Crushing his proud Enemies and the Enemies of his People... burning them up in the Fire of his Wrath, and dunging the Ground with their Flesh: It was the LORD's Doings, and it is marvellous in our Eyes!"[13]

The ruthlessness of the attack appalled most of the colonists' Indian allies: this clearly, was warfare of a kind that they had never seen or imagined before! John Underhill, in his response to them, said,

"I would refer you to David's war. When a people is grown to such a height of blood and sin against God and man... there he hath no respect of persons, but harrows them, and saws them, and puts them to the sword... We had sufficient light from the word of God for our proceedings."[14]

Many of the Pequot not in the Fort at the time of the attack were killed, often in further mass killings over the following months. Captured females were assimilated as slaves into the Mohegan, Narragansett, and Eastern Niantic tribes; the men were sold and sent as slaves to the West Indies. Sassacus was eventually captured and killed by the Mohawk, with his scalp being sent to Hartford.

The Treaty of Hartford

The war officially came to an end in September 1638, with Narragansett, Mohegan and the remaining Pequot sachems signing the Treaty of Hartford, which officially brought about the dissolution of the Pequot nation. The victors, including the allied Indian tribes, portioned out the survivors, while their lands were divided up among the various towns along the Connecticut River valley. The colonial authorities forbade the use of the Pequot name in order, in Captain (John) Mason's words, to "cut off the remembrance of them from the earth."[15]

A small number of the Pequot Tribe, however, did survive, enabling them to reestablish their identity, but as separate tribes in separate reservations: the Mashantucket Pequot (Western) and the Paucatuck Pequot (Eastern). Both successfully gained Federal recognition, though the Paucatuck had it revoked as recent as 2005.

Effects/Analysis of the War

It has been acknowledged that the Puritans "religious rhetoric made their victory over the 'heathens' in the Pequot War a significant factor in the formulation of what became Colonial/American Indian policy over the next three centuries... For the first time, northeastern tribes experienced the total warfare of European military methods, and the English Puritans realized they held the power to dominate the people they saw as Godless savages."[16]

Alfred A. Cave in his book, *"The Pequot War,"*[17] mentions that "the images of brutal and untrustworthy savages plotting the extermination of those who would do the work of God in the wilderness became a vital part of the mythology of the American frontier. A celebration of victory over Indians as the triumph of light over darkness, civilization over savagery, for many generations our central historical myth, finds its earliest full expression in the contemporary chronicles of this little war."

That was undoubtedly a significant moment in my own people's colonial history. As Alden T. Vaughan writes:

> "The effect of the Pequot War on Indian affairs was profound. Overnight the balance of power had shifted from the populous but unorganized natives to the English colonies. Henceforth there was no combination of Indian tribes that could seriously threaten the New England Puritans. The destruction of the Pequot cleared away the only major obstacle to Puritan expansion. And the thoroughness of that destruction made a deep impression on the other tribes."[18]

142

At the end of his *"Brief History of the Pequot War,"* John Mason writes regarding the Pequot:

> "Thus we may see, How the Face of God is set against them that do Evil, to cut off the Remembrance of them from the Earth. Our Tongue shall talk of the Righteousness all the Day long; for they are confounded, they are bro't to Shame that sought our Hurt! Blessed be the Lord God of Israel, who only doth wondrous Things; and blessed be his holy Name for ever: Let the whole Earth be filled with his Glory! Thus the Lord was pleased to smite our Enemies in the hinder Parts, and to give us their Land for our Inheritance; Who remembered us in our low Estate, and redeemed us out of our Enemies Hands: Let us, therefore, praise the Lord for His Goodness and his Wonderful Works to the Children of Men!"[19]

What a profoundly saddening quote to read!

This War not only highlighted a massive clash of very different cultures but sadly it was the beginning of an all too frequently reoccurring theme—the dominance, suppression and subduing of Native American nation after nation. It was, however, as one analyst put it, a "worldview alien to that of the Apostle Paul's, i.e., to be sojourners and **peacemakers.**"[20] A worldview that would sadly resurface again and again within the framework of the Doctrine of Discovery, to be repackaged as Manifest Destiny (see Chapter 16) as it moved increasingly westward.

—ooo0ooo—

The Connecticut Valley was not to see significant "Indian troubles" for another forty years until the outbreak of King Philip's War, also known as the First Indian War (1675-76). With the involvement of many different tribal groupings, it meant that it was fought on several fronts, in a concerted attempt to remove the English from the land.

As it would notably include what is known as the Great Swamp Massacre of the Narragansett Indians in April 1676, now is an ideal time to give some further background information regarding them, before we proceed.

The Narragansett

Because of their isolation in the Narragansett Bay and Island area of New England, the Narragansett appear to have survived the epidemics of diseases (in 1614, and 1620) that laid waste to other tribes across the New England and Canadian Maritimes, due to their contact with European traders. That meant that they became one of the major tribes in the whole of New England making it possible for them to bring some of the smaller tribal groups such as the Wampanoag into submission and exact tribute from them.

As I mentioned earlier, the arrival of the Puritans in 1620 was an attractive contributing factor in causing the Wampanoag to form an alliance with them. It would have been seen by Canonicus (chief sachem of the Narragansett) as a challenge to his authority in the region and led to a period when each side tested each other out. It took the distraction of war breaking out between the Pequot and Mohawk to divert the Narragansett attention away from the Puritans, who continued to consolidate their positions in Plymouth and Massachusetts.

Towards the end of 1636, the relationship between them, the Puritans and the Western Niantic (allies with the Pequot) broke down after they had seized a trading ship off Block Island. That resulted in English reprisal attacks, not only on the Niantic but also on the Pequot in eastern Connecticut. The Pequot tried, without success, to bring the Narragansett into an alliance with them. For what appears to have been strategic reasons, the Narragansett decided to ally themselves with the English, giving them warning of any intended Pequot reprisals. That became a major factor in enabling the English to gain the upper hand at Fort Mystic and the ultimate suppression of any further Pequot resistance following the Treaty of Hartford in 1638.

The power struggles continue

With the demise of the Pequot, there was yet again a disturbance in the balance of power in the region, this time between the Mohegan and a now renewed dominance of the Narragansett. When the Mohegan, under the leadership of Uncas, seized territory from smaller local tribes like the Mattabesic and exacted tribute from them, the Puritans looked upon it favorably. The Puritans were also seeking to strengthen their position by forming alliances with some of the other smaller tribal groups, e.g., the Pocumtuc and Tunxis. To prevent the Narragansett from going to war against the Mohegan, the Puritans coerced them into signing a treaty, stipulating that they wouldn't do so without first consulting the Puritans.

—ooo0ooo—

The Wappinger War (1643-1645)

Irrespective of the treaty, Miantonomo[21], a Narragansett chief, went ahead with plans to enlist other tribes to stand with him against the Mohegan. Along with one hundred of his warriors, he attended councils with the Mattabesic in western Connecticut; the Metoac on Long Island; the Mahican and Wappinger tribes of the Hudson Valley. While such attempts did not appear to be very fruitful, he did, however, succeed in alarming the already edgy Dutch in New Netherlands who were facing growing hostilities in the lower Hudson River region. The Dutch totally misinterpreted Miantonomo's intentions, thinking that a general Indian uprising was being planned. After making their thoughts known to the Massachusetts and Connecticut colonies, the Dutch followed through with an early morning pre-emptive attack on a Wappinger village (referred to as the Pavonia Massacre in which approximately 100 men, women, and children were brutally murdered), hence starting the Wappinger War.

With this increase in tension throughout New England the Massachusetts Bay, Plymouth, Hartford, and New Haven colonies made a defensive alliance with each other. The Rhode Islanders (along with the Narragansett who also lived there), were deliberately excluded because of an internal dispute the Puritans had with one of their members, Roger Williams. A few years earlier, he had publicly challenged the Crown's right to have ownership of Native lands, and as a result, he was banished as a dangerous radical. He went on to procure land from the Indians and lived among them, to develop a solid mutual friendship.

In 1644, the Wappinger War had spread to include nearly 20 tribes. The Dutch found themselves very close to being overwhelmed and turned to the English colonists in Connecticut for help. They responded favorably to a Dutch offer of 25,000 guilders, by providing, under Captain John Underhill's leadership, two companies of soldiers and some Mohegan Scouts, to help quell the uprising.

Meanwhile, Miantonomo, finding himself isolated, also made his move and without consulting the English—who were certain to warn the Mohegan—led 900 of his warriors in a surprise attack on the Mohegan capital of Shetucket. Had it not been for the capture of Miantonomo by the Mohegan they would have most certainly been defeated, but with the loss of their sachem the Narragansett became confused and retreated.

Uncas (the Mohegan sachem) delivered his high-profile prisoner to the English at Hartford, who then secured him in jail while awaiting trial by a panel of five clergymen. Having found him guilty, they recommended that he should be executed and chose that Uncas should be his executioner. Miantonomo was taken to the scene of his defeat where he was tomahawked by Wawequa, the brother of Uncas. This action brought an end to the Narragansett's power in southern New England, and for what was a violation of the treaty, they were also forced to pay an annual tribute of wampum to the Massachusetts Colony.

The New England Confederacy (1643-1684)

Following the Pequot War of 1637, a few of the Puritan New England colonies (Massachusetts Bay, Plymouth, New Haven, and Connecticut) began to look at the possibility of forming a defensive alliance. Not only for protecting themselves from any future attacks by local Indian tribes, as was the case in the defeat of the Wampanoag during the King Philip's War (see below), but also as a means of

146

dealing with any threats coming from the Dutch or the French. It would also have served as a mechanism for sorting out any internal boundary issues and for the returning of fugitives or runaway slaves.

In spite of the wording of the second article of the Articles of Confederation of the United Colonies of New England...

> "The said United Colonies for themselves and their posterities do jointly and severally hereby enter into a firm and perpetual league of friendship and amity for offence and defence, mutual advice and succor upon all just occasions both <u>for preserving and propagating the truth and liberties of the Gospel</u> and for their own mutual safety and welfare." (underlining – *mine*)[22]

... it soon became apparent that it lacked something of true Christian charity. This was a rather weak and elite Puritan club that excluded colonies were most of the settlers were Anglican, who not surprisingly didn't endorse it. From a colonial perspective, a sense of a collective identity was developing, something distinctly separate from being subjects of the British Crown and Parliament.

—ooo0ooo—

The Wampanoags and King Philip's War (June 1675-1676)

Moving forward to 1662 we find that Metacom (also known as King Philip or Metacomet) became the Chief of the Wampanoag Confederacy following the deaths of his father Massasoit (1661) and his older brother Wamsutta (under what was considered as suspicious circumstances). He believed that the English were not only taking their land but also that their missionaries - seeking to convert his people to Christianity - were subverting the traditions and authority of the Wampanoag sachems. Regarding the issue of land, Roger Williams would have agreed with Metacom, when he stated in 1664, "God Land will be (as it now is) as great a God with us English as God Gold was with the Spaniards."[23] Other tribes would also have been in agreement with Metacom's perspective, which meant that he easily found allies as he covertly prepared for a concerted revolt.

The balance of power in the region was also radically shifting, with the population of New England Colonies swelling to 80,000 people, living in 110 towns. Many of these were strongly garrisoned for defensive purposes, with other smaller settlements being stockaded. That included 16,000 men, who with their own weapons had been given a minimum training to serve in a militia. Some of the Indians, primarily the Mohegan's and the Praying Indians, allied themselves with the English, providing what was thought to be about 200 warriors.

On the other hand, the Native American population in the region had, primarily because of diseases, decreased to approximately 11,000, comprising off: 5,000 Narragansett (western Rhode Island and eastern Connecticut); 2,400 Nipmuck (central and western Massachusetts); 2,400 combined Massachusett and Pawtucket (Massachusetts Bay extending northwest to Maine) and 1000 Wampanoag and Pokanoket (Plymouth and eastern Rhode Island). Approximately a quarter of these would have been classified as warriors, mostly equipped with steel knives, tomahawks, and flintlock muskets.

Through a network of informers, the English, very aware that something was about to happen, had summoned Philip on several occasions to give an account of his actions and for him to sign treaties of peace and friendship. Having done so, he then left to resume with his plotting. By 1674 New England's colonists outnumbered the natives two to one, and Philip was acutely aware that he needed to bring the Narragansett's on board if there was to be any chance of success.

The uprising, being originally planned for the summer of 1676, was brought forward to January 1675 because of the murder of John Sassamon, a Native American Christian convert (a "Praying Indian") who acted as an advisor and translator for Prince Philip. He is thought to have been killed for forewarning the English of a pending attack, which led to the arrest, conviction, and hanging of three Wampanoag Indians. Some of the Wampanoag's believed this to be an infringement of their sovereignty, and with Philip no longer being able to restrain them, the Wampanoag warriors attacked Swansea, Massachusetts, thus starting the King Philip's War.[24]

The Narragansett were forced into signing yet another treaty with the English, in which they agreed to remain neutral. With fighting going on all around them, the Narragansett came together for their own protection into a large fortified village in a swamp near Kingston, Rhode Island.

Throughout that summer, Philip was able to elude the English soldiers and yet successfully attack at will many of the outlying homesteads and settlements throughout New England. In total, twelve regional towns were destroyed; the colony's economy almost collapsed, and one-tenth of all men of military service age were killed. To protect his tribe's women and children, Philip brought them to the Narragansett fortification, returning in the late fall of 1675, to take most of them with him to western Massachusetts.

English slaughter of Narragansett–The Great Swamp Fight

In December, the English, having considered that the Narragansett had violated their treaty with them, sent a colonial army of 1,000 men along with 150 Mohegan scouts to lay siege on the Narragansett fort. When Canonchet refused to either surrender any Wampanoags he was protecting in his village or to join them in their fight against Philip, the English attacked. The Narragansett were heavily defeated in this battle, known as the Great Swamp Fight, in which they lost more than 20 sachems and 600 warriors.

Canonchet, however, managed to escape and with a large group of Narragansett joined Philip in western Massachusetts to fight alongside him for the rest of the war. He was to play a significant role in it: beginning in February, he led several attacks against English settlements in the Connecticut River Valley, followed in March by an ambush which almost wiped out Captain Wadsworth's military unit. Shortly after that, yet another ambush saw at least 70 English killed. As Spring approached, two pressing issues arose: food supplies began to run out making hunger a greater enemy than the English soldiers, and Philip's people needed seed corn for planting. It was Canonchet who took up the challenge of returning to Rhode Island to bring back a supply from a secret Narragansett cache, only to be captured by the Mohegan on the return journey. He was then handed over to the English who executed him by firing squad.

Such a loss seems to have had a profound affected on Philip and his allies, who began to desert. He was eventually tracked down by a group of colonial militia and Native American allies. After being shot he was beheaded, drawn and quartered—his head was then taken to Plymouth where it was displayed for the next twenty years. Bar a few isolated skirmishes; the war rapidly came to an end.

The aftermath
It has been estimated that more than 40% of the Native Americans, i.e., approx. 5,000 and 5% of the English colonist, i.e., 2,500 were killed. Because the English population continued to increase through births and immigration, such losses were not as crucial to their future as they would have been for the future of the remaining Native Tribes in the region.

For the Narragansett: After the Great Swamp Fight and the death of Canonchet, it is thought that approximately 3,000 Narragansett women, children, and old people were left defenseless and without adequate food or shelter. They were to be ruthlessly hunted down, with many of them either succumbing to starvation or deliberate massacre. Of those who were captured, the warriors were mostly executed, while an estimated 500 women and children were shipped from Plymouth as slaves to the West Indies, during 1676!

By 1682 there were approximately 500 left to sign a peace treaty with the English. They were also given permission to join the Eastern Niantic, who had remained neutral throughout the war, on their small reservation near Charleston, Rhode Island.

For the Wampanoag: Following the death of Philip, along with most of the leadership, the tribe, now only 400 strong, was close to extinction. Of those taken captive, the men were mostly sold into slavery and ended up in the West Indies, while most of the women and children ended up as slaves to the New England colonists with the remainder being sent to some of the Praying Towns. There were, however, some coastal and island groups of Wampanoag who remained neutral throughout the war. They were treated in a more amenable manner: some were also placed in Praying Towns, and others were allotted lands on a reservation at Cape Cod, where they had self-governance based on an English styled Court and Legal system.[25]

And the Colonists: they were to pay heavily for winning the war by accruing an enormous tax burden, due to the material support they had and were to continue to have from England. They were, despite the decline in the Native American population, never completely free from Indian attacks. Five of the Indian tribes in the Acadia region (part of eastern Quebec along with the Maritime provinces and Maine up to the Kennebec River) formed the Wabanaki Confederacy and entered a political and military alliance with the French. Similar Indian/French alliances would become part of a widening conflict along the whole length of the English colonies western front. Over the next 100 years many frontiers people, including the Scotch-Irish, were to die at their hands during what became known as the French and Indian Wars (1754-1763).

Overall, these last three chapters have not made for good reading. Many negative seeds were sown with a lot of painful fruits ensuing for everyone concerned. The people entity known as the Puritans, with their high spiritual ideals, gradually got compromised and would eventually get absorbed into the broader influx of people coming to New England. Sadly, the Native American tribes experienced the full force of British empire expansion and elements of Christianity that were very unchristian! The legacy still lives on!

We now move on, into Chapter 11, where we begin to look at the development of that people group called the Scotch-Irish and the role they were to play on the western fringes of the colonies leading up to and immediately after the Revolution years in North America.

References:

1. "Although the Netherlands only controlled the Hudson River Valley from 1609 until 1664, in that short time, Dutch entrepreneurs established New Netherland, a series of trading posts, towns, and forts up and down the Hudson River—towns that still exist today."
    Source: http://www.nps.gov/nr/travel/kingston/colonization.htm

History: "In 1602, the government of the Republic of the Seven United Netherlands chartered the Dutch East India Company (*Vereenigde Oostindische Compagnie*), or VOC with the mission of exploring it for a passage to the Indies and claiming any uncharted areas for the United Provinces." During a further voyage "in 1609, the VOC commissioned English explorer Henry Hudson who, in an attempt to find the so-called northwest passage to the Indies, discovered and claimed for the VOC parts of the present-day United States and Canada. In the belief that it was the best route to explore, Hudson entered the Upper New York Bay sailing up the river, which now bears his name."

"In 1614, Adriaen Block led an expedition to the lower Hudson... and then explored the East River... becoming the first known European to... enter Long Island Sound. Block Island and its sound were named after him. Upon returning, Block compiled a map, the first to apply the name 'New Netherland' to the area between English Virginia and French Canada, where he was later granted exclusive trading rights by the Dutch government."

The following year "the first Dutch settlement in the Americas was founded: Fort Nassau, on Castle Island in the Hudson, near present-day Albany. The settlement served mostly as a centre for fur trade with the natives and was later replaced by Fort Orange. Both forts were named in honor of the House of Orange-Nassau."

"In 1621, a new company was established with a trading monopoly in the Americas and West Africa: the Dutch West India

Company (*Westindische Compagnie* or WIC)." Its status as a province was granted in 1623 and three years later Peter Minuit, the Director of the WIC, "purchased the island of Manhattan from the Lenape and started the construction of Fort Amsterdam, which grew to become the main port and capital, New Amsterdam."

"On the Connecticut River, Fort Huys de Goede Hoop was completed in 1633 at present-day Hartford. By 1636, the English from Newtown (now Cambridge, Massachusetts) settled on the north side of the Little River. In the Treaty of Hartford, the border of New Netherland was retracted to western Connecticut, and by 1653, the English had overtaken the Dutch trading post."

"In 1664, the English naval expedition ordered by the Duke of York and Albany (later James II of England) sailed into the harbor at New Amsterdam, threatening to attack. Being greatly outnumbered, Director-General Peter Stuyvesant surrendered... the province was renamed New York (from James's English title). Fort Orange was renamed Fort Albany (from James's Scottish title)."

Source:
http://en.wikipedia.org/wiki/Dutch_colonization_of_the_Americ as

2. Source: http://worldhistoryproject.org/1634/john-stone-is-killed-by-western-niantic-in-retaliation-for-atrocities-he-committed-against-native-americans

3. Source: http://www.claytoncramer.com/unpublished/pequot.htm quoting from John Winthrop, *"The History of New England From 1630 to 1649."* (Boston: Phelps and Farnham, 1825; reprinted Salem, N. H.: Ayer Co., 1992), 1:104, 1:111.

4. The memoir of Capt. Roger Clapp of Dorchester 1630-1680. www.stonefamilyassociation.org/index.php?pr=John_Of_Virginia

5. Francis Jennings, *"The Invasion of America-Indians, Colonialism and the Cant of Conquest."* ((Pub. Norton Library with the University of North Carolina Press, 1976)), Pg. 190.

6. Ibid. Pg. 202.

7. Alden T. Vaughan, *"New England Frontier, Puritans and Indians 1620-1675."* 3rd Edition, University of Oklahoma Press, 1995. Pg. 126. Also, Winthrop Papers III, Pgs. 270-72.
8. Major Mason's *"Brief History of the Pequot War."* (University of Nebraska-Lincoln, Ed. Paul Royster, http://digitalcommons.unl.edu/cgi/viewcontent.cgi?article=1042 &context=etas. Pg. 24. Notes iv.12, 1635 … Capt. Oldham
9. Winthrop, *Journal, I*. Pgs. 186-187.
10. Source: https://en.wikipedia.org/wiki/Block_Island
11. Ibid.
12. Vaughan. Pg. 143; Major Mason, *"Brief History of the Pequot War."* Pgs. 134-135.
13. Ibid. Pgs. 8-14.
14. Vaughan. Pg. 145; Underhill, *"News from America."* Pg. 25.
15. Mason. Pg. 20. Also in, *"Reasoning Together: The Native Critics Collective."* **Edited by Craig S. Womack, Daniel Heath** Justice, Christopher B. Teuton, University of Oklahoma, 2008, Pg. 155.
16. Quoted in http://www.pequotwar.com/history.html
17. Ibid.
18. Vaughan. Pgs. 152-153.
19. Mason. Pg. 20
20. Source: http://www.rapidnet.com/~jbeard/bdm/Psychology/amr/puritan.htm
21. Source: https://en.wikisource.org/wiki/1911_Encyclopædia_Britannica/Miantonomo
22. Source: http://www.let.rug.nl/usa/documents/1600-1650/new-england-articles-of-confederation-1643.php
23. Vaughan. Pg. 311.
24. Source: https://en.wikipedia.org/wiki/King_Philips_War
25. Source: https://en.wikipedia.org/wiki/Wampanoag_people

Chapter 11

The Making of The Scotch-Irish

Introduction

We now move on to the other part of my tribal identity—the Ulster-Scots. I want, over the next few chapters, to develop it like another thread in the tapestry of what eventually became the United States of America. Once again it means details and dates to anchor it into a historical context. Again, I feel it is so important for us to understand something about what shaped them before their journey to America; what made them into the pioneering people living on the western fringes of the Colonies, before and immediately after the War of Independence.

Like the Puritans, the Scots-Irish did not arrive in America as a neutral body of people. They had a history; a deeply traumatic relationship with the English which was shaped both in Scotland and Ireland. There was a lot that was good but yet again, there was also much which gave Satan the footholds that he was looking for, to hinder God's fullest purposes being expressed through them.

Growing up in Northern Ireland, the name "Ulster-Scot" has been used to describe people of Scottish/Borders descent who crossed over the narrow stretch of water from Scotland to the northern Irish province called Ulster, during what became known as the "Ulster Plantation" which started in 1609. The term "Scotch-Irish" is the Americanization of it, used to describe people from within that group who made the additional hop from Ulster to North America to become part of the early colonization process. It has sometimes wrongly included people who went directly from Scotland to America. The first known record of the term in America is found in a written report in June 1695, by the Secretary of Maryland, Sir Thomas Laurence[1] In it he observed: "In the two counties of Dorchester and Somerset, where the Scotch-Irish are numerous, they clothe themselves by their linen and woolen manufactures."

It has also been suggested that the term "Scotch-Irish" was not in a more common usage until after the mass immigration of Catholic-Irish following the potato famine in 1845, with the Protestant Irish Americans using it to make a defining distinction between themselves and the Catholic emigrants. For many Scotch-Irish, Scotland was never a land that they had been to, and so their loyalties were clearly in Ulster the land of their birth. Others from the north England border area, who have been included in the term "Scotch-Irish," preferred the term "Anglo-Irish." Those who migrated directly to America from Scotland saw themselves primarily as Presbyterians of Scottish extraction.

The Scotch-Irish were of two social classes—the majority were poor, mostly tenant farmers, who went to America to become indentured servants. The remainder, the middle classes, were not only able to pay their passage but also purchase land in America. It was from among them that leadership in the farming communities would initially emerge.

By the time of the American War of Independence, it is reckoned that one out of every ten to fifteen people in the thirteen colonies were Scotch-Irish. Following the Revolution, they would also be among the first to cross the Alleghenies into the interior and yet by the early 1800s they were hardly recognizable as a people group outside of Pennsylvania and Virginia, as they intermarried with other ethnic groupings from around Europe.

Both at home in Ulster among the Protestant community and in the United States, we have tended to over-romanticize these ancestors. On both sides of the Atlantic, there are many local historical societies which extoll our forefathers as the paragons of virtue and the bringers of everything that is best to America. We can recite the names of Presidents that have their roots in Ulster, including Andrew Jackson, James Knox Polk, Ulysses S. Grant, Theodore Roosevelt, Woodrow Wilson, not to mention a string of others in the entertainment, literary, sporting and political worlds. While there is nothing wrong in acknowledging these things, I have become increasingly aware that there is a poverty in our knowledge and understanding of this group of people we call the Scotch-Irish.

Some of our good was truly very good, but some was perceived as good only because it was seen through the lens of our cultural blinkers, with our "rose-tinted spectacles" on. Unfortunately, some, as I have been finding out was horrendous. As I have already mentioned, because this is primarily a book on reconciliation, about healing the ancient wounds, it necessitates that I look at the later. Bearing in mind that God is for us—all of us—and because of that, He desires to purify and redeem all our cultures, our "ethnos." In doing so, the result, as of any of reconciliation process, is one of enhancing all that is truly good, truly of Him. It is not about culture bashing!

In this short chapter, I am aware that it is not possible for this to be a comprehensive study. At best, I can but give an overview, drawing attention to a few things that have been highlighted in my spirit as I have researched. What I am after here is to gain a sense of my ancestral roots, an insight into what gave them the character, the drive to pioneer; settle in a new land and cause them to stand against their Quaker hosts, the Native Americans on the frontier and against the English in the War of Independence.

In my research for this chapter, I have greatly appreciated the work of James C. Leyburn in his book, *"The Scotch-Irish, A Social History,"* as he sought to put "flesh and bones" unto the historical details.

As Leyburn says in his Introduction:

> "The starting point of the social history of the Scotch-Irish is in Scotland, long before the name 'Scotch-Irish' was known. Many of the characteristics this people were to show had come into being by the slow process of life in an indefinable part of Scotland in which the qualities of mind, their attitudes, and their loyalties were being shaped by their way of life in the Lowlands and by the manner in which Scottish events impinged upon them."[2]

Pre-Reformation Scotland

Like Ireland, Christianity in Scotland had been Celtic rather than Roman in its formation, but with a succession of wars between Norse Vikings, Britons, Angles and Normans and a lack of strong leadership, the Church suffered. When King David came to the throne (1124-1153) he encouraged the development of the Roman Church, so bishoprics were formed; land was given; monasteries were established, and the old rule of the Celtic, Gaelic-speaking Church was suppressed, just as it was in Ireland.

While this may have given the Roman Church in Scotland a strong institutional power base, it, unfortunately, didn't transfer itself in any significant way into meeting the pastoral needs of the people. By the mid-1500s it had accrued more than one-third of the land and half of the wealth in Scotland.[3] According to Hilaire Belloc, an Anglo-French writer, historian and apologist of the Catholic Church, it had become a corrupt Church. While this may have been the case throughout Europe during the 1600s, it was at its worst in Scotland.[4]

Its clergy were few and well-scattered, with only the most senior clergy having any level of formal University education. With the educational establishments under Church control, it meant that most of the people were illiterate.

That was truly a very different Scotland than the one we know today:

1. The population was thinly spread out over a wide geographical area
2. It was suffering from great economic impoverishment
3. Housing and agricultural methods certainly did not improve the further north you went into the Highlands
4. Society was violent
5. There were practical difficulties in building parish churches
6. Being on the outer fringes of Christendom also meant that it was devoid of the influences of spiritual movements which national scholars or saints had at times provided in other parts of the Church in Medieval Europe

7. Any centralizing influences of Rome were therefore minimal, which the King along with the noblemen used to their political ends
8. In the Lowlands—the land south of present-day Edinburgh and Glasgow, down to the border with England—things were in place for some turbulent changes to take place.

It is worth noting here that the Highlanders do not have any significant place in this story. They would make their own way to America in the 1740s.

Scotland's population was approximately 500,000 people, with most of them living in the Lowlands and except for Edinburgh, there were no towns of any appreciable size. While the best agricultural land would be found there, it was generally badly managed with its open fields and no hedges or walls to define each farm; straying animals; crops trampled on by cattle, etc., which resulted in constant feuding among families, leading only to further social and economic uncertainty. There was also the constant threat of English invasion!

A major underlying problem lay in the fact that from the time of Robert the Bruce (d. 1329) there had been no king strong enough to rule over all the people and provide the ingredients for such unity and stability for law and order to develop. No trained army, police force, civil servants or strong national government. Each nobleman was still very much a feudal Lord, a law unto himself, who saw themselves as equals to any king. The further north you went, things looked worse— in the Highlands, there was a complete absence of any social class structure. Each Clan was very much a family grouping with its leader taking on something of a "father" role. Leyburn makes the observation: "It is the judgment of historians that nation-states could only emerge after feudalism had broken down, for the essence of the feudal system is local loyalty."[5] It was only after Queen Elizabeth I's death in 1603, and James VI of Scotland also becomes James I of England that the Lowlands and English border areas knew a measure of peace and the feudal system was challenged.

Yet, it would be the combination of all these factors that would produce the necessary incentive in 1609 for thousands of Scottish

Protestants to make the break and head for the north of Ireland under King James I's plantation of Ulster scheme. By doing this, they hoped to not only improve their lot there[6] but also civilize and hence quell the rebellious Irish! Interestingly, it was also during his reign that the British colonization of America began in earnest.

The Reformation reaches Scotland

Through the influence of the wider European Protestant Reformation and men like John Calvin (which had started nearly 40 years earlier), John Knox was instrumental in it coming to Scotland. With it, eventually came the birth of the Presbyterian, Church of Scotland. While education remained under its control, there was one key difference—it was fanatical in its desire to have a school in every parish. In the larger towns, schools that taught grammar were established, as they were looking for boys to send to university. They clearly had one purpose in mind, that of developing a growing body of highly educated clergy, who would become the dominant figures to change and shape Scottish society.

That was to have far-reaching consequences not only for Scotland and its relationship with England but also for Ireland and eventually America, as Leyburn records:

> "At the time of the migration to Ulster, Scotland (at least the Lowland part of that country, and especially the south-western region of the Lowlands) was at fierce heat with religious zeal. Because religion was a primary reason for a considerable part of the migration to Ulster, because it gave to the people of the north of Ireland a character they have never lost (one still considered a divisive force in Ireland), and because the fervor was still alive when the Ulster Scots came on the American colonies, it is important to have a reasonably full understanding of religion in Scotland."[7] (underlining – *mine*)

It was men like John Knox and his fellow preachers George Wishart and Andrew Melville, who provided the thrust necessary for such a profound spiritual awakening to erupt. But it should be noted that significant political changes taking place in Britain also had their part to play. "... [O]ne is driven to conclude," writes Leyburn, "that the Reformation would not have come to Scotland when it did except for the noblemen; and further, that the Scottish Reformation actually began as a political movement with economic overtones."

It appears that a few sincere Protestants motivated by the highest interest of religion indicated to the Lords a direction in which they might go and that the low condition to which the Catholic Church had fallen, provided the fertile soil for the Protestant seed. But the transformation of Reform into a movement that touched the people, winning their hearts, engaging their minds, and commanding their fervent loyalty, began to occur after the politicians had already done their work."[8] This mix of religion and politics is a potent one that is still being played out in Northern Ireland today!

As far back as James V of Scotland (1513-1542), his uncle Henry VIII had suggested mirroring his approach of seizing Church property as a means of increasing the exchequer. But due to his relationship with the Catholic Church, James did not follow suit. It would take his Catholic daughter Mary Queen of Scots' turbulent reign to thrust political minded Protestants to the fore following Protestant Elizabeth I's enthronement in England. It has been mooted, in the light of changes in England, which included growth in population, industry, trade, wealth, etc., that it was time for Scotland to change her centuries-old alliance with Catholic France and align herself with her immediate neighbor, Protestant England. To do otherwise was to perpetuate the ongoing cycle of deprivation and conquest and yet in the light of the ancient animosities between Scotland and England, this was a tall order!

Another explosive ingredient was the growing discontentment in Scotland's upper classes with the Catholic hierarchy which came to a head on New Year's Day, 1559. A document known as the Beggar's Summons was posted on the gates of every Catholic religious establishment in Scotland. Though written in a very scholarly way, it reflected the thoughts of many of the ordinary people of the land.

Speaking for "The blind, crooked, lame, widows, **orphans**," the Summons continues:

> "... we wish restitution of wrongs past and reformation in times coming... we have thought good, therefore, ere we enter into conflict with you to warn you in the name of the great God by this public writing affixed on your gates where ye now dwell that ye move forth of our said hospitals, betwixt this and the feast of Whit—Sunday next, so that the lawful proprietors thereof may enter thereto, and afterward enjoy the commodities of the Church which ye have heretofore wrongfully holden from us: certifying you if ye fail, we will at the said term, in whole number and with the help of God and assistance of his saints on earth, of whose ready support we doubt not, enter and take possession of our said patrimony, and eject you utterly forth of the same..."[9]

Strong, fighting words!

It was around this time that John Knox came to the fore. Leyburn sums him up:

> "This dour, passionate, devout, but remorseless Reformer was precisely the leader needed for the Protestant movement. He was a man of the people who had fought Cardinal Beaton, suffered imprisonment for his faith, rowed as a galley slave for the French to whom he had been turned over, and become a friend and colleague of John Calvin in Geneva. To him, the Roman Church was the instrument of the devil, while Reform was the will of God."[10]

What exactly happened is not very clear, but in 1559, following the preaching of a fiery sermon in the Parish Church in Perth, something triggered a riot. The outcome was the destruction of all of its statues, followed by a trail of similar destruction in other places of worship throughout the town.

Mary, who was still the Queen of Scotland at the time, responded by sending in the French army to quell any uprising, only to be met by the Protestants raising up their own army and sending an invitation to Elizabeth I to give them support. Mary was to die before the Treaty of Leith (July 6th, 1560), which saw the French troops leaving Scotland. Four days later Parliament met to pass three Acts, ending the Catholic Church's status of being the national church in Scotland: thereby no longer recognizing the authority of the Pope; condemning all practices and doctrines that were not deemed Protestant and forbidding the saying of the Mass. They also asked the Protestant clergy to draw up a statement of doctrine for the newly established Presbyterian Kirk in Scotland, known as the First Book of Discipline. Remarkably, because they were so ripe for such a radical change as this, most Scottish people appeared to embrace it with ease.

There was nothing comely about much of the religion they championed. Leyburn describes it as,

> "Hebraic and Old Testament in its emphasis, stressing the thou-shalt-nots and the denunciation of sin. It was not a religion of kindness to one's fellows or of gentle manners. Scots, like their fellow-Calvinist contemporaries of the seventeenth century, the Boers of South Africa, regarded themselves as a chosen people, elect of God, and their God as an awful Majesty, given to revenge upon His enemies... It is hopeless to search the records of the Kirk for any signs of a tolerant spirit in these early days—it permitted no dissidents. Scots, like every other people in Western Europe, seemed unable to imagine the existence of one form of public worship unless all others were prohibited. At its inception, the Reformation had seemed to be a call for liberty of mind and of worship; as it developed, the newly established churches became as tyrannical as the ones they replaced."[11]

Like the Boers, the Scots were to further empower their Protestant identity through Covenants: The National Covenant of 1638 and the Solemn League and Covenant in 1643. For me, this was clearly a wrong use of covenants! It had been a means of using God to strongly validate your own power and control games. That is not the Spirit of Christ but rather a sectarian and racist spirit! It is not the way of seeking first God's Kingdom! It had all the hallmarks of the 'empire spirit' traversing across the Reformation, from Catholicism into Protestantism.

There is one more important issue worth flagging up, that flows out of this. When Henry VIII broke England's ties with the Roman Catholic Church, he assumed headship over the new Anglican Church of England. And when the Reformation came to Scotland, and the Presbyterian Church was born, a point of conflict was on the horizon. With the Union of the Crown in 1603, James VI of Scotland also became James I of England. He wanted to be head of both Churches, but the governmental structure of Presbyterianism would not embrace that. Their Covenants not only gave them a national sense of their uniqueness with God but also empowered them to resist militarily any actions by James to bring them into line. Such attempts at domination would play a significant part in reinforcing future actions by the Scots against England. Not only as England sought to impose itself on them in Ireland (leading to immigration to America) but also in America as the Scotch-Irish took a stand with Washington in the War of Independence. The "Spirit of Empire" was alive and well!

We are now ready to embark on the next leg of our journey as we cross the narrow stretch of water called the Irish Sea to the province of Ulster in northeast Ireland.

References:

1. James C. Leyburn, *"The Scotch-Irish: A Social History."* (The University of North Carolina Press, 1962), Appendices, Pgs. 328-329.
2. Ibid. Pg. xviii.
3. Ibid. Pg. 48.
4. Noted in I. M. M. McPhail's review of *"Source Book of Scottish History."* Scottish Historical Review, XXXIII (1954), Pgs. 33, 166.
5. Leyburn, Pg. 14.

6.   Ibid, Pgs. 27 & 29.
7.   Ibid, Pg. 47.
8.   Ibid, Pg. 52.
9.   D. Calderwood, *"History of the Kirk in Scotland."* (Edinburgh, 1842-1849), I, Pgs. 423-424.
10. Leyburn, Pg. 54.
11. Ibid, Pgs. 58-59.

Chapter 12

The Scottish Presbyterians and English in Ireland

Off to Ireland

As you have seen, living on the outer edge of Europe, the Scots were a tough breed! One word has been used to sum them up, a good Scottish one - "dour!" A word derived from Latin to denote an iron-like hardness and durability in character, with an element of stubbornness thrown in! Even their national motto, *Nemo me impune lacessit*: no one attacks me with impunity, is not out of place! Add to that a newly experienced deep religious conviction and zeal; a strong Old Testament-like understanding of God, covenant and land and no love lost regarding the English crown and parliament or the Roman Catholic Church. For such a self-reliant people, even the Presbyterian teaching on predestination suited them, as they religiously sought to live out every aspect of their lives to show God that they were truly His elect.

These were the people who, in 1606, set sail across that narrow stretch of water, which separated them from the north of Ireland. It was a land not so dissimilar in many ways to their own and one that their forefathers had crisscrossed many times over the centuries. There were at least 40,000 of them in the first thirty years. They brought a very clear understanding of how they believed society worked: God had pre-ordered the different social classes and which one you were born into predetermined your status within society; there was a well-defined role for both sexes and the influence of a collective community pressure, with its familiar and traditional ways and values.

One's family ties were also very strong, they were your kin, and among them, you felt secure, everyone knew their place and the part they played. This sense of kinship was also important when it came to defending their rights, and if it went to a fight, issues of allegiance and loyalty were not questioned. It is interesting to note that in the years before the Reformation the Catholic clergy in Scotland did not experience such commitment from the people, while the ministers of the Presbyterian Church did.

The pressure is on

Throughout the whole period of the reign of the Stuarts (1603-1714), the Reformed Kirk of Scotland was to experience quite a "rough ride." As I mentioned in the previous chapter, James I of England (VI of Scotland) sought to enforce religious conformity within his two realms. While he was happy enough that Scotland was Protestant, he had concerns that the governing body of the Presbyterian Church— the General Assembly—might use its power to undermine him. To ensure that this could not happen he wanted them to retain the same type of hierarchical structure, including Bishops, which would bring them under the wider umbrella of the Anglican Church.

His regent in Scotland, the Earl of Morton, attempted unsuccessfully to implement this, no thanks to Andrew Melville, principal of the universities of Glasgow and St. Andrews. He published a Book of Disciplines for the Presbyterian Church, which stipulated that all its ministers were equal and that there should be a separation of church and state. Church government, he said, was something ordained by God with the King as God's temporal servant, subordinate to it. Nothing that James sought to do to counter this was effective, on the contrary, it only reinforced Scottish defiance.

His son, Charles I (ruled 1625-1649), only seemed to exacerbate the situation by further alienating not only the Kirk but also the noblemen and the bulk of the population. Everything was to reach a boiling point in 1636 when he sought to replace Knox's Order of Service with High-Church Anglican ones: The Book of Canons and The Scottish Prayer Book.

To quote from my book, "Heal Not Lightly:"

> "For many Scots, the writing was now on the wall for their Church. The piecemeal reform of religion in Scotland by James and Charles, now seemed to a great

many Scots, and not just a few fanatics, to be leading inexorably back to Catholicism. The response was the National Covenant of 1638... [Covenant] ideas heightened the nationalistic element present in the Church in Scotland, particularly in those inclined to Presbyterianism. For them Scotland was a chosen nation, the Scots an elect people with a great role to play in God's dispensation... Some idea of what the Covenant meant to so many ordinary folk in Scotland is conveyed in the words of John Fleming, Session Clerk of the parish of Galston, Ayrshire: 'In thankful remembrance of the singular mercie of God who was pleased to receave this land into covenant with himself, more formallie than any other people we hear of since the rejecting of his old people the Jews... Signing the Covenant, symbolized Scotland's coming home to God and being received into His special favour, was a highly emotional occasion."[1]

Charles II came to the throne in 1660, and despite promises to the contrary, he sought to remove all ministers from the pulpit who would not embrace Anglicanism. He also forbade public gatherings for worship or groups to meet in homes. That was resisted fiercely by a number of the more radical Covenanters, who armed themselves to fight against the Crown forces. Many ended up either getting imprisoned or hung, but nothing appeared to abate their zeal. Those of a less zealous nature became part of a wave of migration to embrace the more relative peace in Ulster, where they were to become the most dominant expression of Protestantism in six out of the Ulster's nine counties.

This crucial issue of church government continued throughout the reign of Catholic James II until he was deposed in the Bloodless Revolution of 1689, which brought the Dutch, William III of Orange to the throne. He gave the Scots the freedom they were looking for, and the Presbyterian Kirk was firmly established as the Church of Scotland.

The English in Ireland

That must also be put within the context of England's direct involvement in Ireland, where it was seeking to find a solution to its age-old relational conflicts there. So, let's retrace our steps a little to have a look at what eventually brought about the Plantation of Ulster from 1606 for the next century.

Like Scotland, Ireland had known many attempts by the English to subdue it. Ever since the time of Henry II in the mid-twelfth century, successive military campaigns had failed. That was mostly due to a mixture of sheer resistance from the natives and the assimilation that took place as families who had been given Irish land following military operations, intermarried, learned the language and embraced the culture.

By the 1550s and the reign of Elizabeth I, England had managed to secure a region around Dublin, known as the Pale, and establish a Parliament there, though not without it being a constant drain on English manpower and finances. "Beyond the Pale" the rest of Ireland resembled life in the Scottish Highlands: unruly and uncivilized. About religion, Robert Dunlop sums it up when he writes: "there was nothing worthy of being called a Church. To say that the Irish had lapsed into a state of heathenism is perhaps going too far. The tradition of a Christian belief still survived, but it was a lifeless, useless thing."[2]

When faith was eventually stirred up in Ireland, it was not through the Protestant Reformation but rather through a very successful Catholic Counter-Reformation headed up by the tireless energies of the Jesuits. They aligned themselves with the patriotic struggles of the Irish by preaching in their mother tongue; meeting their pastoral needs and instructing the children in the catechism. Clearly, a new strategy needed to be developed if the Irish were to acquiesce!

The Plantation

It came in the form of the Plantation. Elizabeth I had tried to force the native Irish off their lands and give it to the gentry, with the understanding that they would, in turn, settle the land with English people who could both work it as farmers and defend it as soldiers.

However, constant harassment from the dispossessed led to discouragement and many of them returning to England. Resistance was particularly high in Ulster, where, in 1595 the clan chieftains Tyrone and Tyrconnell successfully rallied other chiefs and their clans to rout twenty thousand professional soldiers led by Lord Lieutenant Essex. Just before her death in 1603, Elizabeth ruthlessly responded through her new appointee, Lord Mountjoy, who engaged in a program of destroying food stocks, houses, and livestock, which ultimately caused the submission of the Irish through starvation and death.

A new attempt at plantation became more feasible due to a bit of private enterprise: two Scottish Lairds from Ayrshire, Hugh Montgomery and James Hamilton, did a deal with an imprisoned Irish chieftain who owned much of counties Down and Antrim (just across the narrow strip of the Irish Sea from Scotland). When King James I came to the throne he added his blessings to it, on the condition "that the lands should be planted with British Protestants, and that no grant of fee farm should be made to any person of mere Irish extraction."[3] A combination of good inducements and a few years' good harvest in Ulster ensured a steady flow of people willing to take the risk. In fact, within eight years Montgomery and Hamilton were able to muster two thousand fighting men. Two years later it is recorded that the population had risen to approximately eight thousand people.[4]

In 1607, a series of events known as "The Flight of the Earls" led to Tyrone and Tyrconnell fleeing to Europe. The outcome of this led to much of the remaining land in Ulster becoming the property of the Crown. The success of people like Montgomery and others gave sufficient impetus for the King to engage in a massive colonization program. He allotted the land to three main groups of people:

1. Undertakers. These were lords and gentry from England and Scotland; the Church of Ireland (an expression of the Church of England there); Trinity College Dublin and war veterans. They were to establish large estates protected by castles and other fortifications to be overseen by Protestant farmers.

2. The London Companies. These were the powerful Guilds, which held a lot of governmental influence and power in England. They were also instrumental in establishing the Jamestown Plantation in Virginia and were open to developing other enterprises in Ireland such as creating the city of Londonderry.

3. Servitors. They were Protestant military men who could if necessary be utilized to squash any disturbances that might arise.

It was to be the Scots and people living on the English border with Scotland, with their geographical proximity to Ulster and generous leasing terms, that eventually became the major reason for the success of James's plantation endeavors. As Leyburn observes,

> "Despite every vicissitude, including massacres and war, the Plantation gradually grew strong and proved to be a success. If one cause more than any other can be singled out for its success, it would be the presence, the persistence, and the industry of the Scots in the region."[5]

Whereas, people coming from further south in England were required to forgo all the home comforts of a more established society to make a fresh start in the uncertainties of "savage" Ireland. A very different proposition! This dynamic was equally relevant for the Scotch-Irish going to America!

Although the Plantation of Ulster was a growing success, it nevertheless was challenged continuously on two key fronts:

1. By the Catholic people, whose land they had taken. It should have been no surprise that it did not go unchallenged which in turn kept mutual animosity on the boil. Most of the coming century saw Protestantism as the dominant religion which reflected how Ireland was ruled.

   Throughout the whole period of the plantation the native Irish people, "were to be regarded as little more than local annoyances to be subdued and controlled." Consequently, "[t]hey were summarily driven off the lands [which] they and their ancestors had farmed, however poorly, for generations, and they were to have no right to any of their institutions nor any voice in government. Even "natives of good merit" to whom a tenth of the area was to be granted, were shabbily treated... [and] the Irish gentry were made to feel that their presence was merely tolerated."[6] Rebellion was inevitably and continuously in the air!

On a website dedicated to cataloging British Civil Wars, we read: "During 1641, Irish resentment against the Protestant settlers was exacerbated by an economic recession and a poor harvest. Encouraged by the example of Scotland's defiance of the English government in 1638... disaffected Irish Catholics [started] a rebellion in defense of their interests and to recover the lands they had lost."[7]

In Ulster, "the resentment felt by the Ulster Irish against the settlers soon erupted into violence. Protestants were robbed and evicted from their lands; farms and houses were burnt, cattle stolen. The violence escalated into the widespread killing of settlers." One incident, "a notorious massacre, took place at Portadown in County Armagh in November 1641 where around 100 [Protestant] men, women, and children were thrown off the bridge to drown in the River Bann... Units of the Covenanter army were sent from Scotland to protect Protestant settlers and to extend Scottish territorial holdings... The uprising escalated into the eleven-year Confederate War that was finally ended with Oliver Cromwell's subjugation of Ireland in 1649—53."[8] (see Chapter 6)

The outcome of the massacres and individual killings on both sides only intensified the sectarian feelings, which are still very much kept alive to this day with events like the one mentioned above commemorated, onsite, each year.

Truly horrendous times! Sadly, one could as easily put the name Native American into the narrative instead of Native Irish!

2. By the Anglican Protestant Crown which did not make allowances for any religious difference—even Protestant difference!

During the second year of Queens Anne's reign (William III's sister-in-law), she gave assent to employ the Test Act of 1673, which had originally been drafted "to prevent the further growth of Popery." In itself this was not unusual within European nations: "Most statesmen of Europe at the time agreed that the best interests of the State were served by having all people worship in the same way and that this way should be that of Church established by the government... [indeed] religious wars on the Continent in the seventeenth century had been resolved on the workable principle that the people of any State were required to take on the religion of the monarch."[9] Such a desire for uniformity was just as evident under Queen Elizabeth I; in the Presbyterian Churches of Scotland and Ireland and among the Puritans of New England.

Anne's measures also hit the Presbyterian Church in Ireland hard. They included disqualifications and penalties for the practice of any form of religious worship that was not recognized by herself or the State. The only Sacraments to be recognized were to be those of the English State's, Church of England and to practice your faith in any other way, would mean disqualification from holding any form of public office.

Such legislation caused her to make enemies with a growing body of Presbyterians, known as Protestant Dissenters, as it led to their ministers being denied their pulpits and penalized for the performance of marriages, which were not solemnized by the Established Church. Such unions were "denounced as 'licenses for sin,' the children of such marriages were described as 'bastards,' and the ministers and people were brought before bishops' courts and excommunicated as 'fornicators.'"[10] They couldn't even bury their dead unless an Anglican clergyman took the funeral service.

Other knock-on effects of this included Presbyterian teachers being prohibited from teaching children about their faith, and at local government levels they could no longer hold office—10 of the 12 aldermen were removed from office in Londonderry, while in Belfast the whole Corporation was replaced. By 1716-17,

Presbyterian laity and clergy alike were seriously articulating thoughts of migration to America.

And so, America was on the cards

There had been a few attempts at migration to America before that. It took, however, a combination of their success as Planters in Ulster, along with several other factors such as economic hardship and ongoing English Parliamentary pressures to produce what is known as the Great Migration. It caused a quarter of a million Ulster men to emigrate to the American colonies from then right up to the period of the Revolutionary War. Two pressures are worthy of a mention:

1. **Taxation.** Ulster, as a "plantation," carried something of a different status than the rest of Ireland and gradually developed into something of an economic rival to England, with both the linen and woolen industries in Ulster experiencing rapid growth. As a means of protecting their industrial interests in England and Wales, Parliament's response was to pass a series of Acts. The first of these, introduced in 1661 was the Staple Act, which forbade any direct exporting of goods from Ireland to America, except for necessary provisions, horses, etc. The Woollens Act reinforced this in 1699 by stipulating that all woolen products from Ireland could only be sent to England, with another Act adding further restrictions, this time on goods coming from the colonies into Ireland. To add to that, successive years of drought in Ireland between 1714 and 1719, was to deny the linen industry the essential water for the linen making process.

2. **Rack-renting.** This was the practice by landlords of raising the rent on lands after the lease had expired. It was seen by some as the "straw to break the camels' back." While this may have seemed to be sound economic sense to the landlord, it was crippling to the planters. They had been enticed to Ulster with the lure of readily available land, moderate rents and a thirty-one years' lease which enabled the tenants to make the best of the lands they got. By the 1720s and 30s, these leases were up for renewal. It was then that the process of rack-renting began. For the farmer, there was not surprisingly, a deep sense of injustice,

outrage, and anger. Added to this, many of the farmers were unable to appeal directly to the landlords, as they lived abroad and had handed the affairs of their estates over to agents, who had no scruples regarding obtaining the increased rent for their employers. To make matters worse groups of native Irishmen were known to have banded together to outbid the original tenants for the new lease. A deep pessimism was in the air![11]

—oooOooo—

Blind spots

As an aside, it is interesting how many Protestants here in Ulster would have looked upon the Apartheid Regime of South Africa with disdain, not realizing that the same theological perspective on Covenant that was taken there by the Dutch Reformed Church was also brought by the Scots to Ireland during the Plantation. This Covenantal thinking was resurrected again in 1912 by the Presbyterian Church as a response to the British Home Rule Bill. The outcome was a mass signing of the Ulster Covenant. In the build-up to it, the leadership of the three main Protestant Churches here utilized their hatred and fear of the Roman Catholic Church as a political tool to unite Protestantism in its resistance to the British government, by force of arms if necessary.[12]

Paradoxically, there are many Protestants I know in Ireland who have an interest in all things "Native American." They would, when asked, champion the cause of Native Americans regarding many of the legitimate legal and moral issues related to their suppression over the past 400-500 years. Yet, they are totally blind to the fact that it was their Scots-Irish ancestors who perpetrated so much evil on the Natives in similar fashion to their treatment of Catholics on their historical doorstep! It was wrong in South Africa; it was wrong in the U.S., but it appears not to be wrong here! I get the sense that there are many, on both sides of the Atlantic, who suffer from the same myopia!

—oooOooo—

We are now on the move once again, this time across the Atlantic to see how the various factors that made the Scots/Scotch-Irish into the people they were, influence things on the ground in the ever-expanding colonies.

Let us remind ourselves of some of the things that shaped these people:

- They were clannish frontiers people in Scotland and extremely loyal in their commitment to each other
- As in Scotland, they held a deep animosity towards England
- They also had a deep hatred of Roman Catholicism
- In Ulster, they were not only pioneers, but they also had to defend the native lands they had taken
- They had a rugged faith in God, that bound them together
- That faith was shaped by the Protestant Reformation and Calvinism
- They had a strong sense of being in a special covenant relationship with God which was deeply attached to nationalism.

We are dealing here with a corporate worldview with all the attachments of spiritual strongholds, good or evil, that goes along with them.

References:
1. Harry Smith, *"Heal Not Lightly."* (Pub. New Wine Press, 2006), Pgs. 61-63.
2. Robert Dunlop, MA, *"Ireland, to the Settlement of Ulster."* Cambridge Modern History, III.
3. A full account of this specific venture in Plantation is found in the Montgomery Manuscripts, ed. George Hill (Belfast, 1869). See I, Pg. 27 ff., Pgs. 94, 97.
4. Ibid, Pg. 62.
5. James C. Leyburn, *"The Scotch-Irish—A Social History."* The University of North Carolina Press, 1962, Pg. 97.
6. Ibid. Pg. 96. Brackets – mine.

7. Source: www.british-civil-wars.co.uk/glossary/irish-uprising-1641.htm
8. Ibid.
9. Leyburn, Pg. 165.
10. Rev. Prof. John M. Barkley, *"Short History of the Presbyterian Church in Ireland."* (Pub. The Publications Board, Presbyterian Church in Ireland), Ch. 1, para.16.
11. Leyburn, Pgs. 160-63.
12. This is covered in a lot more detail in my book, *"Heal Not Lightly."* (New Wine Press, 2006). Available from our Website: www.dignityrestored.org

Chapter 13

The Scotch-Irish Head for America

The move is on

The people who ended up leading the first wave of emigration from Ulster in 1717 had done their homework. Virginia and the Carolinas were dominated by the Church of England plantations and "slave-owning"; Maryland, also a plantation colony, was predominantly Roman Catholic, and in New York, it had been reported that the Governors were not so accommodating to dissenters. That left what was known as the Middle Colonies and New England, the later while Calvinist (Puritan) was already well populated and had numerous established industries. Hence the move to Pennsylvania was the "best pick of the bunch." Reports had also been positive enough for preparations to be made, so ships were chartered; land was sold, and five thousand Ulstermen were on the move.

It would also appear that on both sides of the Atlantic expectations were very "upbeat" regarding this move. One of their prospective hosts, Cotton Mather (a leading New England Puritan clergymen, made infamous because of his role in the Salem Witch Trials) had high hopes that "much may be done for the Kingdom of God in these Parts of the World by this Transportation."[1] On writing to one of his friends, he said, "We are comforted with great numbers of our oppressed brethren coming over from the North of Ireland unto us... [they] sit down with us, and we embrace them as our own most united brethren, and we are likely to be very happy in one another."[2] History also records that Mathers along with others, such as Governor Shute and Thomas Lechmere (Surveyor-General of Customs in Boston), had hopes that the Scotch-Irish colonists could be settled on the uncertain frontier of Maine and Massachusetts "as a barrier against the Indians."[3] It was however not to be!

Most of them were to come into either Philadelphia, Chester or New Castle and as their numbers increased they had, via the Savannah

River, immediate access to a seven-hundred-mile sweep of the backcountry. The fact that the land was cheap, plentiful and fertile and that the colonial authorities openly welcomed them, was incentive enough for four further major waves of emigration to follow in 1725-1729, 1740-1741, 1754-1755, and 1771-1775. All of which corresponded, not surprisingly, with the economic highs and lows in Ulster.

It has been estimated that during the first two waves of immigration more than one hundred thousand Scotch-Irish came to America as indentured servants. Some went by such unscrupulous means as kidnapping, but for the majority, their passage was paid, which was from their perspective like an apprenticeship and seen as both practical and respectable. At the end of their indenture which was usually between four and seven years, they were free to move on, having been given for their services a set of tools, some money and often a gun and some cattle. The Quaker Colony of Philadelphia looked after them extremely well, even to the point of giving each of them an entitlement of fifty acres of land.

It is worth noting here that there was also a mass immigration of persecuted Germans: Lutherans, Moravians, Mennonites, etc., pouring into the western fringes of Philadelphia. It has been estimated that around one hundred thousand came, resulting in conflict arising among the culturally and doctrinally different Protestant traditions. Growing conflict between them and the Quaker establishment certainly did not help in producing a sense of cohesion, a working together for the good of all! Up ahead, war acted as something of a catalyst in uniting many, though not even that would persuade the pacifist Quakers to join them. The non-violent religious conviction of the Quakers meant that they found no need to either build forts, establish a militia or train people to fight the Native Indians. Up ahead this would have negative repercussions for them!

Another insight
James Logan (1674-1751), from Lurgan in County Armagh, Ireland, was of Quaker parentage and Scottish descent and in 1699, he sailed to Pennsylvania as William Penn's secretary on board the Canterbury.

Some years later, in his role as the Provincial Secretary of Philadelphia, he extended an invitation to the first group of Ulstermen, whom he saw as his "brave" fellow-countrymen, to join the colony. In 1720, he wrote in a similar vein to Richard Lechmere,

> "At the time we were apprehensive from the Northern Indians... I, therefore, thought it might be prudent to plant a settlement of such men as those who formerly had so bravely defended Londonderry and Enniskillen [*mine*: against Catholics, whose land was taken off them during the Plantation of Ulster!] as a frontier in case of any disturbance... These people if kindly used will be orderly as they have hitherto been and easily dealt with" adding, "They will also, I expect, be a leading example to others."[4]

As a result, he gave them an extensive tract of land in Chester (now Lancaster) County as a buffer zone, which they renamed as Donegal, after a county in the north of Ireland. Yet, by the end of ten years, he had a major rethink! While recognizing their bravery as pioneers, he also noted that,

> "A settlement of families from the North of Ireland gives me more trouble than fifty of any other people..." "troublesome settlers to the government and hard neighbors to the Indians."[5]

He also recorded that,

> "It looks as if Ireland is to send all her inhabitants hither; for last week, not less than six ships arrived, and every day two or three arrives also. The common fear is, that if they continue to come, they will make themselves proprietors of the Province... the Indians themselves are alarmed at the swarms of strangers, and we are afraid of a breach between them—for the Irish are very rough to them."[6]

If this was a prediction, it became a reality, when in 1756 the Quakers lost control of their Assembly!

The main tribes that would have initially been directly affected by this Scotch-Irish intrusion would have been the Lenape (Delaware) and Susquehannock (Conestoga) tribes.

In 1729 James Logan was to temporarily penalize their "audacious and disorderly" habits, by withholding land patents from them. According to Logan, they responded by squatting on approximately one hundred thousand acres of frontier land, reasoning that as it was abundant and because no one else had settled there, it was theirs for the taking if they were willing to do the hard work of clearing the forests and make farms on it.[7] Not all the immigrants were like those described above. There were those described as "the better sort... a Christian people" among them, including Ulstermen "of substance" and those involved in the manufacturing industry.

An increase in their numbers—partly due to a high birth rate—led to a movement of immigrants in a south-westward direction through the Great Valley (sometimes known as the Shenandoah) into Virginia, the Carolinas, Kentucky, and Tennessee. With them also went the sons of the more prosperous settlers from previous migrations, along with those who had completed their service as indentured servants. It is thought, that in the 1740s and 50s, approximately sixty thousand settlers poured into North Carolina, with a further eighty-three thousand into South Carolina—most of them being Scots-Irish. This movement was encouraged by North Carolina's Governors, two of them, Matthew Rowan and Arthur Dobbs, came from Ulster.

The later, born in Carrickfergus, Co. Antrim, had been a member of the Irish House of Commons and became Surveyor General for Ireland in 1730. While still a member of the Irish Parliament he purchased 400,000 acres of land in the Mecklenburg area of N. Carolina. In January 1753, he was appointed its Governor. During his time in office, which was overshadowed by the French and Indian War and the start of the War of Independence, he encouraged the colonists to fight for and defend their land from any French allied Cherokee attacks.[8]

Tensions increase

As more and more people arrived from England and Ireland, looking for and finding a new way of life, and as they by necessity pushed further and further west, tensions were to increase, not only in their contact with the Indians but also in their relationship with the British establishment over land rights. This tended to produce radicalism in many of the colonists. In Colonies like Pennsylvania, where no military support was forthcoming, their contact with the Indians all too often meant, taking the law into their own hands. It goes without saying, that such intrusions into Indian lands inevitably led to a corresponding resistance.

Conflict on the frontier

Initially, their westward advance had been more-or-less trouble-free, as it appears that no Indian tribes inhabited the region in great numbers,[9] using it primarily for hunting. But with such a steady stream of Ulster-Scots and Germans moving on to the frontier, it invariably meant that they would increasingly encroach on Indian territory.

For the radical colonists on the Pennsylvanian frontier, there was in effect no 'law' yet firmly established among them with regards to their unregulated pursuit of land and their insensitive dealings with the Indians. It would appear from all accounts, that these frontier settlers in their insatiable hunger for land, continued to act without regard for either the colonies Proprietors or the Indians. That must have given the Quaker administration of William Penn something of a headache, as tribal chiefs increasingly lodged their complaints with them. From the outset, Penn and his fellow Proprietors had always sought to live peaceably and with integrity among the Indians, which included the fair purchase of any land from them. So, when Ulster-Scots did not wait for official permission to settle, the Quakers were known on occasions to have bought the land retrospectively, so that peace with the Native population could be maintained.

The French and Indian War

That is the name given to the war that broke out in 1754 between Britain, France, and their Indian allies. It was also widely known as the Seven Years' War, which connected it to a much wider war in Europe between the English and the French with Prussian and Austrian involvement.

One of the key elements of it was the sectarian-fueled hatred and fear. The predominantly Protestant English colonists feared the influence of the Roman Catholic hierarchy over New France and its administration. While the French equally feared the strong anti-Catholic sentiments held by most of the English colonies. Not so different from what was happening in Ireland at the time! In America, it could have been understood from four unique perspectives:

1. France: stopping English expansion into what they saw as their colonially gained lands under the Doctrine of Discovery. France not only owned Canada but they also laid claim to the rich arable and fur-bearing trading land of the Ohio and Mississippi valleys.

2. England: they saw the Catholic French wanting to become the primary power in North America and therefore had to be strongly resisted at both a political and a religious level.

3. English/Scotch-Irish colonists: on the "coal face," saw it as a war against Indian brutality—though they also saw the Indians as allies of the French. Nevertheless, it was their families, homes, and property that were under attack, which produced incredible fear among them as well as a growing frustration at the lack of Quaker military support.

4. Native Americans: they became easy allies of the French, having been promised, that success against the English/colonists, i.e., pushing them back to the coast, would restore former territories to them.

Initially, the war went very much in favor of the numerically smaller French forces and their Indian allies, primarily due to the British colonies not operating as a single unit, which led to disunity among them as to how they handled the conflict. This was to change in 1756 when William Pitt became the British Secretary of State, and he poured more resources into the War; which lead to the capture of a growing number of French forts. In 1759, Quebec was to fall to them following the Battle of the Plains of Abraham. The following year, after the capture of Montreal, the War on American soil was ended.

The Treaty of Paris

On February 10, 1763, the Treaty of Paris was signed, and the wider war was officially over. In it, France lost not only all its lands in North American, east of the Mississippi, but also all of Canada to Britain except for two small islands off Newfoundland (Saint Pierre and Miquelon), but it gained the British occupied Caribbean islands of Guadeloupe. That made sound economic sense for the French: the war had been costly; the Islands yielded an abundant harvest of sugar cane, and they were easier to defend. France was also to cede French Louisiana (west of the Mississippi River) to its Spanish ally as compensation for Spain's loss to Britain of Florida, which had earlier been ceded by Spain to Britain in exchange for the return of Havana, Cuba. All in all, Britain fared well as far as land acquisition goes, ending up as the prevailing colonial power in the eastern half of North America!

Paul Johnson in his book, *"A History of the American People"* described the Treaty as,

> "one of the greatest territorial carve-ups in history... This was a momentous geopolitical shift... because it made Britain the master of North America, no longer challenged there by the most formidable military power in Europe. Suddenly, in the mid-1760s, Britain had emerged as proprietor of the largest empire the world had seen since Roman times—in terms of territorial extent and global compass."[10]

The war did, however, have negative repercussions for Britain and its colonies—economically, politically and relationally—as it went deeply into debt. As a means of trying to solve this, the Crown chose to exact taxes from the colonies. This proved to be an increasingly contentious solution, which became a significant component that ultimately led to the American Revolutionary War.[11] For the Scotch-

Irish, it undoubtedly stirred up memories of similar English actions against them in Scotland and Ireland!

One of these taxes, introduced in 1765 by the British Parliament, was the Stamp Act, which helped to pay for the soldiers that were stationed in the newly established forts on the American frontier after the Seven Year War. These forts had the dual purpose of acting as trading posts and as garrisons to deal with any skirmishes between local tribes and land-hungry colonists. The later saw such taxation as a massive violation of their rights, especially as they had no representation in Parliament to give them a say in what taxes should be raised and how they should be spent.

These colonists saw this as a restriction being imposed upon them from a distant Parliament, one that had the counter-productive effect of alienating them. That was undoubtedly **Robert Williams Junior's** perspective, who saw America as "a New World of abundant and cheap land, free of [Norman-derived] feudal constraints and governed according to the revered, natural-law inspired principles of an ancient, **defeudalized Saxon constitution...** The tyranny of a government devoted to destroying individual property, rather than rightfully preserving it, demanded the fiercest resistance."[12]

—oooOooo—

The Revolutionary Era

We are now entering what has become known in American history as the Revolutionary Era. It was becoming increasingly clear that things between the Scots-Irish and English in America and London were not going well, they were certainly not "singing from the same hymn sheet" regarding their discourse on colonization. Some of the colonies, like Massachusetts, called for joint resistance to Parliament's decisions, which in turn only served in it turning up the tone of its own rhetoric. Not surprisingly opposition was intense, violence ensued, and Britain found itself, with its troops spread out across the frontier, unable to readily quell it.

Alongside any physical struggle, one of the major discourses on resistance to British power in America, which regularly came up in my research, was grounded in the thinking of John Locke. He held, that if you have worked hard to acquire a piece of land, the government should be there to protect that acquisition, not oppose it. Let's look at him in a bit more detail.

John Locke (1632-1704)

Born into a Puritan family, he was, as a young man, sent to an academic establishment in Oxford, called Christ Church. Finding that he was increasingly frustrated with the undergraduate classical curriculum of the time, he turned to the works of modern philosophers such as René Descartes. He was later to be introduced by a friend to medicine and experimental philosophy, which were part of the curriculum of other English universities and also at the Royal Society, of which he eventually became a Member.

Before the French and Indian War, the British American colonists had been developing their societies in what was a very hostile environment, without much assistance from a very distant Crown and Government. With that came the growing feeling that restrictions to their independent development were being forced on them. Their response was in part to latch on to John Locke's words in his *"Second Treatise of Government,"* in which he expounded on natural law and property.

In the early part of it he speaks of a "state of perfect freedom," a state in which everyone was at freedom to "order their actions, and dispose of their possessions, and persons as they think fit, within the boundaries of the Law of Nature, without asking leave, or depending upon the will of any other man."[13] This is exactly how these radicalized colonists saw themselves. Locke was both articulating and legitimizing their right to claim the American wilderness as their own, under natural law.

In another passage within this treatise he writes:

"To which let me add, that he who appropriates land to himself by his labour, does not lessen but increase the common stock of mankind. For the provisions serving to support human life, produced by one acre of enclosed and cultivated land, are (to speak much within compasse) ten times more, than those, which are yielded by an acre of land, of an equal richnesse, lyeing waste in common. And therefore he, that encloses land and has a greater plenty of the conveniencies of life from ten acres, thus he could have from hundred left to nature, may truly be said, to give ninety acres to mankind. For this labour now supplys him with provisions out of ten acres, which were but the product of an hundred lying in common."[14]

This stood in opposition to the 1763 Kings Proclamation (see the heading: "The Proclamation Line" in Ch. 14) which "prevented English Americans from appropriating the Indians' 'waste' lands and increasing the 'common stock of mankind' [and]... even worse from the English Americans' 'common sense' perspective, the Proclamation reserved the western frontier to savage tribes of Indians."[15]

Mindful that Locke had served as secretary to the legal owners of the Carolina Company and had assisted in drawing up their first constitution, we read that his western worldview (influenced by English colonizing discourse on Discovery, which he was very familiar with) led him to describe the Indians as

"rich in land and poor in all the comforts of life; whom nature having furnished as liberally as any other people with materials of plenty, i.e., a fruitful soil, apt to produce in abundance what might serve for food, raiment, and delight, yet for want of improving it by labor have not one-hundredth part of the conveniences we enjoy. And a king [Indian] of large and fruitful territory there, feeds, lodges, and is clad worse than a day-laborer in England."[16]

-oooOooo-

Irrespective of these opposing views, the Doctrine of Discovery continued to influence the thinking and practice of both the English and Scotch-Irish colonists (though perhaps not as consciously so, by the later). As Williams observes,

> "the utilitarian justifications for dispossessing the American Indians that had emerged in early seventeenth century English colonizing discourse had, by Locke's time, hardened into the assumptions of ideological argument... [and also] judging by the Revolutionary era's reception of Locke, the continuity in English colonizing discourse of the thematic of Indian deficiency had been completely integrated into the 'common sense' of the late eighteenth century English Americans."[17]

Regarding the English government's involvement on the frontier, pragmatism would continue to be the order of the day. The restriction on the colonists obtaining more land had little to do with a change in its overall relationship or attitude towards the Indians—as a Christian European nation, they had the superior right of conquest through Discovery and therefore, over non-Christian people to the land. While Discovery may have recognized that the Indians had a right to occupancy—albeit a diminishing one—the Crown continued to exercise its authority when it came to the issue of selling land.

—oooOooo—

This seems as good a place as any to take a slight side-step and look at a few landmark legal decisions that would have huge repercussions for all concerned, white and Indian. These would clarify in law how they saw the legal status and rights of the Native Americans regarding land. Ultimately the United States would have superior rights to the land and the Indians natural-law rights to sovereignty regarding it, did not need to be recognized. This superior title would be determined in 1823 through a landmark legal case by Chief Justice John Marshall, the case of *Johnson v. McIntosh*.

188

Johnson v. McIntosh[18]

In 1773 and 1775 Thomas Johnson bought some land from the Piankeshaw Indians (part of the Miami Tribe). The plaintiffs, Thomas Johnson's descendants, had inherited the land and the defendant, William McIntosh had at a later date also obtained a patent for an overlapping part of it from the United States federal government. [See 18, Note 3] There is, however, some evidence available which contradicts this; that the two parcels of land did not overlap and that the facts were purposely misrepresented to the court so that a ruling could be procured. [See 18, Note 4]

McIntosh's "lawyers unashamedly relied on the feudally derived argument that the Indians lacked natural law rights to the land they occupied and that the superior title to the soil of America was vested in the European nation that had first discovered and occupied the territory claimed by the savages. Citing a long list of authorities, including Locke and Jefferson... McIntosh's counsel stated that the Law of Nations as adopted by civilized European states had always 'denied the right of the Indians to be considered as independent communities, having a permanent property in the soil, capable of alienation to private individuals. They remain in a state of nature and have never been admitted to the general society of nations.'"[19] "Discovery," they argued, "is the foundation of title, in European nations, and this overlooks all proprietary rights in the natives. The Indians were 'destitute' of the basic, essential rights belonging to 'citizens in the ordinary sense of that term.' They were regarded under the law of all the colonies, and of the United States, 'as an inferior race of people... under the perpetual protection and pupilage of the government.'"[20]

Seeking to avoid the moral and emotive aspects of the case, Marshall "instead focused his opinion exclusively on the need for rationalizing the process of land acquisition in a country originally inhabited by a savage people but gradually overtaken by a foreign invader." "The inquiry," he said, "therefore, is, in a great measure confined to the power of Indians to give, and of private individuals to receive, a title which can be sustained in the courts of this Country."[21]

Williams makes it clear that Marshall certainly had a working knowledge of the Doctrine of Discovery:

> "Marshall's opinion in Johnson held that under the "Doctrine of Discovery," assertedly recognized as part of the Law of Nations by virtually every European colonizing nation, discovery of territory in the New World gave the discovering European nation "an exclusive right to extinguish the Indian title of occupancy, either by purchase or by conquest." This title which England had acquired under the Doctrine of Discovery, had devolved to the United States as a result of its victory in the Revolutionary War."[22]

That is undoubtedly one of the most influential cases in United States legal history as it "lays down the foundations of the doctrine of aboriginal title in The United States, and the related discovery Doctrine."[23] In it, the U.S. Supreme Court held that private citizens were not allowed to purchase lands directly from Native Americans, it had to be done through the federal government, thus ruling in favor of McIntosh.

Reference to the *Johnson* ruling has constantly been used for over 200 years in either state or federal cases related to Native American land title. Nearly all of the cases have been land disputes between two non-Native parties.

Another landmark decision, also overseen by Chief Justice Marshall, was a case directly involving Native Americans:

Cherokee Nation v. Georgia (1831)
This was

> "a United States Supreme Court case in which the Cherokee Nation sought a federal injunction against laws passed by the state of Georgia depriving them of rights within its boundaries, but the Supreme Court did not hear the case on its merits. It ruled that it had no

original jurisdiction in the matter, as the Cherokee was a dependent nation, with a relationship to the United States like that of a ward to its guardian... Chief Justice Marshall said: 'The court has bestowed its best attention on this question, and, after mature deliberation, the majority is of the opinion that an Indian tribe or nation within the United States is not a foreign state in the sense of the constitution, and cannot maintain an action in the courts of the United States.'"[24]

Williams observes that "this... Supreme Court opinion is regarded as the textual source of the basic principles of modern federal Indian law" and goes on to say that the "acceptance of the Doctrine of Discovery and its denial of territorial sovereignty to American Indian nations... represent a point of closure, not a point of origin, in United States colonizing discourse."[25] In this ruling Marshall was merely setting in concrete the results of a political struggle that the Founders had faced some years earlier in the Proclamation, indeed something that was deeply rooted centuries before, in the developing medieval colonizing discourse in Europe before and after the Reformation.

I finish this Chapter with an excerpt from the Conclusion of Williams' book...

"The conquest of the earth is not a pretty thing when you look into it too much. The history of the American Indian in Western legal thought reveals that a will to empire proceeds most effectively under a rule of law. In the United States, and in other Western settler-colonized states, that rule begins with the Doctrine of Discovery and its discourse of conquest, which denies fundamental human rights and self-determination to indigenous tribal peoples... This medievally grounded discourse reaffirmed in Western colonizing law by Chief Justice John Marshall in *Johnson v. McIntosh,* vests superior rights of sovereignty over non-Western indigenous peoples and their territories in European-descended governments. The Doctrine of Discovery

191

and its discourses of conquest assert the West's lawful power to impose its vision of truth on non-Western peoples through a racist, colonizing rule of law.

In the United States, the doctrine has proved itself to be a perfect instrument of empire. Under the rules and principles of federal Indian law derived from the doctrine, the United States acquired a continent 'in perfect good faith' that its wars and acts of genocide directed against Indian people accorded with the rule of law. Supreme Court decisions interpreting the doctrine have extended to the federal government plenary power to control Indian affairs unrestrained by normal constitutional limitations. In case after case, the Supreme Court in the late nineteenth and early twentieth centuries simply refused to check Congress's free rein in matters where it was thought that broad discretionary powers were vital to the solution of the immensely difficult 'Indian problem.' Treaties promising tribes a reserved homeland in perpetuation were wantonly violated; tribes were relocated to distant, barren regions to accommodate white expansion; and tribal lands and resources were repeatedly confiscated to satisfy the needs and destiny of a superior civilization."[26]

Williams then gives us some examples of things denied to the Native Americans because of the United States embracing the Doctrine of Discovery as an instrument of conquest:

- Violent suppression of Indian religious practices and traditional forms of government
- Separation of Indian children from their homes
- Wholesale spoliation of treaty-guaranteed resources
- Forced assimilative programs
- Involuntary sterilization of Indian women ...

… things that regarded tribal peoples as being "normatively deficient and culturally, politically, and morally inferior." Because they were seen as "infidels, pagans" they were presumed under the law "to lack the rational capacity necessary to assume an equal status or to exercise equal rights under the West's medievally derived colonization law."[27]

The Doctrine of Discovery was nothing more than the reflection of a set of Eurocentric racist beliefs elevated to the status of a universal principle—one culture's argument to support its conquest and colonization of a newly discovered, alien world.[28]

One thing is clear, what we have read here, that was supposedly done for the "public good," did not include the good of the American Indian!

Now, where was I? Oh yes, the Scots-Irish!

References:

1. Cotton Mather, *"Diary of Cotton Mather, 1709-1724."* Massachusetts Historical Society Collections, 7th ser., 8 (Boston, 1912), Pg. 549, qu. in Bolton (1967), Pg. 136.
2. Patrick Griffin, *"The People with No Name: Ireland's Ulster Scots, America's Scots Irish, and the Creation of a British Atlantic World. 1689-1764."* (Princeton University Press, 2001), 1689-1764, Pg. 90.
3. Henry J. Ford, *"The Scotch-Irish in America."* (Princeton, 1915), Pg. 222.
4. John H. Finlay, *"The Coming of the Scot."* (New York, 1940), Pgs. 58-59.
5. George Chambers, *"A Tribute to the Principles, Virtues, Habits and Public Usefulness of the Irish and Scotch Early Settlers of Pennsylvania."* (Chambersburg, 1856), Pg. 10.
6. James Logan, The Logan Papers, III, Pg. 303.
7. James G. Leyburn, *"The Scotch-Irish – a Social History."* (The University of North Carolina Press, 1962), Pgs. 192-193. Cited in *"Colonial Records of Pennsylvania, 1683-1790."* (Harrisburg, 1851-1853), IX, Pg. 380.
8. Source: http://www.fortdobbs.org/news13.htm

9. Leyburn, Pg. 223-224.
10. Paul Johnson, *"A History of the American People."* (Harper Collins Publishers Inc., New York, 1997), Pgs. 128-129.
11. Sources: http://historycentral.com/Revolt/french.html
    http://en.wikipedia.org/wiki/French_and_Indian_War
12. Robert Williams, Jnr., *"The American Indian in Western Legal Thought."* (Oxford University Press, New York, 1990), Pg. 228.
13. Williams, Pg. 247. Note 54 (Pg. 282) links it to J. Locke, *"Two Treatise of Government."* Pg. 309.
14. Ibid, Pg. 248. Note 61 (Pg. 282) links it to J. Locke, *"Two Treatise of Government."* Pg. 336.
15. Ibid, Pg. 248.
16. Ibid. Note 62 (Pg. 282) links it to J. Locke, *"Two Treatise of Government."* Pgs. 338-339.
17. Ibid, Pgs. 248-249.
18. Source: https://en.wikipedia.org/wiki/Johnson_v._M'Intosh
    Background:
    Note 3. Kades, 148 U. Pa. L. Rev. at 1092 ("Mapping the United Companies' claims alongside M'Intosh's purchases, as enumerated in the district court records, shows that the litigants' land claims did not overlap. Hence there was no real 'case or controversy,' and M'ntosh, like another leading early Supreme Court land case, Fletcher v. Peck, appears to have been a sham.").

    Note 4. Kades, 148 U. Pa. L. Rev. at 1093 ("M'Intosh did not contest a single fact alleged in the complaint, jurisdictional or otherwise. Perhaps he participated in framing the complaint, which became the stipulated facts of the case. Neither the district court nor the Supreme Court questioned any of these facts. Everyone involved, it seems, wanted a decision on the legal question of the validity of private purchases from the Native Americans").
19. Williams, Pgs. 310-311. Johnson v. McIntosh, 21 U.S. (8 Wheat) at Pgs. 565-567.
20. Ibid. Pg. 311. Johnson v. McIntosh, 21 U.S. (8 Wheat) at Pgs. 567-571.
21. Ibid. Pg. 312. Johnson v. McIntosh, 21 U.S. (8 Wheat) at Pg. 572.
22. Ibid. Pgs. 312-313.

23. Source:
    https://en.wikipedia.org/wiki/Aboriginal_title_in_the_United_Sta
    tes
24. Source:
    http://en.wikipedia.org/wiki/Cherokee_Nation_v._Georgia
25. Williams, Pg. 231.
26. Ibid. Pg. 325.
27. Ibid. Pg. 326.
28. Ibid. Pg. 326.

Chapter 14

On the Western Frontier

A formidable force

Back on track again! However, one saw it, throughout the whole period of turmoil of The French Indian War and the War of Independence, the Scotch-Irish rose up almost to a man, to defend everything they believed, by a God-given right, to be theirs! With the policy of appeasement promoted by the Quakers seen as an irrelevancy, the Scots-Irish took the war to the Indians, often wreaking havoc on both white and Indian communities wherever they went.

On the frontier, the Scotch-Irish also quickly learned to abandon the "proper way" to fight, by adopting the guerrilla warfare tactics practiced by the Indians (i.e., surprise attacks on their villages, burning, butchery, scalping). They were later to successfully utilize such tactics against the English Military Redcoats during the War of Independence, who were used to the more conventional warfare methods of two opposing forces facing each other in combat.

As one historian noted in his journal, the Scotch-Irish were

> "… impatient of restraint, rebellious against anything that in their eyes bore the resemblance of injustice, we find these men readiest among the ready on the battlefields of the Revolution. If they had their faults, a lack of patriotism or courage was not among the number. Amongst them were to be found men of education, intelligence, and virtue."[1]

Before the Revolution, there is also no doubt that the Scotch-Irish played a significant role in the defeat of the French and as a result the frontier Indians (The French and Indian War, 1754-1763). This led in 1760 to the British gaining possession of the whole of Canada. That was followed by the Treaty of Paris in 1763, in which France formally ceded to Britain all its territory east of the Mississippi. Included was the establishment of a temporary boundary called the Proclamation Line to separate the colonies from Indian Territory (more about this later).

The Paxton Boys

Towards the end of the French and Indian War, the pacifist Pennsylvanian Assembly had to reluctantly respond to the frequent Indian attacks upon the Scotch-Irish settlements by authorizing, for defensive purposes, the formation of a 700-strong militia. It was made up of two units, the Cumberland Boys, and the Paxton Boys. The latter, a group of Scotch-Irish rangers from the Paxton Township in Dauphin County, was soon to overstep their mandate and show another side of their character - impulsiveness. In December 1763, based on a non-verified rumor that the peaceful Conestoga Indians (Susquehannock) in the neighboring Lancaster County had been passing information on to hostile Indians, the Paxton Boys attacked their settlement, killing twenty of its inhabitants in a most brutal and barbarous manner. They then went on, in a more premeditated way, to slaughter a further 140 Christian Indians (converts of the Moravians), who had been taken to a prison on Province Island on the Schuylkill River for their safety.[2] That sadly was a contributing factor in bringing about the extinction of the Conestoga tribe.

Below are two written accounts of that period, the first by William Henry of Lancaster regarding the second attack and the second by the Rev. Elder (one of the Paxton Boys leadership):

> "I saw a number of people running down the street towards the gaol (jail), which enticed me and other lads to follow them. At about sixty or eighty yards from the gaol, we met from twenty-five to thirty men, well mounted on horses, and with rifles, tomahawks, and scalping knives, equipped for murder. I ran into the prison yard, and there, O what a horrid sight presented itself to my view! Near the back door of the prison, lay an old Indian and his squaw (wife), particularly well-known and esteemed by the people of the town,

because of his placid and friendly conduct. His name was Will Sock; across him and his squaw lay two children, of about the age of three years, whose heads were split with the tomahawk, and their scalps all taken off. Towards the middle of the gaol yard, along the west side of the wall, lay a stout Indian, whom I particularly noticed to have been shot in the breast, his legs were chopped with the tomahawk, his hands cut off, and finally a rifle ball discharged in his mouth; so that his head was blown to atoms, and the brains were splashed against, and yet hanging to the wall, for three or four feet around. This man's hands and feet had also been chopped off with a tomahawk. In this manner lay the whole of them, men, women, and children, spread about the prison yard: shot-scalped-hacked-and cut to pieces."[3]

While the Rev. Elder was not directly implicated in either attack, he nevertheless wrote in their defense to Governor Penn, on January 27, 1764:

"The storm which had been so long gathering, has, at length, exploded. Had Government removed the Indians, which had been frequently, but without effect, urged, this painful catastrophe might have been avoided. What could I do with men heated to madness? All that I could do was done. I expostulated, but life and reason were set at defiance. Yet the men in private life are virtuous and respectable; not cruel, but mild and merciful. The time will arrive when each palliating circumstance will be weighed. This deed, magnified into the blackest of crimes, shall be considered as one of those ebullitions of wrath, caused by momentary excitement, to which human infirmity is subjected."[4]

They also made threats to kill Quakers in Philadelphia, whom they saw as "Indian-lovers" that stood in the path of any further opening up of the frontier. That caused Benjamin Franklin to muster the militia to defend the city. While he was no lover of the Indians, he was nevertheless disgusted enough with the actions of the Paxton Boys to write a pamphlet which strongly condemned these "Christian White Savages."[5] Within the Scotch-Irish community the actions of the Paxton Boys were by-and-large justified, while other residents of the Pennsylvania colony feared that with so many radical Scotch-Irish around, the stability of their lives and institutions could be severely undermined.

In his book *"Peaceable Kingdom Lost"* Kevin Kenny writes,

> "In the aftermath of the Paxton affair, social order on the Pennsylvania frontier disintegrated. With no effective means of law enforcement, much of the frontier was ungovernable. Indian affairs were in disarray. The boundary line set by royal proclamation in 1763 had little effect in stemming the westward tide of migration and the seizure of Indian lands. Also, the provincial government had lost control over the aggressive vanguard of Ulster settlers in the lower Susquehanna Valley. In the Assembly, leaders of the still dominant Quaker party insisted that the chaos on the frontier arose directly from John Penn's failure to pursue the Paxton Boys, who had not been investigated, let alone arrested, tried, or punished; they were free, it seemed, to do as they pleased, and the lesson was not lost on other western settlers."[6]

In September 1766, based on information given to John Penn that,

> "many ill-disposed persons, in express Disobedience of his Majesty's Proclamation and Royal Instructions, and regardless of the rights of the Proprietaries, or the Indians in Alliance with the English," had settled, "without any License or Authority... upon Lands within this Province, not yet purchased of the Nations."[7]

he tried to restore some of his authority, by forbidding any further settling on Indian lands that had not been legitimately purchased, very conscious that ongoing provocation of the Indians could lead to another Indian War.

The Paxton Boys were to continue to wreak havoc on the "Establishment." Counter to many nineteenth and early twentieth-century historians, who portrayed them as "harbingers of the American Revolution, frontier democrats fighting against the quasi-feudal privilege of the Penn family," Kenny saw them as not having such lofty reasons but rather more of a local concern even in their siding with the Patriots in the Revolution. "What they wanted," Kenny believed, "was land, personal security, and vengeance against Indians." In their pursuit of these their fight was "against proprietary privilege, but scarcely in the interest of liberty and equality for all." Counter to many earlier historians, he would hold that it was this rather than patriotism that influenced their decisions to fight against the English in the Revolution.[8] What he saw demonstrated among them was a fiercely independent spirit, that would serve both for good or ill in the coming years, as they moved further west into the Ohio Valley.

Pontiacs War (1763-1766)

At a time when the pioneering colonists now had the possibility of peace, it all ended abruptly. The British hierarchy had hoped that the Proclamation Line would have procured peace with the Indians, but decisions on the ground caused things to turn out very differently. Silver comments:

> "They [the British] made a hash of it. With the eclipse of French power and the British takeover of Canada, ill-timed economies and humiliations—Gen. Sir Jeffrey Amherst, the commander in chief at war's end, felt that truckling to Indian allies was now beneath the empire's dignity—estranged the region's Indians and helped spark Pontiac's War."[9]

In response, Pontiac, Chief of the Ottawa tribe and former ally of the French, brought many other tribes together in a concerted fight against the British along more than one thousand miles of frontier stretching from Niagara to Virginia, to stop their ongoing encroachment into its territories. Every fort, except those in Detroit and Pittsburgh, was destroyed.[10] In Pennsylvania, with Indian attacks taking place within sixty miles of Philadelphia, it is believed that at least 2000 settlers were killed, with many more having to flee east. It was to take three years, at considerable British military and financial expense, to quell this uprising. Again, history reveals that the Scotch-Irish proved to be very "able soldiers, rough, ingenious, adaptable [and] ready to endure hardship."[11] Little mention is made, however, of how many Indians died and what they thought about their lands being infiltrated and taken off them.

—oooOooo—

The War of Independence

In the light of what I have shared over the last few chapters about the national character of my Scottish ancestors and their lack of love for the English, they were, not surprisingly, acknowledged as one of the most effective elements in what is known as George Washington's Continental Army,[12] during the War of Independence (1775-1783). Here are a few of the numerous quotes I came across regarding the Scotch-Irish Presbyterians and the critical role they played:

- "Call it not an American Rebellion, it is nothing more nor less than an Irish-Scotch Presbyterian Rebellion." Captain Johann Heinrich, a German mercenary serving with the British.

- "There is no use crying about it. Cousin America has run off with a Presbyterian parson, and that is the end of it." Horace Walpole, Westminster MP, to his colleagues.

- "Presbyterianism is really at the Bottom of this whole Conspiracy, it has supplied it with Vigour and will never rest, till something is decided upon it." In a letter sent to Lord Dartmouth from his agent in New York.

- "Itinerant Presbyterian preachers traverse this country Poisoning the minds of the People—Instilling Democratical and Commonwealth Principles into their minds… Especially that they owe no Subjection to Great Britain—that they are a free People." Excerpt from a report sent from Charles Woodmason, an Anglican clergyman who was loyal to the Crown.

- Colonel Banastre Tarleton, on considering that several Presbyterian ministers had made the journey south from Pennsylvania to urge the Scotch-Irish to support the rebellion and join George Washington's rebel "Continental Army," described Presbyterian churches as "sedition shops."[13]

It is reckoned that up to 80% of the Scots-Irish settlers were persuaded that their interests were best served by breaking their constitutional links with the British Crown and bring about independence for their new homeland. That was surely shaped, as I have already mentioned, by their bitter experience of religious discrimination and economic deprivation in Ireland and Scotland before that. Undoubtedly, one could also add to that the English Parliament's taxation policies in the American colonies, e.g., the Stamp Act of 1765. Their introduction, to help pay for the high costs incurred during the French and Indian War, would have been reminiscent of the heavy taxations they had experienced back home.

The historian Froude eluded to this when he saw that it was because of England's "short-sightedness interests" and "the cupidity of the landlords that damaged Ulster [that] ultimately gave added power to the Revolutionary cause in America [and] led to England losing her colonies."[14]

Such a depth of bitterness, resentment, and anger is not difficult to harness. Perhaps one of the most effective means of doing that was found in the pulpits of the Presbyterian ministers, whose politicized sermons frequently denounced both the Anglican Church and King George III for his Royal Proclamation (1763) in which he tried at setting the limits of white expansion to the west of it.

Interestingly, in Ireland in 1912 during the Home Rule crisis, the Presbyterian Church also stirred up rebellion against the British Government in a most effective way which led eventually to the signing of the Ulster Covenant; the Easter Rising (1916) and the partitioning of the Island (1922). Over the past 50 years, our Catholic and Protestant separateness has at times been reinforced on both sides for political ends, as people live and act out of the stories from their histories. Many key events have been kept alive in our corporate psyches through songs, wall murals, flags, parades, sermons, political speeches, etc., Once again, this illustrates my interpretative position regarding history—it is the stuff that Satan can take and use effectively to set people groups against each other. Neither group being capable of reaching their God-intended potential!

—oooOooo—

On the western front

As I researched for this chapter, I became aware of a tension arising within me. I began to see emerging two different narratives regarding the Scotch-Irish pioneers in America. One was that of a people who heroically "laid the foundations of democratic faith and practice" and the other was totally opposite—of a people, who the further west they went, appeared to lose not only something of their faith foundation but also the civilizing influences of the European institutions and standards they left behind. The next few pages will reflect something of that. For many of these Scotch-Irish immigrants, coming to America must have been tainted with a touch of déjà vu. It had not been that long in the past that their Scottish relatives, grounded in Calvinistic theology, had made covenants with God in their stand against the British Crown and the Anglican Church. And again, when during the Plantation of Ulster, having removed the native Irish from the productive lands in counties like Down and Antrim, they also had to establish their homes and culture in a very hostile environment. Their Presbyterian faith, with its strong sense of right and wrong, undoubtedly bound them into a tight, cohesive unit. So, when social, political and spiritual persecution came yet again through the Crown, Government, and Church in England, they left for America with a clear sense of God's calling on their lives. There was certainly no love lost for the English nor as it turned out, for the "savage" on the land or for that matter—the Quaker establishment!

The Proclamation Line

As I mentioned earlier, with the ending of the French Indian War by the Treaty of Paris in 1763, an initiative called the Royal Proclamation was introduced by the British to bring the land speculators under control—known as the Proclamation Line, it followed the east-west watershed of the Appalachian Mountains. The British colonies were situated on the Atlantic coast with the American Indian on the other side of the mountains, on land designated as the Indian Reserve. This was considered by the British as a temporary boundary which allowed for a more ordered westward expansion to take place later. It was also meant to give the Crown full control of any future lands that may be purchased from Native Tribes, as well as allowing time through trade agreements for the civilizing process of the Indians, who were seen as "languishing in a savage state."[15]

That didn't go down well with any colonists who had already settled on or were in the process of doing so on lands west of the Line. The circumstances also saw the rise of people known as 'land jobbers'[16] on the frontier, who worked for speculating elites (which included George Washington) in the east to obtain quality land deeds of the Indians.

One of the chief architects of the Proclamation Line was Irish born William Petty, Earl of Shelburne. Born in Ireland, he made many connections in his thinking between Britain's past in Ireland and its current presence in America. (Interestingly, it was his great-grandfather who played a prominent role in England's plantation and subjugation of Ireland under Cromwell a century earlier, by developing the means of surveying the land that was to be confiscated and then given to Cromwell's soldiers as payment for services rendered. For his services, he was granted a 30,000-acre estate in Kenmare, West of Ireland.)

Petty subscribed to his ancestor's views of the "savage" Irish he grew up around, who required a firm hand. He fondly recalled his English ancestors who had "kept that barbarous country in strict subordination." Such ideas had legitimated the conquest of Ireland.[17]He served as British Home Secretary and then as Prime

Minister (1782-83) during the final months of the American War of Independence. He was also a friend and patron of Adam Smith, one of the Scottish thinkers to embrace what was called the Stadial Theory (see below).

Joined in agreement to the principal of a Proclamation Line was a fellow Irish immigrant, Sir William Johnson. He was a convert to Anglicanism from Catholicism, a huge thing to do in those days, and a member of the strongly anti-Catholic Anglican mission, the Society for the Propagation of the Gospel (SPG). He served as a military commander during the Seven Year War and as a diplomat to the Six Nations Iroquois Confederacy. Out of the experience gained he informed the Board of Trade that the Indians "will never be content with our possessing the Frontiers, unless we settle limits with them, and make it worth their while."[18] He felt the Proclamation Line gave the necessary space and that by developing trading relationships with the Indians, they could through civilizing influences [especially Christianity] eventually be prepared for subjecthood. (again, see Stadial Theory, below).

Thomas Barton, an Anglican minister (also from Ireland) working on the Pennsylvanian frontier, backed up the belief that "True religion… had a critical role to play in the imperial civilizing scheme."[19] As did another advocate for the SPG's civilizing mission, the Scots-born, William Smith (Provost of the College of Philadelphia). He had first-hand experience of England's brutal suppression of the "barbarous" Scottish Highlanders and their cultural values, during the Jacobite Rising (1745).

Stadial Theory

Patrick Griffin, in his book, *"American Leviathan"* mentions the development of the Stadial Theory which sought to make sense of why people like the Indians lived in ways that were alien to Western sensibilities. It was developed by an Ulster-Scot, Francis Hutcheson (Father of the Scottish Enlightenment), who argued "that the pursuit of benevolence" was "an innate 'moral sense'" every bit as real as the more physical senses which "encouraged virtue and made man a social creature, pressing him to join others in the common good."[20]

Such an observation was meant to have "revolutionary implications for understanding those with alien ways." English and Scottish thinkers were to take Hutcheson's understanding of humanity and use it to explain the difference, for example, between Lowland and Highland Scots.

At its most basic,

> "... [it] posited that societies moved through discrete and observable stages of development, hence the term 'stadial.' Each society began at a hunter-gatherer stage, proceeded over time to become pastoral and then agricultural and eventually evolved into a commercial stage. As a society progressed through each level, the manners and morals of the people shifted to reflect the appropriate stage, from savage to the barbarian to the sophisticated. The theory, therefore, could survey all societies through space and time, plotting each along a different stage of the developmental path."[21]

It was seen by some, as the main hope for Indians to become civilized.

What was not anticipated, however, was the possibility that white colonists could climb back down the stadial ladder! It appears to have been a sad but true reality, that by leaving behind their social and spiritual structures, potentially positive character traits took on a darker side. Rugged individualism and incredible courage, which one might say were essential out there on the frontier, were tainted by a disregard for the law and the high social values they had grown up with. Lynch law, violence, coarseness and lack of sexual restraint were pervasive. Griffin speaks of it in graphic terms when he suggests that they climbed back down the Stadial ladder to become "white savages"; worse than the Indians! "If men and women could ascend the ladder from savagery to civility, they could just as easily descend it."[22] Griffin writes in terms of the Kentuckians, not only tolerating Indian killing but rather celebrating it.[23]

That was borne out in a footnote on frontier society in Leyburn's book:

"a most graphic account of the shocking effects upon a conventional mind of this primitive life... recorded in the Journal of the Reverend Charles Woodmason, an itinerant Anglican minister among the settlers in South Carolina from 1766-1768... Population increase had far outstripped institutions. There were families, of course; but many couples lived together and had children without being married, for who was there to perform the ceremony? No courts were present to secure justice nor were there schools or churches. Lawlessness, vile manners, ignorance, and slovenliness were commonplace, with people unaware of how far they had sunk from 'civilized' life... it was a simple tragedy that so many of the people had moved so far, and so often, from civilized society that thousands had never even heard of God, religion or church. Often where religious institutions had made their start, bigotry and denominational animosities were so rampant that one sect would try to drive another from the region."[24]

Unless one had a solid Christian faith, it was easy for a steady insidious deterioration of moral standards to set in. That was especially so for the younger generation and for those who had moved away from their families. Yet sadly, I read of Clergy who were more than very supportive of actions, such as the those perpetrated by the Paxton Boys mentioned above! They were white!

—oooOooo—

Both Barton and Smith were, however, to be greatly challenged in their thinking. Would their project of seeing the civilizing influence of Christianity upon the Indians be possible?

Griffin records:

"The 'sudden, treacherous and unprovoked attack, made by Indians upon the frontiers of Pennsylvania, Maryland, and Virginia, soon after the publication of the general Peace,' made William Smith reconsider the whole civility project. Instead of the civilizing influence of religion flourishing in the West, he beheld 'savage enemies afresh on our frontiers, ravaging and murdering with their usual barbarity.' He did not doubt that religion, in theory, could civilize. The issue was one of time.

If Indians lived in the West unmolested, then they would have the time and space necessary to develop. But if whites crossed the line—as they were doing—time was no longer on the side of the Indians. In other words, if white and Indian worlds kept colliding, Indians would remain in a savage state and continue to kill, capture, and torture whites. In such circumstances, stadial time literally stood still, and cultural development stalled, dooming any civilizing mission to failure..."[25]

Following an Indian attack in 1764, Barton called them, "faithless wretches." Indeed, in that same year he had written an apology on the Paxton Boys, in which he labelled the Indians as "perfidious Villains," "heathens," "idle vagabonds," "Cruel Monsters" and "barbarians," while holding the view that it was right for the Paxton Boys to kill the Conestoga, who had "not embrace civility, and for that they received their just deserts. These 'treacherous Savages... by their perfidy, had forfeited their Lives.'" In addition, they had turned "free born subjects of Britain" and the "brave and Industrious Sons of Pennsylvania" into a people "naked and defenseless," robbing them "of their tokens of civility and their mantle of subjecthood."[26] That's some rationalization!

That was not the first time he had expressed his position. He firmly believed that "Indians who cooperated with the civilizers could be redeemed," but that "recalcitrant ones who refused to allow whites to civilize them had to be chastised." It was during the Seven Years' War when Indians from the Ohio Country were decimating white settlements on the frontier that he wrote an infamous pamphlet called *"Unanimity and Public Spirit."*[27]

In it, his portrayal of the Indians was not unlike that made about the rebellious Irish Papists and Scottish Highlanders at the height of Catholic-Protestant tension in Britain. According to Griffin, Barton had plagiarized it from a sermon "published in London, Dublin, and Belfast during the 1745 Jacobite invasion." Sadly, it bore so many parallels with Presbyterian and Church of Ireland sermons that were preached during the 1912 Home Rule crises in Ireland. Griffin continues,

> "By likening Indians to savage, plotting Papists or barbarous clans, he was equating them with bogeys easily identifiable to his contemporaries. By viewing Indians like these groups beyond the pale (see an explanation of the term at 28), Barton was tapping into a deep well of myth and collective memory from which the stadial notions that he had subscribed to, had sprung. Just as the English had treated such recalcitrant groups in the past, so men and women in the present were justified in treating Indians."

It called for the

> "'Support of our common protestant cause... in this time of Public Danger." The Indians in this piece come off as savages engaged in an 'inhuman' enterprise inflicting 'the Horrors of a Savage War' on 'our pure Protestant Faith, our equitable Laws, and our sacred liberties.' Their 'resentments' he found 'implacable,' and their cause 'unrighteous.' To complicate matters, the French had whipped Indians into this frenzy. 'Romish artifice and Knavery' lay behind 'savagery.' The Catholic 'Sons of Violence' had corrupted the 'Savages' beyond the point of redemption. Such a combination promised to do the same to Protestant settlers in America, turning them into 'Brutes' and rendering 'reason useless.'" [29]

Barton felt that as Protestants they needed to unite to defeat the common foe. If they didn't, they ran the risk of degenerating to become like them! Sadly, for many, this is exactly what did happen. They did unite, but in a savagery that turned out to be worse than that of the Indians! And such was their solidarity, which when it came to people being tried in court for murdering Indians, neighbors refused to stand as a witness against them. Such defiance would continue as settlers crossed over the protective Proclamation Line.

It seems to me that they were all - English, Scots-Irish, French and Indian - puppets in the one play, in which Satan was the one manipulating all the strings!

References:

1. James G. Leyburn, *"The Scotch-Irish—a Social History."* (The University of North Carolina Press, 1962), Pgs. 192-193. Cited in *"Colonial Records of Pennsylvania, 1683-1790."* (Harrisburg, 1851-1853), IX, Pg. 11.
2. Paul Johnson, *"A History of the American People."* (A Phoenix Giant Paperback, Harper Collins Publishers Inc., New York, 1977), Pg. 141.
3. Quoted in Jeremy Engels, *"Equipped for Murder: The Paxton Boys and The Spirit of Killing All Indians in Pennsylvania, 1763-1764."* Rhetoric & Public Affairs, Vol. 8, No. 3, 2005, Pgs. 355-382.
4. Ibid. Pg. 230.
5. Narrative of the Late Massacres in Lancaster County, Franklin Papers xi.
6. Kevin Kenny, *"Peaceable Kingdom Lost—The Paxton Boys and the Destruction of William Penn's Holy Experiment."* (Oxford University Press, 2009), Pg. 205.
7. Ibid. Pg. 120.
8. Ibid. Pgs. 230-231.
9. Peter Silver, *"Our Savage Neighbors."* (W. W. Norton & Co, Inc. New York, 2008) Pg. 35.
10. Johnson, Pg.140.
11. Leyburn, Pg. 230.
12. The Continental Army was formed by the Second Continental Congress after the outbreak of the American Revolutionary War by the colonies that became the United States of America.

Established by a resolution of the Congress on June 14, 1775, it was created to coordinate the military efforts of the Thirteen Colonies in their revolt against the rule of Great Britain. Source: https://en.m.wikipedia.org/wiki/Continental_Army

13. Dr. Jonathan Bardon, An essay, *"An Irish-Scotch Presbyterian Rebellion."* Source: http://www.bbc.co.uk/ulsterscots/library/a-narrow-sea-episode-41

14. James Anthony Froude, *"The English in Ireland, II."* General Books LLC, 2012, Pgs. 146-148.

15. Patrick Griffin, *"American Leviathan-Empire, Nation and Revolutionary Frontier."* (Hill & Wang, 2007), Pg. 22.

16. Land jobbers: "part squatter, part entrepreneur, these men went west to scout out the best sites for the companies [in the east – mine]. In the bargain, they gained fair-sized holdings for themselves." "These men went to great lengths to 'seduce' Indians, offering even guns as concessions for land." Griffin, Pg. 61.

17. Griffin, Pg. 32.

18. Johnson to Board of Trade, 25 Sept. 1763, CO5/65, Pgs. 117-122.

19. Griffin, Pg. 37.

20. Ibid. Pgs. 28-29.

21. Ibid. Pg. 29.

22. Robert Williams, Jnr, *"Savage Anxieties, The Invention of Western Civilization."* Palgrave McMillan, 2012, Pg. 39.

23. Ibid. Pg. 194.

24. Leyburn, pg. 268. Cited from Woodmason, *"The Carolina Back-country on the Eve of the Revolution."* ("The Journals and Other Writings of Charles Woodmason, Anglican Itinerant," ed. Richard J. Hooker, Chapel Hill, 1953.)

25. Griffin, Pg. 66.

26. Ibid. Pg. 66.

27. Ibid. Pg. 67.

28. Beyond the Pale: The Pale was the part of Ireland that was directly under the control of the English government in the late Middle Ages. By the late 15th century it was an area along the east coast stretching from south of Dublin, in an arc northwards, up to the garrison town of Dundalk. The phrase "beyond the pale" meant that anyone who traveled outside of that boundary left behind all

the rules and institutions of English society, which the English considered synonymous with civilization itself and enter the realm of the Irish savage.

Source: https://en.wikipedia.org/wiki/The_Pale

29. Griffin, Pg. 67.

Chapter 15

Time to Decide!

On the other side of the coin

It soon became clear that the Imperial plan, which also required the Indians to act in good faith, was failing. For a bi-lateral system to work efficiently, the Indians had to embrace a stark reality—they might have ownership of the land west of the Proclamation Line, but ultimately the British had sovereignty over it. They were also expected to buy into Britain's civilizing mission for them. As I mentioned earlier in the book, regarding the Puritans coming to New England—we were still very much the superior race!

Inevitably the Indians were going to question the set-up while Indian haters continued to pour over the line; the actions of land grabbers and unrestrained trade. William Johnson was right when he recognized that continued disorder in the West has "made us look less in the Indian eyes than ever... They are greatly disgusted at the ill-treatment of their own People, alarmed at the specious Words of Subjection and Dominion, and astonished at the granting of Lands within their Rights." Little wonder that "they rejected the paternalistic logic of a system they had no hand in drawing up and the civilizing mission it entailed."[1]

And probably most alarming of all were the actions of the frontier settlers. Having "[begun] under the specious pretense of Revenge, but in violation of the British faith," they went on "to murder, Robb and otherwise grossly misuse all Indians they could find." For the Indians, all they had to do was look eastward and see what Britain intended— "to plant colonies in the heart of their country."[2]

We tend to forget, in the reading of most historical accounts, that under such ongoing pressure from Britain and the settlers, the Indians had little choice but to rise up and defend not only their lives but also their families, freedom, lands and hunting grounds. Little wonder the younger Indians were hard to restrain! And when the authorities did try to protect the Indians, they were caught in the middle, with colonists vociferous in their complaint, that the army was not there to protect them.

At the end of the American Revolutionary War, in the 1783 Treaty of Paris (not to be confused with the 1763 Treaty), Britain was to cede the land West of the Proclamation Line to the United States. On the ground, things didn't change—violence was to continue. By 1790, the first in a series of what were called the Indian Intercourse Acts were made law, enabling the regulation of travel and trade within Native American lands. In 1823, the landmark U.S. Supreme Court ruling in *Johnson v. M'Intosh* firmly established that the U.S. government (not private individuals) was the only body that could purchase Native American lands.

The internal conflict continues:
The Regulator Movement (1765-1771)
A series of events in the Carolinas was to precipitate unrest leading to outright war:

- In the 1760s, there was a dramatic increase in the population of people from the eastern cities including lawyers, bankers, and merchants
- Increasing numbers of Scots-Irish immigrants filled up the back-country
- The western edges of these colonies had, up to then, been mostly made up of planters who relied on agriculture
- Due to a season of drought they had been experiencing an economic depression, which caused among the farming community, a reliance on the merchants and going into debt
- The Court system, heavily weighted towards the new well-educated newcomers, produced a growing number of them losing both home and property
- Correspondingly a clique of wealthy officials grew, along with an element of corrupt practices
- The majority backcountry/agricultural people rose up to purge the governmental system of this corruption and control, to

bring some semblance of order, by what became known as the Regulator uprising.[3]

They included many Christians from a predominantly evangelical, pietistic persuasion which produced "an individualistic approach to church, salvation, and personal morality that profoundly influenced their understanding of public relationships and economic issues."[4] Officially, they were seen as opposing the local British authority, something that had to be confronted by the government militias, a confrontation which proved to be counter-productive in the end, as similar conflicts in the 1630s and 40s in Scotland between Covenanters and the English had shown. Some historians saw it as a major catalyst which precipitated the Revolutionary War.

At such points in history, it is not unusual for prominent figures to emerge, as we are only too aware of in Northern Ireland. In North America, one such person came to the fore. He was the Rev. Alexander Creaghead (sometimes referred to as Craighead), a Scotch-Irish minister originally from Donegal who lived in Mecklenburg County, North Carolina. Right from the outset of the 1760s, when armed conflict between the Crown forces and the frontier colonists (known as "over-mountain men") broke out in the Carolinas, he was promoting independence from England.

The Covenants
Such "promoting" did not come suddenly to the fore. I was fascinated to read in *"Our Savage Neighbors"* that some years earlier in 1739-40 Creaghead led "group re-swearings" of the Scottish National Covenant of 1638 and the Solemn League and Covenant of 1643 in which "participants publicly renounced the reigning king." Silver continues:

> "Amid naked, upraised swords, **Creaghead's** crowds chanted out declarations of war against the **church's** enemies and proclaimed that George I, George II, and any other members of the royal house of Hanover had no shadow of a 'legal Right to rule over this **Realm**'... They wanted not simply to redo the acts of their ancestors but in a sense, actually to *be* them once more:

215

to dredge up out of the clear well of Presbyterian history 'in its former **Purity**' their real nature as a church and a chosen people—that 'unspeakable Dignity,' with which Creaghead told them only the Jews and they had ever been honored." [5]

This is the same stuff that could rouse thousands of men to sign the similar politically motivated "re-swearing" in the Ulster Covenant of 1912. Both were a clear misuse of biblical covenants and an act of rebellion against the British Government! Need I say it? This is the stuff that gives Satan massive footholds into Church and nation! Not a good foundation!

Along with other clergy and their congregations who had joined him throughout the coming decade, the Regulator movement was birthed. Creaghead's leadership and preaching were to earn him the title "**Father** of Independence," and by May 1775, as the rebellion in Piedmont reached its peak, his followers signed the Mecklenburg Resolves. Some historians see the Resolves as being closely associated with what is known as the Mecklenburg Declaration of Independence (as no original documentation of the later has ever been found, it has left others to question if it ever existed). Nevertheless, it has been claimed by many, to be the first Declaration of Independence made in the 13 colonies during the American Revolution.

Such measures of dedication and resolve of these men made it impossible for the British forces to subdue these provinces. And, it was also this resolve, along with their skill in using the long-range rifle in guerilla warfare that decisive victories were made possible at King's Mountain and Cowpens, which ultimately paved the way for Lord Cornwallis to surrender at Yorktown in October 1781. It was indeed at the battle at King's Mountain that another clergyman, the Rev. Samuel Doak, raised a rallying call to these over-mountain men to take up "the sword of the Lord and of Gideon." Thomas Jefferson was to call it "The turn of the tide of success."

Gnadenhutten

216

Following the War of Independence things on the western front remained highly sensitive and at a governmental level, both confederated and state, they were not yet very well organized. It is understood that at this time the Continental Army only consisted of approximately eighty men, so, with government approval, it was left to local volunteers to fight local tribes, with revenge and plunder their only pay!

For many on the front, the war was not over. The English may have been defeated, but some of the Indian tribes did not see it that way; there were also those who felt that the Indians had not suffered enough at their hands. It was during this time, in April 1782, that another horrendous atrocity by the Scotch-Irish took place. At Gnadenhutten (The Tents of Grace) on the Muskingum River, west of present-day Pittsburgh, 96 Moravian Ohio Delaware Indian pacifists were systematically and brutally murdered.

Without going into the detail that Silver in *"Our Savage Neighbors"* affords to the event, it is sufficient to record that throughout the War of Independence these Christian Indians tried to maintain neutrality, ministering to whoever came through their villages. As a result, they tended not to be fully trusted by either side! In the previous year, the British and their Wyandot allies had marched them north to the Upper Sandusky plain on the edge of Detroit for their own safety, which as it turns out, was unable to sustain them with enough food. That led some of them to return to Gnadenhutten, Salem, and Schoenbrunn in the Fall of 1781, to harvest their crops.

In Spring, the following year, word got out in Pittsburgh of the kidnapping of a number of people including Robert Wallace, whose wife and children were murdered by a Wyandot and Delaware raiding party, who with their prisoners had passed through Gnadenhutten. From what appears to have been a catalog of misinterpreted information, a company of 150 - 200 men, without the local commander Col. John Gibson's knowledge (from a Presbyterian family in Antrim, Northern Ireland), set out for it. Close to the town, they apprehended a few people, not Moravians, one of whom they murdered and scalped. By finding the body lying on the road, most of the residents of Schoenbrunn somehow escaped what unfolded next. Silver picks up the story:

> "The volunteers took everyone [left] in Gnadenhutten prisoner without resistance, going through the fields around the town and 'b[idding] them come into the town, telling them no harm should befall them,' news at which 'they seemed very glad.' The mission's residents, and perhaps many of the men collecting them, must have thought they would have been taken captive to Fort Pitt... but having been disarmed and bound, and urged to locate all their possession for the trip ahead... as night fell, the twenty-odd congregants who had been in the fields were sorted by sex and confined in frightened groups to two buildings at the center of the settlement, the cooper's shop and the meetinghouse."[6]

It was then ascertained that there were more Indians at Salem, who were brought over and similarly joined to the others. Silver continues:

> "That evening a 'Council' was held, at which David Williamson, the militia's elected leader (again, of Scotch-Irish origin. – mine), 'told his men that he would leave it to their choice, wither to carry the Indians as Prisoners to Fort Pitt, or to kill them; when they agreed that they should be killed.'"

It would seem, that this decision, was neither unanimous or quickly reached. At least a tenth of them were objectors and took no further part in it.

> "Two men were sent to tell the Indians that they would all be killed the next morning. The brethren, who found themselves separated into their familiar choirs of male and female voices, started singing 'Hymns and Psalms all Night... and kept sing[ing as long as there were three alive'... When morning came, a Mahican man named Abraham was pulled out of the men's and boy's

218

building by a cord around the neck and felled with a mallet from the cooper's shop... [T]wo men alone accomplished the whole murder after the Indians had been bound... kill[ing] them one after the other with the mallet, [then] moved inside for the rest of the killings, and apparently made more use of tomahawks to stove in their victims' heads."[7]

"With scalping substituted for throat slitting, this was the same two-step process used at harvest time to slaughter cattle... Killing the Moravians inside the mission buildings, 'which they called the Slaughter House,' was a way of saying that the Indians there were like dumb beasts... After the men were all slaughtered... the women and girls in the other building were tomahawked, with '[m]any children... killed in their wretched mothers' arms.'"

"The killing went on in serial, with a small number of men doing the work at any moment in an agonizingly slow, abattoir-like procedure. In each house, the singing, praying victims watched one another die and be scalped for the space of perhaps a quarter hour... It seems very clear the massacre was not the passionate outburst of a few of the militia... The men at Gnadenhutten were acting on a powerful post-war distaste for Indians as Indians, a feeling that in this instance was by itself so clearly pivotal and indiscriminate as to be worth labeling racist."[8]

That leaves me speechless!

Following the War of Independence, the restless Scotch-Irish would be at the forefront of the incessant push west into the Ohio Valley. Eventually, through intermarriage, their cultural identity would begin to merge into an ethnic mix to become 'Americans,' but during their initial move west they were still very much, in heart and thought, Scotch-Irish!

Conflict continues

A clear irreconcilable gulf began to form along the Alleghenies, as people living in the West began to turn their backs on Eastern governmental authority for not providing them with adequate protection from Indian attacks. That was especially the case in Western Pennsylvania, possibly arising from the pacifist Quakers having no standing army to fight for them. They were seen as being too "liberal to Savages, and at the same Time not contribut[ing] a single Farthing as a Society to help [them in their] Distresses." In general, the American government at this time was committed to the civilizing approach of the stadial theory, regarding the Indians; choosing to chastise misdemeanors rather than conquest. Ultimately, peace would only be possible when the East submitted to Western pressure for their protection, which would mean both the conquering and removal of the Indians from their midst.[9]

Harry Innes (eventually to become the first U.S. Federal Judge in Kentucky) voiced the thoughts of many to Henry Knox when he said that the "Indians have always been the aggressors," and that "any incursion made into their country have been from reiterated injuries committed by them."[10] In the minds of the people, Indians, not settlers, inhabited a space somewhere between "savagery" and nonhuman status. He called for a general war, and if Knox did not act, westerners would. It was patently clear that very few frontiers people were up for embracing any idea that Indians were redeemable!

Nevertheless, Government officials were to continue with their policy of "treating with the enemy" which only had the effects of further alienating the westerners who were bent on war. One negotiator argued that the key to pacifying the West lay in "mak[ing] known" that the United States "in no wise desired to wage a bloody war with them, but on the contrary, were ready and willing to make a peace which should in every respect be in accordance with the laws of justice and humanity."[11] Settlers, on the other hand, could not tolerate the ongoing accommodation of what was regarded as "a cruel savage enemy."[12]

Added to the Indian problem was also the internal one widely felt beyond Pennsylvania, into Ohio and Kentucky, that of Property rights.

The thinking continued to prevail that if settlers had claimed the land, cleared it, developed it and protected it from the Indians, then clearly it was theirs for the keeping! Counter to that, this was a region overrun with unresolved conflicts between them, the jobbers, and eastern speculators. (The latter were closely connected to wealthy patrons and local government who were looking after their own interests in the Ohio Valley.) Procurement of land was something all sides were prepared to use violence over, either civil war or war for independence were possible outcomes![13]

Following the War of Independence, many westerners were still struggling over with these issues—even with ideas of separate nationhood, which were fostered by the ongoing inability of the east to govern them efficiently and provide protection from Indian attacks.

In the light of that, 1792-94 would prove to be watershed years regarding Government, Westerner Settler, and Indian affairs. In 1793 Harry Innes received a letter from the serving Secretary of State, Thomas Jefferson which reflected that:

> "It is very interesting to the U.S. to see how this last effort for living in peace with the Indians will succeed. If it does not, there will be a great revolution of opinion here as to the manner in which they are to be dealt with."[14]

The Greenville Treaty
Griffin puts it well when he writes,

> "the gulf between western concerns and Atlantic interests... had grown so wide that no reconciliation on the terms of easterners seemed possible. Only if the East bowed to western demands for protection, especially when it came to conquering and displacing Indians, could peace come."[15]

This impasse would eventually be resolved by the firmer military and political action which commenced in 1792 when George Washington commissioned Anthony Wayne. At his disposal was a highly-trained force of five thousand soldiers, many like Wayne were hardened veterans of the Revolutionary War. He describes it as "no army of chastisement... created to conquer."[16] The defeat of the confederation of Indian nations (Miami, Chippewa, Wyandot, Shawnee, Pottawatomie, Kickapoo, Delaware, Wea, Piankashaw, Kaskaskia and Eel River) and their British allies saw the drawing of a new line well north of the Ohio River. Unlike the former British Proclamation line, which kept the whites out of Indian land, this one was designed to keep the Indians far away from land settled by the whites. The formal Treaty of Greenville and its Demarcation Line was signed in August 1795. Along with another treaty signed with the Spanish, the Mississippi became available for American navigation, and as a result, the West opened up to further expansion! While the Native Americans observed the terms of the Treaty, sadly, the Americans didn't. That would lead to further tensions in the early 1800's involving the infamous Shawnee leader, Tecumseh.

—oooOooo—

Further Presbyterian insights

People who did not go to America in family or congregational units, more often than not, formed relationships with others on the voyage over and set out together on their new life. In so doing, they already had the makings of a small Presbyterian congregation. As I have previously mentioned, the only element - so often missing - was a clergyman. For someone to go to America in that role, over and above the intense training, he would have needed nothing short of the zeal, vision, and passion of a pioneer missionary. Such an ardor seems to have been scarce in Ulster—pastoral care was minimal; many of the clergy were content to oversee the sacraments and defend their own denominations theological stances. Life was also comfortable and being salaried they did not need to do any form of secular employment to supplement their income, whereas in America they would initially have had to be willing to take up something very manual such as pioneer farming.

In America, a lack of spiritual vitality was also becoming increasingly apparent: their early zeal and energy had dissipated leaving much of Puritanism, Presbyterianism, and Anglicanism as something 'nice,' social, formal and legalistic. Things had become predictable, staid, serious, settled.

It was to take the Great Awakening in 1738 to stir things up, though even that appears to have had a lesser impact on the Western fringes! With people like John and Charles Wesley and George Whitefield at the helm, colonial America was ablaze with religious fervor. Yet, as in any new outpouring of the Spirit of God, there were those who stood in clear opposition to it. Within Presbyterianism, this was to ultimately lead to a thirteen-yearlong schism (1745-1758) and the formation of the Old Side (those who opposed it) and the New Side. With the latter being very mission-minded, a transformation was underway; an American Church was emerging. 1746 saw the establishment of Princeton College in New Jersey, a clear declaration from within Presbyterianism that it was no longer dependent on England or Scotland. Nevertheless, there was still a gross shortage of ordained clergy, meaning that up to two hundred thousand Scotch-Irish in the back-country were still not having their spiritual needs sufficiently met.

Unlike the other major churches in Britain and America, the Presbyterian Churches governmental structure was federal. That was similar to the political institutions developing in America. It had also been Calvin's belief that the churches elders (Presbyters) should seek close links with their local magistrates for the purposes of effectively maintaining public order. And so it was, through such a governmental system, that the Scotch-Irish in their Church Session and Courts had been developing skills in legal and judicial matters, which were to hold them in good stead upon their arrival in America. Not surprisingly, there were those among the new colonists who readily got involved in the local political and legal processes. In Pennsylvania, this was to have a marked effect on the colonial assemblies, which up to then had been dominated by the Quakers.

A personal reflection

Destiny denied! I have become more acutely aware that the Puritans and Ulster—Scots came to America with their destinies in England, Scotland, and Ireland being denied. Their histories, including the persecutions they had experienced back home, became a part of their corporate identities, which negatively shaped how they saw themselves and others when they came to North America. One could also add to that the theological, legal and political perspectives within the Doctrine of Discovery which they had consciously or otherwise imbibed. These invariably influenced their perceptions of and responses to the Roman Catholic Church and Native American communities, determining their actions. I write "otherwise imbibed" because I am aware that the Scotch-Irish, in coming to America, would not have been as directly influenced by the DOD in the way the Puritans and Anglicans were a century before. Yet, both the Puritans and Scotch-Irish most certainly had a strong sense of being "exceptional," set aside by God and sent to America by Him. For the Scotch-Irish, this would have been primarily embedded in them by their understanding of being a Covenant people. My sense is that by the time they arrived in America, the DOD was so deeply embedded into colonial life, and especially that of its leadership, that it would have been unconsciously absorbed by them.

I have found in Ireland that ownership of the painful aspects of "our history" has been an essential prerequisite for the healing of these things deep within our personal and national psyche. Sadly, for many, they see themselves in the right and project the problems of their own history unto "them"—God is on our side, so "they" must always be in the wrong! If we don't personally know and own these negative aspects of our history, we cannot experience Christ's healing ministry of reconciliation to be worked out in us, nor can we embrace the part God wants us to play in the healing in the nation. This is something I will pick up on in the second part of this book – "A Dignity Restored." Before that, I want us to look at two other issues: Manifest Destiny and the Residential Boarding Schools.

References:

1. Patrick Griffin, *"American Leviathan—Empire, Nation and Revolutionary Frontier."* (Hill & Wang, 2007)

2. Ibid. Pg. 69.
3. Ibid. Pg. 69.
4. Source: http://en.wikipedia.org/wiki/War_of_the_Regulation
5. Source: http://uncpress.unc.edu/nc_encyclopedia/regulator.html
30. Peter Silver, *"Our Savage Neighbors."* (W. W. Norton & Co, Inc. New York, 2008) Pgs. 25-26.
6. Silver, Pg. 269.
7. Ibid. Pg. 270.
8. Ibid. Pg. 27.
9. Griffin, Pgs. 213-214.
10. Ibid. Pg. 215.
11. Ibid. Pg. 216.
12. Ibid. Pg. 217.
13. Ibid. Pg. 214.
14. Ibid. Pg. 240.
15. Ibid. Pg. 214.
16. Ibid. Pg. 246.

Chapter 16

Manifest Destiny

The term "Manifest Destiny" is also one that repeatedly came up in my research. So, let's take a closer look at it!

Anders Stephanson in his book, *"Manifest Destiny—American Expansion and the Empire of Right"* points out that the Puritans came to America seeing

> "The world as God's 'manifestation' and history as a predetermined 'destiny.' These 'had been ideological staples of the strongly providentialist period in England between 1620 and 1660, during which, of course, their initial migration to New England took place.'"[1]

This could equally be said of the Presbyterians in Scotland during this period, with their understanding of God's covenanted relationship with them! The Puritans, as we saw earlier, went to North America with a very clear sense of a "Divine calling to separateness." To quote Stephanson again:

> "In the early sixteenth century, the normative community of Christian Europe was driven by the Protestant Reformation and the religious wars it induced. In the very same epoch, as it happened, the Americas were being *'discovered'*: and it was, of course, a particularly fierce and uncompromising phalanx within the Reformation —namely the Puritans—that eventually colonized the region known as New England... English Protestantism, early on, had developed a notion of England as not only spatially but also spiritually separate from the European continent, as the bastion of true religion and chief

source of its expansion: a place divinely singled out for higher missions. The Separatists who crossed the Atlantic were part of this tradition, only more radical. Old England, in their eyes, had not broken in the end with the satanic ways of popery. Divine purposes would have to be worked out elsewhere, in some new and uncorrupted land."[2]

Add to that, the Doctrine of Discovery and the belief that the Indians, which they encountered in New England, were the outsiders, savage, profane, to be overcome, conquered and you have a potent mix!

These were, as I have already mentioned, my tribal identities (English and Scotch-Irish) that came to America in the 17th and early 18th centuries, with a sense of divine calling, having had their destines denied through persecution back home. David Pletcher made a similar connection, seeing **Manifest Destiny** as "a conviction that God intended North America to be under the control of Americans [i.e., Euro-Americans – *mine*]. It's a kind of early projection of Anglo-Saxon supremacy, and there's a racist element there."[3]

While Michael T. Lubrage writes,

> "The idea of **Manifest Destiny** is as old as America itself. The philosophy sailed with Christopher Columbus across the Atlantic. It resided in the spirits of the Jamestown colonists and it landed at Plymouth Rock with the Pilgrims. It also traveled with the fire and brimstone preachers during the Great Awakening...
>
> ... To some, the Manifest Destiny Doctrine was based on the idea that America had a divine providence. It had a future that was destined by God to expand its borders, with no limit to area or country. All the traveling and expansion were part of the spirit of Manifest Destiny, a belief that it was God's will that Americans spread the entire continent, and to control and populate the country as they see fit. Many

expansionists conceived God as having the power to sustain and guide human destiny. 'It was white man's burden to conquer and Christianize the land.' (Demkin – see note 4) For example, the idea that the Puritan notion of establishing a 'city on a hill' was eventually secularized into Manifest Destiny—a sort of materialistic, religious, utopian destiny."[4]

They, along with other writers, were clearly making a connection between the Doctrine of Discovery and Manifest Destiny. From such perspectives, any victory over the Indians was seen as Providential, as was the devastating effects of smallpox/leptospirosis in the 1630s. John Winthrop concluded, "God hath consumed the natives with a miraculous plagey." This was not all that much different to what Benjamin Franklin was to say 100 years later when he proclaimed that rum was "'the appointed means' by which 'the design of Providence to extirpate these savages' was fulfilled, 'in order to make room for the cultivators of the earth.'"[5] Now, try and get your head around either of those two analyses!

John O'Sullivan

Contrary to my first understanding, Andrew Jackson was not the name primarily attached to the words "Manifest Destiny." Jackson had indeed spoken in 1843 of expansion in terms of "extending the area of freedom," just as other Presidents before him had elaborated on its underlying principles. But it is generally accepted that John O'Sullivan (yet, another Irishman!), co-founder and editor of the *Democratic Review* and the *New York Morning News* that penned it. He had already used the phrase earlier in connection with the annexation of Texas, but without much notice being taken. It was its second mention in an Editorial of the *Morning News* (December 27th, 1845) that caught people's attention. Entitled "The True Title," it was written to advance the annexation of Oregon Country to the United States:

> "Away, away, with all these cobweb tissues of rights
> of discovery, exploration, settlement, contiguity, etc.
> [The American claim] is by the right of our **manifest**

destiny to overspread and to possess the whole of the continent which Providence has given us for the development of the great experiment of liberty and federative self-government entrusted to us."[6]

Stephanson, in the Prologue to his book, in saying "it was anything but new," goes on to give a quote from a colonization agent's information to prospective English emigrants in 1616, "What need wee then feare, but goe up at once as **a peculiar people** marked and **chosen by the finger of God** to possess it?"[7]

Jefferson also alludes to this sense of choosiness and being sent by God in his second inaugural address when he spoke of, "our fathers, [being sent] as Israel of old, from their native land and planted them in a country flowing with all the necessities of life."[8]

In an article written on the issue by Robert E. May, he describes Jackson as "the hero of the Democrats in the mid-1840s... who lent glamor" to it. He also observes, "that most of the concepts attached to the phrase had been espoused by O'Sullivan in only slightly different language prior to this, and that his arguments drew on the ideology of earlier U.S. expansionists such as John Quincy Adams"[9] and "that many of his ideas can be traced back even further—to, for instance, the sense of destiny of the Puritans who settled in colonial New England and the thoughts about empire taking a westward course..." as expressed in the last four lines of a poem written in 1726 by the Anglo-Irish clergyman and philosopher, Bishop George Berkeley. He entitled it, "Verse on the Prospect of Planting Arts and Learning in America"[10]

> Westward the course of empire takes its way:
> The four first acts already past,
> A fifth shall close the drama with the day:
> Time's noblest offspring is the last.

Such "westward" thinking certainly seems to be in keeping with the religious reflections of others around that time. In a sermon preached by the Reverend Thomas Brockaway in 1784, he said,

"'Empire, learning, and religion, have in past ages, been traveling from east to west, and this continent is their last western state... Here then is God erecting a stage on which to exhibit the great things of His kingdom.' What had originally been, for the clergy, a satanic space to be conquered was by now an alluring, pastoral emptiness to be exploited."[11]

Ralph Waldo Emerson (1803-1832) likewise expresses such a belief, that over and above any territorial expansion, a providential destiny was guiding individuals, states and nations and that this was especially so regarding the model republic of the United States.

Miguel Angel González Quiroga in an article entitled *"The Power of an Idea,"* summed it up well when he wrote,

"... the die was cast when the United States was born as a nation and began its slow but inexorable expansion to the west... Expansion was an historical process that, like a westward wind, swept all before it... European immigration led to an explosive growth of the population of the United States and this inevitably led to expansion. Expansion led to war."[12]

Robert Sampson, in his book *"John L. O'Sullivan and His Times,"* comments that O'Sullivan's *Morning News* had another lead article in it, purported to have been crafted by him. Quoting from it, he writes:

"'Yes, more, more, more will be the unresting cry, till our national identity is fulfilled and 'the whole boundless continent is ours.' Texas, Oregon, California, even Canada were fated to be 'embraced within the ever-widening circle' of the United States. Rather than an empire, he envisioned a 'peaceful union,' joined by a 'common constitution, a common nationality, a common sentiment of Patriotism, a common pursuit of the great American idea of free development of humanity to the best and highest results it may be capable of working out for itself.' To achieve this 'great destiny,' the United States must have 'the whole... [W]e shall have it, we must have it, we will have it.'"[13]

And so, West they went, again!

—ooo0ooo—

Following the Treaty of Paris in 1783, which marked the end of the Revolution between Britain and the U.S., a series of key events brought this westward move about:

- The Louisiana Purchase in 1803. Through it, Thomas Jefferson bought the Louisiana Territory from France for a sum of 15 million dollars (approx. $233 million today). In so doing the U.S. practically doubled in size as it gained land from the Mississippi River to the Rocky Mountains.

- On February 28, 1845, the U.S. Congress passed a bill authorizing the United States to annex the Republic of Texas. The March 1 saw President John Tyler sign an annexation resolution, followed in mid-December by President Polk signing a Joint Resolution enabling it to become the 28th State on December 29. In "*Manifest Destiny and Mission in American History*," Frederick Merk writes, "Texas was a perfect example of how Manifest Destiny would work, a pattern to be copied by the remainder of the continent. Prior to American occupation it had been a raw wilderness, rich in resources, not unused, or misused... It's people... had formed a state and had applied to the Union for admission. They had persisted, despite rebuffs, in applying, and at last, had succeeded. Here was a plan, favored by God, for North America."[14]

- Oregon. There were at the time approximately 3,500-4,000 American citizens living there, who not only wanted American law to be applied but also saw themselves as something of a vanguard for the nation.[4] Following border disputes with Britain regarding the northernmost limits of Oregon, which neither side wanted to go to war over, the 49th parallel was settled upon by President Polk in the Oregon Treaty in 1846.

- The Mexican–American War (or the U.S.-Mexican War), followed on from the annexation of Texas (1846-48), as Mexico still considered Texas part of its territory. Its end saw President James K. Polk's vision of American territorial expansion to the Pacific coast realized. Sadly, there were advocates of Manifest Destiny who, not unlike the British involvement in Ireland, believed that the United States had a responsibility, a mission among the Catholic Mexicans, to bring both the Protestant faith and cultural progress to people under the control of the Catholic Church and their equally repressive secular leaders.

- In a process that began in the seventeenth century, the U.S. also obtained vast cessions from Native American tribes. In turn, they were relocated to reservations on what was at the time, unwanted remote regions.

Frederick Merk made an observation which follows on from what I mention above regarding the ending of the Mexican War, that it was "the duty of the United States to regenerate backward peoples of the continent." He comments that,

> "It acquired importance only when Mexico moved, in the mid-1840s, into the focus of American expansionism. Regeneration had not been part of the thinking of the American government in dealing with the red man of the wilderness. The Indian was a heathen whose land title passed, according to canon well established, to the Christian prince and his heirs who had discovered or conquered them. Natives retained only rights of occupancy in their lands. Numbering but a few thousand in the latitudes of the United States they were provided for by concentration on reservations."[15]

Although he doesn't use the words, this is nevertheless an articulation of an aspect of the Doctrine of Discovery!

He continues,

> "There was a vague, uneasy sense, in some quarters, of an insufficiency of good land. It was a new note in the national life. The old note was expressed by Jefferson in his inaugural address. He had assured the nation (bound still by the Mississippi) that it possessed, 'a chosen country, with room enough for our descendants to the thousandth and thousandth generation.' But already by 1845 western settlement was at the bend of the Missouri. Beyond lay serried rows of Indian reservations and far west, semi-aridity... Yet a vast surplus of arable land would be needed if a refuge was to be kept open for the oppressed of the world. The answer to the need was obvious. It was given by O'Sullivan: 'Yes, more, more, more... till our national destiny is fulfilled and... the whole boundless continent is ours.'" (New York Morning News, Feb. 7, 1845)[16]

Stephenson also writes about this,

> "A more precise elaboration of this was found in the natural law tradition. Here the essential aspect was the connection between possession and productivity, as considered conceptually in the idea of *vacuum domicilium* (i.e., a Doctrine of Discovery term – *mine*). Emerich de Vattel, the eighteenth-century thinker, offered the standard reference (though Locke was also cited). On what grounds, Vattel had asked, can one 'lawfully take possession of a part of a vast country, in which there are found none but erratic nations' which cannot 'people the whole?' His response ran as follows. There was a given 'obligation to cultivate the earth'—it was natural to improve nature—and these people manifestly could not do that: hence the title to the land was not true legal possession. The cramped European, by contrast, could make real use of the land, *subdue* it; and thus, they were justified in establishing full legal title...

233

...In vulgar form, this argument boiled down to the dual proposition that Indians were hunters and gathers and that the land was therefore empty, a 'waste' there for the taking. Plentiful evidence showing that Indians were not in fact nomads, was willfully ignored. And when it could not be ignored, other ways were found, as in the notorious case of the Cherokee nation...

... After abandoning his erstwhile notion that Indians would become dark—skinned versions of Enlightenment whites, Jefferson had in fact designated the Louisiana Purchase for resettlement purposes. This was at a moment when that vast space still appeared to be the 'great American dessert.' When, in the 1840s and 50s, the reality was found otherwise, the tribal remnants were once again pushed aside. Americans wanted land to exploit, not indigenous people to assimilate. For Jefferson, at any rate, his original (1786) 'certainty that not a foot of land will ever be taken from the Indians without their own consent' was duly replaced with a somber realization that government could not control white intrusion and expropriation, even had it so wished. Assimilation projects along Christian-humanitarian lines went on until the 1820's but generally failed. There remained expulsion or extermination...

... In the Jacksonian epoch, Senator Benjamin Leigh of Virginia would express the spirit of either/or with admirable lucidity: 'It is peculiar to the character of this Anglo-Saxon race of men to which we belong, that it has never been contented to live in the same country with any other distinct race, upon terms of equality; it has, invariably, when placed in that situation, proceeded to exterminate or enslave the other race in some form or other or, failing that, to abandon the country.' But no one was about to abandon this particular country."[17]

The wider context

O'Sullivan's "more, more, more" of Manifest Destiny was also set within the wider context of several other factors. A key one being a series of economic depressions (1818 and 1829) which led to a growing number of people seeking a better life on the frontier: inexpensive land; the lure of self-sufficiency; independence and for some commercial and political position/power. It was also a time, a season of tremendous and exciting change in the western world: industrialization and technological advances such as the railroad; the rotary printing press and the magnetic telegraph.

Within a few decades, the Statue of Liberty would be erected on a base of what was originally Fort Wood on Ellis Island, during "Tecumseh's War" in 1812. In his book *Sign Language*, Terry Wildman quotes from the website of "The Statue of Liberty—Ellis Island Foundation."

"The Statue of Liberty is more than a monument. She is a beloved friend, a living symbol of freedom to millions around the world..."[18] He goes on to say,

> "The Statue faces eastward toward Europe holding high a torch representing the light of freedom. On a plaque attached to the base of the statue is the famous quote from the poem of Emma Lazarus... 'The New Colossus,' 'Give me your tired, your poor, your huddled masses yearning to breathe, the wretched refuse of your teeming shores. Send these homeless; tempest-tossed to me, I lift my lamp beside the golden door!'"[19]

Unfortunately, the "the poor... wretched... homeless" of Europe, in coming to America were to make its original inhabitants "poor... wretched... homeless," instead! The persecuted became the persecutor; the wounded became the "wounder!"

As I mentioned above, with the United States boundaries remorselessly moving west, it inevitably led to clashes with the Native American tribes as they sought to defend their homelands. History records many of these encounters; with major ones standing out, such as Red Cloud's War; Custer's Last Stand; the Massacre of Wounded Knee...

The "city upon a hill" – Manifest Destiny?

It was with interest that I read while researching this chapter, that a number of U.S. presidents during my lifetime have cited John Winthrop in some of their rallying calls.

Here are two of them:

1. President-elect John F. Kennedy. "In an address to the Massachusetts Legislature on January 9, 1961, 'During the last 60 days, I have been engaged in the task of constructing an administration... I have been guided by the standard John Winthrop set before his shipmates on the flagship Arabella [sic] 331 years ago, as they, too, faced the task of building a government on a new and perilous frontier. 'We must always consider,' he said, 'that we shall be as a city upon a hill—the eyes of all people are upon us.' Today the eyes of all people are truly upon us, and our governments, in every branch, at every level, national, State, and local, must be as a city upon a hill-constructed and inhabited by men aware of their grave trust and their great responsibilities."[20]

2. President Ronald Regan. Speaking at the first Conservative Political Action Conference in January 1974, shortly after the return of John McCain, Bill Lawrence, and Ed Martin as POWs from North Vietnam, he quoted:

   "For we must consider that we shall be as a city upon a hill, the eyes of all people are upon us. So that if we shall deal falsely with our God in this work we have undertaken, and so cause Him to withdraw His present help from us, we shall be made a story and a byword through the world..."

He then declared,

"Well, we have not dealt falsely with our God... We cannot escape our destiny, nor should we try to. The leadership of the free world was thrust upon us two centuries ago in that little hall of Philadelphia. In the days following World War II, when the economic strength and power of America was all that stood between the world and the dark ages, Pope Pius XII said, 'The American people have a great genius for splendid and unselfish actions. Into the hands of America, God has placed the destinies of an afflicted mankind.' 'We are, indeed, and we are today, the last best hope of man on earth.'"

Reagan's last lines explicate the meaning of Winthrop's words in modern times: America must help to maintain freedom in this world.[21]

The creator is still our hope-another way!

There is so much within the Western Church that has not been a demonstration of the "true body of Christ"; an expression of Creator's love. It has been Christendom (the spirit of Empire) rather than Christianity! One thing is certain. The United States of America, and for that matter the U.K., is not and never has been a Christian nation! They are both products of Christendom! There is much that has been done in God's name that needs to be repented of!

I finish this chapter with a poem I wrote during a ministry trip to the west coast of the United States back in 2009. For me, it was very clearly a "download" from Creator and as such, expresses His heart for the Native American peoples, what I felt from Him in my spirit. What you read is very much as I wrote it down. It came as quickly and took not much longer to write.

He walks the land.

In Ireland, and here also,
    I step on to your land.
A land and hearts scarred...
    as you were moved, coerced, forced towards the

setting sun.
Like a great earth-mover we pushed, pushed, pushed you before us…
    ripping, tearing at your very roots.
The blood cries out!

I sit among you listening.
In some strange, profound way,
    I feel your pain, His pain.
At times gentle, quiet,
    at others…
        gut-wrenching, agonizing—PAIN!

In their thousands, they came
    —my people, my tribe,
        to fulfill their destiny,
            yet destroying yours.

They knew not, that God had also put "eternity in your hearts."
They knew not, that He wanted to redeem you and your cultures too
    —another way!
"Father forgive them"—did they truly know not what they did?
"During the days of His life on earth, He offered up prayers, petitions,
    with loud cries and tears… and He was heard."
He still does…
    walking your land, my land, still crying, weeping, still heard—
        through those He finds, to share it with… to stand among you, and weep.

There is still a destiny, a dignity for you.
Still available, now being restored—IN HIM!
        © Harry Smith, November 2009

Conclusion

There has been much here in this and in the former chapters that need to be owned, and responded to, some of which we will look at in the second section of this book, "A Dignity Restored." But there is one specific outworking of it, that still lives on in a very real way today, in the surviving victims of the Residential Boarding Schools era, in the USA and Canada. It is this that we now briefly turn to, as we come to the end of this section of the book—A Destiny Denied.

References:

1. Anders Stephanson, *"Manifest Destiny—American Expansion and the Empire of Right."* (Pub. Hill & Wang, 1995), Pg. 5.
2. Ibid, Pg. 3.
3. An Ideal or a Justification—A Conversation with David M. Pletcher, Indiana University.
4. Michael T. Lubrage *"Manifest Destiny—The Philosophy that Created a Nation."* Source: http://www.let.rug.nl/usa/essays/1801-1900/manifest-destiny/ (Sub-section: "The components of Manifest Destiny"). He also quotes here from Stephen R Demkin's Lecture Notes, Delaware County Community College.
5. Stephanson, Pgs. 10-11.
6. Frederick Merk, *"Manifest Destiny and Mission in American History."* (Random House, 1966), Pgs. 31-32. (emphasis – mine)
7. Stephanson, Prologue Pg. xii. (emphasis – mine)
8. Ibid. Pg. 5. (parenthesis – mine)
9. Robert E. May, *"Manifest Destiny."* Source: http://www.pbs.org/kera/usmexicanwar/prelude/md_manifest_destiny2.html
10. Source: http://math.berkeley.edu/about/history/viewpoints/berkeley
11. William R. Handley, *"Marriage, Violence and the Nation in the American Literary West."* (Cambridge University Press, 2002) Pg. 27. Also, Stephanson, Pg. 19.
12. Source: http://www.pbs.org/kera/usmexicanwar/prelude/md_power_of_an_idea.html

13. Robert Sampson, *"John L. O'Sullivan and His Times."* Kent State University Press, 2003, Pg. 201.
14. Merk, Pgs. 46-47.
15. Merk, Pg. 33.
16. Ibid, Pgs. 51-52.
17. Stephanson, Pgs. 25-27.
18. Terry Wildman, *"Sign Language—A look at the Historic and Prophetic Landscape of America."* (Great Thunder Publishing, Maricopa, Arizona, 2011), Pgs. 81-83.
19. Source: http://www.statueofliberty.org/Statue_of_Liberty.html
20. Source: http://www.enotes.com/homework-help/what-does-saying-city-upon-hill-mean-many-392535
21. Source: https://satyagraha.wordpress.com/2013/04/18/john-winthrops-city-on-a-hill-speech-1630/

Chapter 17

The Residential Boarding Schools

In the Summer of 2013, Dorothy and I were in Harbor Springs, Michigan, with Terry and Darlene Wildman (Rainsong). It was there that I was confronted, full-on, with the issue of Residential Boarding Schools for Native American children. I knew about them before that, but never in the way, I unexpectedly experienced them that day!

There had been a Residential School in Harbor Springs run by the Catholic Sisters of Notre Dame. It was one of the earliest in existence, having opened in 1829 in a small log cabin, it went through a series of expansions (1885, 1913 and 1928) to become one of the largest Indian Mission establishments in the United States, closing as recently as 1983. Over those years, it accommodated approximately 3,500 boarders as well as many day pupils.

The Boarding School is no longer there, having been replaced by a modern multi-functional building for the Parish. Neither was there any obvious visible sign of a plaque acknowledging the history of the School. All we saw was a simple white Cross in a shaded area close to the nearby Church. As I stood there before it, a weeping rose up from within my spirit. A few days later, I felt the prompting to write a poem, simply called, "Listen!" I was very conscious that I was identifying with something of God's heart, a deep wound within the Native American people regarding the legacy of these Boarding Schools. A wound that for many, still needs to be healed.

Listen!

It stands alone in a tree-shaded place,
beside a church in Harbor Springs.
A white, wreathed, Indian feathered, cross.
I stand there and listen.

Listening to a cry, not only in the heart of God
but also to another, rising up from the ground.
For over one hundred and fifty years,
on a nearby plot of land,
ever enlarging walls engulfed the lives of Native young—
The Holy Childhood of Jesus Residential School—
thousands, in an unholy embrace.

Listen!
As they were torn from their homes,
transported,
debraided,
language and culture suppressed.
Many died, to be placed in unmarked graves!
Others, still alive,
are left still dying,
in so many different ways – on the inside!

Listen!
Creator's Son, with arms stretched out,
embraces the wounds of history.
His blood also cries out, better than that of Abel.

The Father hears…
and…
folding you in His arms,
He releases redemption, healing, forgiveness, dignity, hope!
Be still! Listen!
Can you hear the blood,
His heart—for you?

—oooOooo—

The Boarding School's history

Schooling on reservations and the subsequent development of
Boarding Schools were initially introduced from the late 1820s by
Catholic Orders, Episcopalian, and Methodist missionaries to provide
educational opportunities for Indian children who had no other means

of obtaining it.

By 1880 the Government's Bureau of Indian Affairs was to establish many more Boarding Schools, as it was thought that schooling on the reservations did not sufficiently remove the pupils from the tribe's influence. "Assimilation through total immersion"[1] became a central tenant of what became known as a hugely misguided social experiment.

They were the brain-child of Army Captain Richard Pratt, who was known for his infamous speech in 1892:

> "A great general has said that the only good Indian is a dead one, and that high sanction of his destruction has been an enormous factor in promoting Indian massacres. In a sense, I agree with the sentiment, but only in this: that all the Indian there is in the race should be dead. Kill the Indian in him, and save the man."[2]

In 1879, he established what has become the most well-known of these, the Carlisle Indian School in Pennsylvania, of which he was its Headmaster for 25 years. It is thought that approximately 500 Boarding Schools were established overall, that followed the Carlisle model.

In a comprehensive article by Kay Porterfield she writes:

> "In order to assimilate American Indian children into European culture, Pratt subjected them to what we would call brainwashing tactics today. These are the same methods that cult leaders use to coerce recruits to commit completely to a new way of thinking."[3]

Education became mandatory in 1893, which empowered government agents on the reservations to enforce any federal regulations. Carolyn Marr, an anthropologist who has studied the boarding schools, writes:

> "If parents refused to send their children to school the

243

authorities could withhold annuities or rations or send them to jail. Some parents were uncomfortable having their children sent far away from home. The educators had quotas to fill, however, and considerable pressure was exerted on Indian families to send their youngsters to boarding schools beginning when the child was six years old. Fear and loneliness caused by this early separation from family is a common experience shared by all former students. Once their children were enrolled in a distant school, parents lost control over decisions that affected them."[4]

It is believed that approximately 100,000 Indian children, between the ages of 7-14, were sent to them, many having been forcibly removed from their families. There they experienced the humiliation of having their braided hair cut; their Native clothing replaced with a uniform; being punished for speaking their Native language to each other and military-style discipline. The simple non-Indian diet, the cold austerity of the buildings and cramped dormitory accommodation left them susceptible to communicable diseases. Many were to die in these schools to be placed in unmarked graves. The exact number has never fully been determined! In many of the schools, they were registered with English names, having had their Indian name taken away. That led to some parents not knowing of their child's death, thus making it impossible for them to be buried within their tribal lands.

It was assumed by the reformers that it was essential to "civilize" these children by making them embrace white values and belief systems. History was taught with a clear white bias:

> "Columbus Day was heralded as a banner day in history and a beneficent development in their own race's fortunes, as only after discovery did Indians enter the stream of history. Thanksgiving was a holiday to celebrate "good" Indians having aided the brave Pilgrim Fathers... George Washington's birthday served as a reminder of the Great White Father. On Memorial Day, some students at off-reservation schools were made to decorate the graves of soldiers

sent to kill their fathers."[5]

Anne Stanton, a reporter for Northern Michigan's Northern Express Newspaper, wrote an article in which she refers to the School I visited in Harbor Springs, called *"They Came for the Children."* In it she mentions Professor David Wallace Adams and his book *"Education for Extinction,"* in which he refers to John Oberly's philosophy back in 1888 when he was Superintendent of Indian Schools:

> "The curriculum taught the basics, but also Christian beliefs and the moral imperative of becoming an American consumer, Adams wrote. And Indians were clearly not 'consumers' in the late 1800s. They lived communally and traditionally, and that was a problem in a capitalistic society... Indian schools needed to wean students from 'the degrading communism of the tribal reservation system' and to imbue him 'with the exalting egotism of American civilization, so that he will say, 'I' instead of 'We,' and 'This is mine,' instead of 'This is ours.'"[6]

Gleaning from an Annual Report of the Commissioner of Indian Affairs, she also mentions that, "By 1900, there were 153 government and private boarding schools in the country, attended by nearly 18,000 children."[7] Nevertheless, attitudes were changing—a harrowing report in the 1920s gave the conclusion that "children at federal boarding schools were malnourished, overworked, harshly punished and poorly educated."[8] In 1969, another report stated that the Indian education system was a "national tragedy." What was a solution to the so-called Indian problem was for thousands largely remembered as a time of the abuse and desecration of their culture. Add to that the results of recent investigations, which have revealed documentation of sexual, physical and mental abuse.[9]

"It was not until 1978 with the passing of the Indian Child Welfare Act that Native American parents gained the legal right to deny their children's placement in off-reservation schools."[10] Yet even in 2007, while most of the Schools had closed down, there were still 9,500 children in attendance.[11]

As part of a healing process, The National Native American Boarding School Healing Coalition's website reports that "In May 2016 the Northern Arapaho and the Sicangu Lakota met with Army representatives to discuss the repatriation of their children buried at the Carlisle Indian Industrial School cemetery. The Army agreed to voluntarily send these children home and pay for their exhumation, transport, and internment. Thus, began the first boarding school repatriation effort in U.S. history that we know of." May it be the first of many![12]

—oooOooo—

A Native reflection

On a no longer existing website (www.nativenewsnetwork.com) there was an article written about Jennie Blackbird. She was described as "the grandmother of the Walpole Island First Nation, Bkejwanong Territory that straddles the US/Canadian border." It continued:

> "As a child, she spent six years at an Indian residential school in Bradford, Ontario. At an Annual Anishinaabe Family Language & Culture Workshop, she shared about her experiences there. It was clear from the memories that 'lingered in her mind and heart, that they were still profoundly painful... At one point, she was overcome with emotion, choked up, and tears welled in her eyes.'
>
> Blackbird told a story of a woman on Walpole Island who went to the grocery store and came home to discover that some governmental Indian agent had shown up and taken all of her children from the home and placed them in Indian residential school. 'Can you imagine your children being snatched away from you?' she asked. 'Well, that is what happened to us.'
>
> She continued, 'It has taken me a long time to even do this workshop. When [I was] first asked to do a workshop on Indian residential schools, I could not

because I was not ready... I think many of us lived in denial about it. My own husband, who spent 11 years at a residential school, would never talk about it. We were married for 24 years before he died about 20 years ago and he would never talk about it with even me.'

She has sisters who cannot remember what month or year they were taken from their home. It is like they have blocked them out. She said she and her sisters do not talk about attending the Indian residential school. 'One time I asked one of my sisters about school and she put her head down and told me she did not want to talk about it,' recounted Blackbird.

Even though her language (Anishinaabe) was forbidden at the school, Blackbird was, fortunately, able to retain her tribal language. 'I remember so many things my grandfather taught me,' Blackbird said. 'He taught me that our language was the first language. It was here thousands of years before the Europeans arrived. My grandfather told me 'language speaks to who we are.' There are no swear words in our language. There are no dirty words.' 'He also taught me that Truth was here before the air. The creator is Truth. He put us here,' she told the workshop participants. She also said her grandfather taught her that when tears come, it means we are to speak with our hearts."

—oooOooo—

Two days after that experience in Harbor Springs, I was speaking at a meeting in the Indian River House of Prayer and shared with them my recent encounter with God. Towards the end of that sharing, a Native American lady stepped forward and hugged me. We stood there together weeping, my spirit connecting with a pain in hers. She spoke to me, thanked me for acknowledging the hurts of many who attended that School, finishing with the words, "I was there!" My prayer is that this was an important step in her own healing process and will also be so for others who may read this.

Back to the poem—here are some related scriptures that also came to mind:

Genesis 4:10. In which God is speaking to Cain regarding the murder of his brother Abel, "*Listen! Your brother's blood cries out to me from the ground.*"

Hebrews 12:24. It speaks of Christ's death in terms of, "*... the sprinkled blood that speaks a better word than the blood of Abel.*"

And Exodus 3:7-9, in which God is speaking about the Jews and their 400 years of captivity in Egypt, says: "*I have indeed seen the misery of my people... I have heard them crying out... I am concerned about their suffering... The cry of the Israelites has reached me...*"

Indeed, because of their suffering, God says in v.8. "*I have come down.*"

Clearly, nothing goes unnoticed by our Creator God!

The word "Listen," caught my attention. Although it had always been there, I had never seen it before! God sees, He hears and draws near! He is concerned about injustice, the spilling of innocent blood, yet we can read about and encounter injustices like those carried out in the Boarding Schools and act with indifference. God is calling us in these days to "listen!"

Such listening can take the form of my experience in Harbor Springs; as we read the Scriptures; hearing the experiences of others or through reading "your" and "their" history with a heart and mind open listen to what God thinks of our cultural interpretations—they may not line up with His! It is often out of the place of listening that He begins to reveal His plans to individuals (including Tribal Elders, Church, and political leaders), showing a way forward, through the development of initiatives enabling personal or corporate healing and reconciliation.

That goes for many other sites across the United States. I am thinking of the Wounded Knee massacre of the Lakota Sioux, and The Great Swamp Massacre of the Narragansett, because I have been to them. Those are places where the blood still cries out. I don't confess to understand it, but despite the many prayers of repentance, and reconciliation initiatives, there is still unfinished business surrounding such places! I sense something still needs to be broken in the heavenly realms over them for God's healing power and presence to flow freely in these Nations. We will know – when the weeping stops!! We now cross-over to the next section of this book: **"A Dignity Restored."**

References:

1. Charla Bear, *"American Indian Boarding Schools Haunt Many."* Part 1, NPR, 12 May 2008.
2. Source: http://www.npr.org/templates/story/story.php?storyId=16516865&ps=rs
3. Source: http://www.kporterfield.com/aicttw/articles/boardingschool.html
4. Carolyn Marr, *"Assimilation Through Education: Indian Boarding Schools in the Pacific Northwest."* Source: http://content.lib.washington.edu/aipnw/marr.html
5. Source: www.nrcprograms.org/site/PageServer?pagename=airc_hist_boardingschools
6. Source: http://www.northernexpress.com/michigan/article-3658-they-came-for-the-children.html
7. Ibid.
8. The Miriam Report. Source: http://www.nativepartnership.org/site/PageServer?pagename=airc_hist_boardingschools
9. Amnesty International USA, *"Soul Wound: The Legacy of Native American School."* Retrieved Feb. 8, 2006
10. Source:

http://www.nativepartnership.org/site/PageServer?pagename=air
c_hist_boardingschools

11. Source:
https://en.wikipedia.org/wiki/American_Indian_boarding_school
s

12. Source:
https://boardingschoolhealing.org/advocacy/carlisle-repatriation/

Bridging the Gap

A bridge: *A structure spanning and providing passage over a river or road.*
In music: a transitional, modulatory passage connecting sections of a composition.

As I finished, what I hoped was the last draft of the chapters of this book, under the heading of "A Destiny Denied," my thoughts turned to the second section: "A Dignity Restored," aware that our dignity and our destinies, individually and corporately, are integrally connected. I wanted it to be encouraging, affirming and a host of other positive adjectives. Instead, little did I realize that it would be fraught with difficulties. Not bad difficulties but above all, I wanted to communicate something of God's heart for the Native American people (and for that matter, the English, Ulster-Scots, and Euro-Americans). The reality is that I felt so inadequate for the task. How does one do justice to communicating God's love for them, especially as an Irishman, living thousands of miles away, across the "big pond?"

There have been times on this journey, that I have so profoundly felt the heart of God, such as during our trip to Michigan in August 2013, with Terry & Darlene Wildman. Towards the end of our time there we went to see the newly released film, "The Butler." Everyone else in the auditorium was watching a film about race discrimination within a black/white context, but for me, I didn't see "black" I saw "Indian." I don't think I was ever so undone in my spirit and in my emotions by anything in that way before. There was so much pain welling up in my heart—pain for what we had done to the Native Americans but also a pain, which touched on something deep in the heart of God for them. Experiences like that, as I have said, are difficult to communicate adequately.

Nevertheless, in the second section of this book, I want to "cross-over," and look at some of the issues pertaining to healing/reconciliation—our **Dignities Restored**! We have looked at some horrendous stuff in the first section of this book. And even though I have just scratched the surface, I trust that your heart, mind, and spirit have been sufficiently touched by God, to realize afresh, or in a deeper way, that the foundations, and what has been built on them, have at times been incredibly bad. God is longing for us to be firmly established in our covenant relationship with Himself, within ourselves and with others; to build His Kingdom together; difference is okay, how we worship Him—issues connected to contextualization v. syncretism; what is on God's heart regarding His Church within a nation; our corporate identity; re-finding/discovering our identity in Him…

I believe that God is wanting to raise up a people after His own heart for the United States of America that includes every Native American tribe and indeed, all the ethnicities that make up its population. I believe He wants to reveal to them what their tribes' current destiny is meant to be, from His perspective and therefore fully realizable in Him. Satan has been the robber, the destroyer of this—mankind has been his instrument. Satan very clearly, still has power, but at the Cross, he was divested of his authority. The only authority he now has, enabling him to use this power, is the authority we give him through broken and wrong covenants, fear, hatred, suspicion, power trips, unrepentance, unforgiveness, nationalism, sectarianism, denominationalism…

"Greater is He who is in us…" He is the restorer, the healer of our wounded histories!

Part 2

A Dignity Restored

Chapter 18

Creator's Plumb Line

In the first part of this book, we looked at some of the negative aspects of what wrong covenants or treaties can do to a nation. We also looked at how my tribes came to America firmly convinced that being in a special covenant relationship with God gave them license to establish what they perceived was His Kingdom in the Colonies, with devastating consequences for the original people of the land. Now I want to give you some good news. In fact, more than good—IT'S WONDERFUL NEWS!

While writing "*Heal Not Lightly*," I was reading in my daily devotions from the Prophet Amos's book in the Old Testament. In it, God was speaking to the tribes of Israel about how they were building the nation and therefore their lives, in ways that did not align with the original plans that He had drawn up for them:

> "*This is what he showed me: The Lord was standing by a wall that had been built true to plumb, with a plumb line in his hand. And the Lord asked me, "What do you see, Amos?" "A plumb line," I replied. Then the Lord said, "Look, I am setting a plumb line among my people Israel: I will spare them no longer. "The high places of Isaac will be destroyed and the sanctuaries of Israel will be ruined; with my sword I will rise against the house of Jeroboam."* (Amos 7:7-9)

Unlike the wall, they were from God's perspective, clearly "off-plumb!"

As I reflected on these verses, I sensed that God was using them to speak to me regarding the Ulster Covenant, as it was not aligning itself with what the Scriptures were teaching us about covenant.

Time and time again, God has used the Bible as His plumb line for my life, as He uses a verse or a chapter to confirm something, guide/direct me, get me back on track. If only the Christians coming to America from England, Scotland and Ireland had fully understood this; especially those, who as spiritual leaders, prided themselves on their biblical knowledge. They would not have justified genocide in Jesus' name; they would not have allowed the "spirit of Empire" enshrined in the "Doctrine of Discovery" to have shaped their spiritual and political lives, and they would not have allowed covenants/treaties to continually manipulate the natives off their land.

The wonderful news

In "*Heal Not Lightly*" I wrote, "Throughout the whole of the Bible, God relates to people by means of covenants (sometimes called treaties or pacts)."[1] In the context of writing this chapter, I realized that I was experiencing a pain and weeping in my spirit regarding that sentence, as the misuse of treaties had pushed countless Native Americans away from a fuller revelation of their Creator. If I were to tell someone who had experienced a lot of physical abuse from an earthly father, that God their Heavenly Father loved them, they would find that extremely hard to emotionally and intellectually accept, as their frame of reference regarding "fatherhood" had been so painfully distorted! So, what does the above sentence, put into the context of covenant, convey to Natives Americans, regarding the ongoing legacy my ancestors left them, through hundreds of broken covenants and treaties?

Irrespective of how my ancestors and Euro-Americans have abused covenants, it does not change the absolute truth that God is not only a covenant-making God, but He is also a covenant-keeping one. My hope and security as a Christian depend entirely upon God's revealed character and His faithfulness to the promises He made in the Old and New Covenants (Testaments) and on my ability to appropriate and enjoy the benefits of them as I respond in repentance, faith, and obedience. Grasping the true nature and significance of this covenant relationship with God is not only the key to unlocking many Scripture passages but also to transform our understanding of the nature of the relationship He wants to have with us.

At the heart of every covenant which God made, was His desire to have an intimate relationship with us. That is what we were made for! When Adam and Eve sinned, we read that they broke covenant: *"Like Adam, they have broken the covenant—they were unfaithful to me there."* (Hosea 6:7) I am so thankful that God did not leave it there, that He began His redemptive search to restore our broken relationship with Him. This restoration was all-embracing because God wanted every area of our lives to know His wholeness—physical, moral, spiritual, intellectual, emotional, in our families, our life vocation and our relationship with each other. He wanted it to extend to the temporal and the eternal; the spiritual and the secular; the private and the public. In today's world, when so many people are looking for a sense of identity, security, and belonging, the good news is that it can be found in ever-increasing measure as we embrace God's heart towards us, as expressed through covenant.

He chose to model this through entering a relationship with the tribes that made up the nation of Israel. It is worth pointing out that He did not choose them because they were particularly any more special than other people groups. Nevertheless, because He chose them, that made them special. That can equally be said of anyone who has chosen to enter a relationship with Him by appropriating what Christ did on the Cross. I can confidently say today, "I am also **special!**"

The Hebrew word for covenant is *b'riyth*, which means "to bind." In the Scriptures, there are many examples of this mutually taking place between two people: David and Jonathan, *"And Jonathan made a covenant with David because he loved him as himself."* (1 Samuel 18:3); Laban and Jacob, *"Come now, let us make a covenant, you and I, and let it serve as a witness between us."* (Genesis 31:44); between a husband and a wife, *"This is why a man will leave his father and mother and is united to his wife, and they become one flesh."* (Genesis 2:24) and Israel with the Gibeonites, *"Then Joshua made a treaty of peace with them to let them live, and the leaders of the assembly ratified it by oath."* (Joshua 9:15)

In the light of that, I want us to look at this plumb line regarding covenant, adapting it from a chapter in my first book. It reveals something of God's nature and heart towards all of mankind. Many people have told me how helpful this has been to them!

A closer look
Throughout the Scriptures we find three constants regarding God and covenant:
1. I will be your God (Genesis 17:8)
2. I will take you as my people (Exodus 6:7)
3. I will dwell among you (Exodus 29:45-46)

In Leviticus 26:12 we find all three of them mentioned:

> *"I will walk among you and be your God, and you will be my people."*

As do other scriptures:

> *"I will establish my covenant as an everlasting covenant between me and you and your descendants after you for generations to come, to be your God and the God of your descendants after you."* (Genesis 17:7)

> *"You are standing here in order to enter into a covenant with the Lord your God, a covenant the Lord is making with you this day and sealing with an oath, to confirm this day as His people, that He may be your God as he promised you as he swore to your fathers, Abraham, Isaac, and Jacob..."* (Deuteronomy 29:12-13)

> *"For we are the temple of the living God. As God has said: "I will live with them and walk among them, and I will be their God, and they will be my people."* (2 Corinthians 6:16)

Notice the "I will's" and then the "they will." This is good news from the Creator and Sustainer of all! Good news for every Native, Black, Hispanic, Euro-American, English, Scottish and Irish person. To embrace this means that we can, in Christ, begin a journey of

257

embracing God's reconciliation program into our wounded personal and corporate histories.

In his book, *"The Holy Wild,"* Mark Buchanan writes:

> "Through Abraham, He chose a people for Himself, a people to walk in His ways, live by His grace, trust His word, display His character. He promised all this. But here's the rub: He guaranteed the promise by His own faithfulness, not Abraham's... It needed God's faithfulness."[2]

The Abrahamic Covenant

He is speaking about the narrative in Genesis 15:7-18 that describes the process whereby God enters into a covenant with Abraham. He understood what God was saying to him because it closely followed a ritual that was already practiced in his day (see Chapter 19), during which people entering a covenant with each other by sacrificing an animal and cutting it into two halves. The severed pieces were laid out facing each other with a pathway between. The partners of the covenant then walked between the bloody halves of the carcass. This was to solemnly enact two things: a pledge to walk within the bounds of their promise and a willingness if they didn't, to suffer the same fate as the animal, to be hewn and scattered. Within the Hebrew context, this was known as "cutting" the covenant. Interestingly, it was also during this solemn act that God spoke to Abraham about His commitment to them regarding a specific piece of land (vs.13-14).

Significantly, when God entered this covenant with Abraham there was one very noticeable and big difference, only one covenant partner walked the path—GOD! This covenant, the vastness of its promise, depended on God alone! It was in the sacrifice/the shedding of blood mentioned above, that God put His seal on the covenant, making it a very solemn and serious occasion.

The Mosaic Covenant

At the time of Moses, God entered another covenant with Israel. In it, Laws were given which included the Ten Commandments. They also included a host of civil and ceremonial laws, regarding how they should live in a right way with each other and God. This Mosaic Law also gave instructions regarding the means of dealing with the breaking of those laws and the restoration of the relationships. This culminated in an annual Day of Atonement (Leviticus 16), with the sacrificing of an unblemished goat and the presenting of its blood before the Mercy Seat in the Holy of Holies.

—oooOooo—

In the New Testament, we discover that Christ fulfilled this once and for all through His death on the cross. He became the Sacrificial Lamb! Significantly this happened on the Day of Atonement, at the same time as the High Priest was performing the sacrificial ritual in the Temple. His blood became the blood of a New Covenant.

Just a few days before this, Jesus instituted amid a Passover Meal with his disciples, what we now call the Eucharist or The Lord's Supper. During it we read that *"he took the cup, gave thanks and offered it to them, saying, 'Drink from it, all of you. This is my blood of the covenant, which is poured out for many for the forgiveness of sins.'"* (Matthew 26:27-28)

Here we see that covenant and forgiveness are linked: forgiveness is possible only through atonement, atonement is only possible through sacrifice and sacrifice means the shedding of blood. *"Without the shedding of blood, there is no forgiveness."* (Hebrews 9:22)

—oooOooo—

It is the serious nature of "cutting" the covenant, that really strikes me. They entered the covenant by death, which the sacrifice represented. They gave up their rights to live any longer for themselves. They acknowledged that they had to die to their rights and from then on, live for, and if needs be, die for the other party to the covenant. Whatever the other partner needs or asks for, they will supply. How lightly we understand this in our western society today when we can so readily turn a marriage covenant into a contract, to be terminated at ease.

259

Other aspects of the nature of God's covenant relationship with man

Because it is God's initiative, His gift to us, it is founded and maintained entirely by grace. It is totally undeserved: there is nothing in us that gives us any exclusive claim on His attention whatsoever. It is an expression of God's generous, forgiving and gracious character. In fact, it is within the context of covenant, that God's character is most fully revealed:

> *"And He passed in front of Moses, proclaiming, 'The Lord, the Lord, the compassionate and gracious God, slow to anger, abounding in love and faithfulness, maintaining love to thousands, and forgiving wickedness, rebellion, and sin.'"* (Exodus 34:6-7)

At the very core of this verse is the Hebrew word *"hesed."* It is consistently used in the Old Testament regarding God's love. It can also mean "steadfast love" or "everlasting kindness," and it is linked to His faithfulness to the covenantal bond:

> *"Know therefore that the Lord your God is God; he is the faithful God, keeping his covenant of love (hesed) to a thousand generations of those who love him and keep his commandments."* (Deuteronomy 7:9, NIV)

Like the passage above in Genesis 17:7, where we find the word everlasting attached to it, everlasting means everlasting!

There are also two other significant elements worth noting regarding the making of a covenant: a promise and an oath.

A Promise—the commitment of covenant, is an undertaking to do or to give something to someone. Equally, it can be an undertaking to not do or give something in the future. It is not just a proposal or an intention: it is saying, "I am making a serious and earnest commitment as to how I am going to act in the future. I intend that commitment to be taken and relied on, and I will act in the way I have declared. I am also taking on myself an obligation to fulfill my pledged word. I am acknowledging that I am limiting my freedom of action in that particular situation, making myself duty bound to do or to act exactly as I said I would." In Psalm 89:33-34 we read, *"I will not take my love from him, nor will I ever betray my faithfulness. I will not violate my covenant or alter what my lips have uttered."* What fantastic news!

Yes, God takes His promises very seriously. When He makes a promise, He has committed himself to that course of action, and we are meant to take His promise as a pledge or guarantee that He will do precisely what He has said. Paul, in writing to Titus puts it this way: *"... the knowledge of the truth which is according to godliness, in the hope of eternal life, which God, who cannot lie, promised ages ago."* (Titus 1:1-2. NASB)

An Oath is a further confirmation of the covenant, giving it an even greater seriousness or solemnity. The person is not only calling on God to bear witness to his words, but he is also saying "I hold myself answerable and accountable to God." *"Men swear by someone greater than themselves, and the oath confirms what is said and puts an end to all argument."* (Hebrews 6:16) They are acknowledging that their honor and reputation is at stake. In a Court of Law, the breaking of an oath would make us guilty of perjury.

God's covenants are based on His promise confirmed by an oath:

> *"Then Joseph said to his brothers, 'I am about to die. But God will surely come to your aid and take you up out of this land to the land promised on oath to Abraham, Isaac and Jacob.'"* (Genesis 50:24)

> *"You are standing here in order to enter into a covenant with the Lord your God, a covenant the Lord is making with you this day and sealing with an oath, to confirm you this day as his people, that he may be your God as he promised you and as he swore to your fathers, Abraham, Isaac, and Jacob."* (Deuteronomy 29:12-13)

"And it was not without an oath! Others became priests without an oath, but he became a priest with an oath when God said to him: 'The Lord has sworn and will not change his mind: 'You are a priest forever.' Because of this oath, Jesus has become the guarantee of a better covenant.'" (Hebrews 7:20-22)

When God makes an oath, He is not making an appeal as we would, to a higher authority; He is appealing to His own holy character. He is putting His deity, His character, His holiness on the line, as a guarantee of His faithfulness to His promises. *"When God made his promise to Abraham since there was no one greater for him to swear by, he swore by himself, saying, 'I will surely bless you and give you many descendants.'"* (Hebrews 6:13-14)

As I mentioned earlier, it is God as the stronger party who sets out the conditions under which the covenant obligations are fulfilled. He alone sets the terms. For our part, we can accept or reject them, but they are not open to debate or negotiation. This is a fundamental principle for us to understand. One of the main reasons for not entering the blessing of our covenant relationship with God is that we have considered the terms too demanding for us. As a result, we tend to try and side-step them, partially obey them or make attempts at offering to God something which is more amenable to us.

I think by now; you know that we are dealing with something that is relationally very secure and very serious.

In the Old Testament there were, however, several critical issues that stood in the way of God achieving His desire for an intimate relationship with people. There was a need for a final solution to the sin problem. While the law of God could show us what we should or should not do, it could not enable us to do it. We lacked the power to obey the law along with the motivation or desire to obey it. This produced an enormous gulf between a holy God and us.

It is in this context that the prophets began to speak about a new covenant. Not new in the sense that it replaced what had gone before, but new in the sense that it represented a radical breakthrough that would finally achieve the purposes of the covenants, in a new way.

> *"The days are coming," declares the Lord, "when I will make a new covenant with the house of Israel and with the people of Judah. It will not be like the covenant I made with their ancestors when I took them by the hand to lead them out of Egypt, because they broke my covenant, though I was a husband to them,"* declares the Lord. *"This is the covenant I will make with the people of Israel after that time,"* declares the Lord. *"I will put the law in their minds and I will write it on their hearts. I will be their God, and they will be my people. No longer will a man teach their neighbor, or say to one another, "Know the Lord," because they will all know me, from the least to the greatest."* declares the Lord. *"For I will forgive their wickedness and will remember their sins no more."* (Jeremiah 31:31-34)

Our Creator God was speaking here prophetically of the coming of His son Jesus Christ to earth and of a new era, following his death and resurrection, when His Spirit would come and dwell within us. Yes! Jesus is the fulfillment of God's plan of salvation. He is the fulfillment of all the "types" in the Old Testament—what the temple, the offerings, and the priesthood represented. The problem of sin had been dealt with, once and for all, through *covenant!*

—oooOooo—

The power of wrong covenants

In the light of what I have written in this chapter, it has become increasingly clear to me that, without exaggeration, this is one of the most powerful truths communicated by our Creator God, about Himself, to us. It could also be said, in the light of that, that there is nothing Satan, God's archenemy, hates more.

It seems logical to me, that if I were a high-ranking angel like Satan, who because of an act of rebellion, was forever cast out of the immediacy of God's glory, I would choose to get my revenge by seeking to undermine and distort something that was closest to His heart. There is nothing closer to God's heart than what He has purposed to do through covenant.

On the downside, if Satan can get two people or two people groups to be covenanted against each other, as is the case in Rwanda among the Hutu and Tutsi tribes, it can have far-reaching detrimental effects which lead to anything from alienation to murder or genocide. That will have catastrophic consequences regarding the future dignity and destiny of each group. I am also convinced that this is why marriage, the church, and Israel (people and land), which are all expression in Scripture of covenants ordained by God, have been under such a sustained attack down through history.

I have dealt in this chapter with the issue of covenant, as it pertains to God and how He reaches out redemptively to man, but I am also of the increased conviction that the dynamics of covenant are the foundation upon which all relationships between heaven and earth and on earth are meant to be established. Interestingly covenants have also been used in many cultures around the world, as a means of making relational commitments to each other. Entered with integrity, it produces deep, lasting relationships at all levels, even among people(s) who do not have a relationship with God. This is one of His eternal principles for all mankind! Many cultures around the world embrace the use of covenants/pacts/treaties as a means of establishing this relational stability within them. It is what all the covenants/treaties made with the Native Americans should have aspired to.

An Irish example
Once again, this takes me back to the issue of the 1912 Ulster Covenant, mentioned in Chapter 1. To recap: The leadership of the three main Protestant denominations, which were in the majority in the Province of Ulster, instigated what I believe was fundamentally a wrong covenant. Through it, they used God's name, the power of covenant and their hatred and fear of the Catholic Church to unite Protestantism against the British Government's Home Rule Bill.

Equally wrong was another covenant made in 1916 by an Irish nationalist group called Sinn Fein. In it, they were committing themselves to total severance from British rule. Both invoked deity (one regarding God and the other one regarding God and the Irish goddess Eire), both called for either written or verbal consent which amounted to taking an oath, and both called for blood sacrifice, shown by their willingness to die for their cause. In fact, according to Celtic mythology, Eire required it.

This brings a different understanding of what became known as "the troubles" which started in Northern Ireland in 1969 and the ensuing "peace process" of today. People, around the world, look at Northern Ireland and think that we are a powerful example, to other divided nations, of peace and reconciliation. But if you were to ask the average person on the street, they will tell you that you only must scratch the surface, and the same negative attitudes are still very much present.

In the Government at Stormont (the Northern Ireland Assembly), an innovative power-sharing Assembly, we have two people groups: Irish/Catholic/Nationalist and Ulster/Protestant/Unionist, that are in a continual counter-covenantal relationship with each other; both are looking for totally opposite outcomes from the political process; the collapse of the Assembly has constantly been a possibility. Today as I write this (August 2018) that has become a reality—we have not had a sitting Assembly for the past 20 months! Satan has been given the legal right to operate in the life of our churches, government, and society!

Having looked at the power of covenants and how God looks at them, can peace in Ireland be permanent? I, along with many others hope so, but I am conscious that the Scriptures tell us, *"If a kingdom is divided against itself, that kingdom cannot stand."* (Mark 3:25) Mega ownership and repentance are needed!

In the United States

The history of the United States sadly records that so many Treaties with Native American Tribes were also made and signed, only to be broken—some say as many as 500! Take for example:

- The Indian Removal Act of 1830: Having forcibly removed Tribes off the land in the southeast, they were moved west of the Mississippi River on what is known as the "Trail of Tears," with the understanding that these new lands would be "theirs forever." Only to find that the Government did not honor it as white westward expansion continued unabated.

- The 1868 Treaty of Fort Laramie with the Sioux Nation which was violated in 1874 when gold was found in the Black Hills of South Dakota.[3]

- The Curtis Act of 1898 (an extension of the Dawes Severalty Act which provided for the allotment of the Indian Territory and the sale of any "surplus" land), was strongly opposed by the Oklahoma tribes who saw it as a violation of previous treaties. When they brought their objections to the U.S. Supreme Court two significant decisions were made by it: *Cherokee Nation v. Hitchcock* (1902) and *Lone Wolf v. Hitchcock* (1903), which empowered Congress to either modify or terminate treaties without any Native American consent.[4]

Again, mega ownership and repentance are needed!

—oooOooo—

Embracing God's Covenant for your life

To be in a right relationship with God is to be "in covenant" with Him. We do nothing to earn this. Jesus has done all the work required for us to enter it, by his sinless life, sacrificial death, and resurrection. Nevertheless, there are a number of responses to be made which enable us to enter into and maintaining this Covenant Relationship with God:

1. **Believe.** To believe means to trust in the power and the promises of God and Jesus. We trust that Jesus is who He says He is, and that He does everything He says He does. (John 3:16; Galatians 2:16) He has dealt with the issue of our sin which separated us

from God. The way has been opened for us to enter a dynamic relationship with God.

2. **Repentance.** To repent means to make a U-turn in your life. It is a change of mind which involves a turning from sin and a turning to God (Vines Complete Expository Dictionary). (Acts 2:38; Acts 20:21)

3. **Confession.** To publicly acknowledge our faith response to Jesus. (Romans 10:9)

4. **Obedience.** To follow God's commands every day. We have been called by God to live each day in covenant relationship with Him. We, in turn, are being transformed into Christlikeness in nature, character, lifestyle. (1 John 3:24)

By entering a covenant relationship with God, Scripture explicitly tells us that we receive two things that allow us to have a right standing before Him:

1. **Forgiveness.** Forgiveness means that God lets go of the sins that have separated us from Him, and God expects us to let go of the sins that separate others from us. (Matthew 6:14-15; Colossians 3:13)

2. **The Holy Spirit.** We receive Jesus' Spirit to guide us in our new life and to gift us for service in His Church. (Galatians 5:22-25; 1 Corinthians 12:7; 1 John 3:24)[5]

—oooOooo—

The good news is that our covenant making and keeping God has made a provision for the reversal of the wounds of history. Reconciliation is possible. Granted, it is a bit more of a challenge at a national level, where layers of wounding, pain, broken treaties, etc., are involved. But most certainly I have seen it at an individual level, many times over, between Catholics and Protestants in Ireland. Again, bearing in mind Paul's words to the church in Corinth: *"Christ... gave us the ministry of reconciliation."* We as Christians, as the church in the United Kingdom and the United States, have been called by Christ to this ministry. All of us! We are meant to be His agents of healing in our nations. Bottom line! Let us look a bit deeper at this as we move into the next chapter!

References:

1. Harry Smith, *"Heal Not Lightly."* New Wine Ministries, 2006, Pg. 69.
2. Mark Buchanan, *"The Holy Wild."* Multnomah Publishers, 2003, Pg. 59.
3. Source: https//www.smithsonianmag.com/blogs/national-museum-american-indian/2018/10/31/treaty-fort-laramie
4. Source: http://law.jrank.org/pages/22787/Native-Americans-Congressional-Control-after-1871.html
5. Adapted from: http://www.cccpitt.org/becoming-a-christian-nav/

Chapter 19

Reconciled to Reconcile

During our 18 years in the Christian Renewal Centre, there were plenty of opportunities to both explore and live out reconciliation—both between God and us and each other in our divided society. To embrace God's heart for Ireland and the healing of the ancient wounds, meant that in prayer, conversation, and historical research we had to be open to remove the blinders off our own culture and ask God to help us to see both our history and theirs from His perspective! That can enable us to begin a journey of both understanding and owning the wrongs and painful actions of our tribe towards "the other." It also allows us to not only look for the good in both cultures but also to ask ourselves: "What is there, that is a reflection of God's intent in them?" Satan is not a creator, He takes what is of God our Creator, and distorts them. One clear example of this stands out within the UK and Irish reconciliation networks. As a nation, England was seen to have been given by God a fatherly, protecting, nurturing role among the nations; instead one sees, as it built an empire around the world, the opposite characteristics manifesting themselves! It nevertheless points us in the direction as to what can be redeemed!

If we are not prepared to embark on that journey, how else can we reach out in reconciliation? The good news is that we are not called to go it alone. We have a God who leads the way. Reconciliation is, after all, His idea! It began in Him! Right at the very beginning of the Jewish (and Christian) scriptures we find that we are its pinnacle, everything else He created was "*good,*" but after He had made the man, He pronounced that we are "*very good!*" We were made in His image; made for communion and fellowship with Him and made to rule over, subdue, have dominion over creation (Genesis 1:26, 28). These are words that are often misunderstood, e.g., Dominion is not meant to be something negative, it is more in keeping with God telling us that we were to responsibly manage and use the earth's resources in our service of each other and God.

We were also made to live in perfect harmony with Him, with others and ourselves. How incredibly wonderful that must have been! However, for this to happen, God took the risk of incorporating freedom of choice right at the center of how we relate to Him and each other. We had to choose to love and to walk in right relationships. In Genesis, we read that Adam and Eve choose the way of disobedience and of the fracturing of that relationship, which ultimately led to physical death and separation from God. As a result, disharmony came into our bodies, our souls, and spirits which would become increasingly manifest at both personal and societal levels, bringing with it, corruption and ultimately death.

Thankfully, when we blew it, God did not write us off! Indeed, He tells us that He is not far from any of us, that He *"set eternity in the hearts of men..."* (Ecclesiastes 3:11). As there is something of a God-orientation within us all, He has established a recovery program that would enable us to be restored and reconciled to Him. As I have already mentioned in the last chapter, God chose to model that through developing a relationship with a nation of people, made up of twelve tribes, called the Jews. Through them, He would show us how we could live individually and collectively in right relationship with Him and others, even to the point of giving them laws that would embrace family life, legal issues, community health and their spiritual life—indeed, every aspect of life! That importantly included how they were to deal with any wrongs committed against Him and others, which culminated in an annual blood sacrifice called Passover. It was a very comprehensive package, one that was to be a foreshadow of the reconciliation He would make available to us through His Son, Jesus Christ, the perfect blood sacrifice. He was the final, the complete revelation of our Creator and His Great Spirit, to us all.

I mentioned earlier that we were made to rule over, subdue, have dominion over creation; bring God's Kingdom reign to earth. This original intent still stands. The Scriptures, however, clearly tell us that when we live in disobedience to God, this can directly affect the earth and creation in corresponding negative ways—through control, dominance, fear, war, etc., Romans 8:22, talks about it in terms of the whole of creation groaning.

Hosea 4:1-3 says:

> *"Hear the word of the Lord, you Israelites, because the Lord has a charge to bring against you who live in the land: 'There is no faithfulness, no love, no acknowledgment of God in the land. There is only cursing, lying and murder, stealing and adultery; they break all bounds, and bloodshed follows bloodshed. Because of this, the land dries up, and all who live in it waste away; the beasts of the field, the birds in the sky and the fish in the sea are swept away.'"*

Thankfully, when our relationship with Him is put right by accepting the salvation He offers through His Son's death and resurrection, He calls us to partner with Him in the restoration process: not only for ourselves and our fellow humans but also for the earth. There are ample stories of whole communities being transformed; of rain, fish, crabs, caribou returning, as communities have repented of generational wrongs, murders, etc.,

—oooOooo—

Reconciliation—what is it?

According to the Merriam-Webster dictionary, it is the act of causing two people or groups to become friendly again after an argument or disagreement; the process of finding a way to make two different ideas, facts, etc., exist or be true at the same time.[1]

The Oxford Dictionary similarly states that it is the restoration of friendly relations; the act of making one view or belief compatible with another; the act of making financial accounts consistent; harmonization.[2]

However, in the Greek (Vines Complete Expository Dictionary – computer based) we find two very different and clarifying words:

1. *"Diallassomai."* That refers to two parties who are mutually hostile toward one another being reconciled – it "denotes mutual

concession after mutual hostility." It is only found in Matthew 5:23-24 when Jesus says,

> *"Therefore, if you are offering your gift at the altar and there remember that your brother has something against you, leave your gift there in front of the altar. First, go and be reconciled to them, then come and offer your gift."*

This is a universal principle!

2. *"Katallage."* Meaning, to reconcile two parties where only one party is hostile toward the other. That is the word used in the New Testament regarding us, as the separated, guilty party, being reconciled to God. It shows God's favor towards us! God was never hostile towards us; he has done everything necessary through the death of His Son to make that reconciliation possible. However, it does not happen if we do not embrace it.

It is also used for our commissioning to be reconcilers—helping to bring others into that reconciled relationship with God:

> *"All this is from God, who reconciled us to himself through Christ and gave us the ministry of reconciliation: that God was reconciling the world to himself in Christ, not counting people's sin against them. And he has committed to us the message of reconciliation. We are therefore Christ's ambassadors, as though God were making his appeal through us. We implore you on Christ's behalf: Be reconciled to God."* (2 Corinthians 5:18-20)

We see this again in Romans 5:10-11,

> *"For if, when we were God's enemies, we were reconciled to him through the death of his Son, how much more, having been reconciled, shall we be saved through his life! Not only is this so, but we also boast in God through our Lord Jesus Christ, through whom*

we have now received reconciliation."

Regarding Jewish/Gentile reconciliation, Paul uses the same word again, when he writes,

> *"For he himself is our peace, who has made the two groups one, and has destroyed the barrier, the dividing wall of hostility, by setting aside in his flesh the law with its commands and regulations. His purpose was to create in himself one new humanity out of the two, thus making peace, and in this one body to reconcile both of them to God through the cross, by which he put to death their hostility... For through him we both have access to the Father by one Spirit."* (Ephesians 2:14-18)

These were foundational scriptures for our Reconciliation Community in Ireland. As Catholics and Protestants, we found that when we were first reconciled to Christ, we were then positionally made one in him! Understanding that oneness was a great motivator to work on the healing of our cultural, historical and theological differences and wounds! These verses clearly tell us, that reconciliation is not a specialist ministry. It is God's call to everyone who is a follower of Jesus. We have been reconciled to reconcile! It is more than what many of us grew up to believe: being brought into a right relationship with God, salvation.

The verses quoted above from Ephesians tell me that it is a complete package deal that is being appropriated. Our different cultural expressions of faith (Jewish and Gentile; Catholic and Protestant; Native and Euro-American) are not to stand in the way of us becoming as one in Christ. We have been united in Christ; the barrier has been destroyed; the dividing wall of hostility is gone; the ground at the foot of the Cross is level; our hostility has been put to death, we are reconciled to God – PERIOD!

Perhaps not yet a reality for everyone but it is done, completed in Christ. What a starting point. It is something that we are meant to move out from and yet appropriate, travel towards! We are bringing

God's Kingdom reign to earth. It embraces a lifelong process of being reconciled to each other and within ourselves, as we become more and more like Christ (what we call sanctification).

—oooOooo—

How different our histories may have looked if my Christian forefathers: Puritans/Scotch-Irish, English/Irish and Irish/Euro-Americans, had consistently lived out the message of reconciliation (both meanings!) among the Irish Catholics and Native Americans. No longer living solely for ourselves and Empire, but for God. No longer seeing people from different ethnic groups as inferior but as all made uniquely different yet equal, before Him. The new creation has come, Christ had made it possible, we were to walk it out! The tragedy is, history shows that we haven't always been too good at it! All too often we turned people away from Christ, not reconciled them to Him! It's certainly a far cry from forcing people at the point of a sword to embrace the Christian faith!

The reality is, that for many reasons we may never fully cooperate with God, and therefore enable Him to do this unifying work in us. We may be reconciled to Him so far as we have become Christians, but we may allow other issues in our histories: fear, negative experience, cultural prejudices, etc., to get in the way of us fully embracing this level of reconciliation for ourselves, another person or ethnic group. That is unfortunately still true for many people in Northern Ireland today. There are too many members of my tribe, my brothers and sisters in Christ, who hold cultural and historic beliefs that allow bigoted non-Christian, anti-Catholic sentiments to determine their actions towards them. That brings us back to the nature of strongholds that I wrote about in Chapter 2, a reminder that we are all "a work in process," in need of others to show us our blind-spots! It also requires our "yes," at every stage of the journey!

Sadly, as we look back, the same could be said about the Puritans who also had a relationship with God. They had embraced the salvation Christ made available to them on the Cross, but the 'Spirit of Empire' and the prevailing worldview regarding Catholicism won out when it came to their actions in Ireland, actions that could justify horrendous exploits of brutality and genocide. That sadly, along with the "Protestantization" of the Catholic Doctrine of Discovery, would continue to inform their attitudes and actions towards the Catholic French and the Indians when they went to America.

If we individually and corporately are reconciled to God, in Christ, (*katallage*), we should not be able to live together without at times needing to be reconciled to each other (*diallassomai).* I am sure that is why Paul is calling upon divided Christians in Corinth to be reconciled to each other. That was understood to be an integral aspect of their witness to the non-Christian world around them and in keeping with Christ's prayer in John 17, *"that we may be one, so that the world might know"* him. One gets the sense that Paul also knew that this isn't always easy when he had to write, *"Make every effort to keep the unity of the Spirit through the bond of peace."* (Ephesians 4:3; underlining – *mine*)

What a challenge! If I am not walking in a right relationship with someone (and especially if they are not a follower of Christ) and I do not seek to reconcile myself to them, then I am not living the life of one who is God's earthly representative, invested with His authority to act on His behalf. Philip Yancey commenting on this, writes:

> "When God 'makes his appeal through us'... he takes an awful risk: the risk that we will badly represent him. Slavery, the Crusades, pogroms against the Jews, colonialism, wars... all these movements have claimed the sanction of Christ for their cause. The world God wants to love, the world God is appealing to, may never see him; our own face may get in the way."[3]

Strong words to us, His followers. Our lives are the message! There is no integrity in me saying to someone "Be reconciled to God" if I am not seeking to be reconciled to my fellow man! There is, on the other hand, something very compelling being demonstrated to people as we live out a lifestyle which shows God's reconciling, healing love to them. That was certainly our challenging experience, time and time again when we lived in community.

That was clearly the message of Jesus Christ in his infamous Sermon on the Mount, in which he cut through the mediocracy and hypocrisy of faith in his day, among the spiritual leaders. I quote Jesus' words in Matthew 5:23 again, to highlight another issue He is addressing: *"If you are offering your gift at the altar and there remember that your brother has something against you. Leave your gift there in front of the altar. First, go and be reconciled (diallasso) to your brother; then come and offer your gift."* Jesus is taking reconciliation to a higher plain. He is not just talking about ME being in the wrong and doing something to sort it out. Here he is saying IF *"your brother has something against you."* He was implying that we are to be the prime movers in the reconciliation process! Again, He is our example. He was without sin and yet took the initiative by dying on the cross so that we could be reconciled to the Father!

We also see this demonstrated in what we call The Lord's Prayer. In it he teaches us to pray, *"Forgive us our debts, as we also have forgiven our debtors."* (Matthew 6:9-13) We see here that God is clearly calling us to take the initiative in being made right with others; forgiving anyone who has sinned against us. We also see that this releases God's forgiveness towards us. Indeed, His forgiveness of us is conditional on us first forgiving: *"Forgive us our debts AS we have..."*

That is revolutionary! If we are honest, when somebody hurts us, we generally wait for them to come and say "Sorry" to us. We rationalize that it was their fault; that they should make the first move. And again, if we are honest, our thoughts towards them are not exactly going to be pure! But for the healing of a relationship, God calls us to go and say, "I'm sorry, my heart has not been right towards you. I want a healthy relationship with you. Will you forgive me?" That places them in the position of having to deal with the primary cause of their break in the relationship and respond, "Well, actually it was really my fault... Will you forgive me?" If they don't, then no reconciliation takes place, but you have operated with integrity, you have been obedient to Christ! You are at peace with Him and in yourself. Granted you may grieve over the unhealed status of that relationship—but, that is how it should be!

—oooOooo—

Identification – embracing God's heart

I have found, time and time again, that right at the heart of reconciliation is the word, identification. God identifies with our plight, and He calls us to identify, not only with His heart for people but also with them in their pain and woundedness. In the light of that, let's look at a few words from the Prophet Nehemiah in the Old Testament. In chapter one of his book, the scene unfolds with the tribes of Israel in exile, because of generations of disobedience to God. Despite this, God's heart towards them was set on reconciliation and restoration. Nehemiah's heart was also open and available to God, enabling him to become an instrument through which it could happen.

Invariably, God always looks for someone who will embrace the Nehemiah stance; someone through whom He can respond. A partnership with the Divine is an incredible privilege! And, before there is any visible action on the ground, there is invariably the hidden action of intercession. One is seen, the other is so often, unseen!

At the beginning of his book, we read that Nehemiah was already identifying with God's heart. When some of his friends came to Susa in Babylon and shared with him the plight of Jerusalem and those that remained there, there was a spontaneous deep response rising out of his innermost being,

> *"When I heard these things, I sat down and wept. For some days I mourned and fasted and prayed before the God of Heaven."* (Nehemiah 1:4)

Out of this came a prayer of repentance, a confession of sin:

> *"I confess the sins **we** Israelites, including **myself and my father's family**, have committed against you. **We** have acted very wickedly towards you. **We** have not obeyed the commands, decrees, and laws you gave your servant Moses."* (vs. 6-7; bold – *mine*).

277

My sense is, that such a response came out of an already prayerfully concerned heart for Jerusalem and its inhabitants.

Russ Parker, in his book "Healing Wounded History," hits the target when he says that "at the core of true intercession stands a weeper rather than a warrior."[4] Weeping is a weapon! Notice also Nehemiah's inclusive wording: "I" and "We." He was standing before God representing the generations. He could have said, "Oh, those poor people back in Jerusalem; it isn't my problem; that's the fault of my parents; it's nothing to do with me!" But instead, he felt it deeply; it cost him something to identify with God's heart for the issue! That is an excellent example of what has been called "Identificational Repentance," or what others have called, "Identificational Confession." For me, the dynamics of repentance and confession are so closely allied, as Jim W. Goll puts it when he says that,

> "confession of sin goes far beyond a mere verbalizing or admitting of wrong. 'It is a deep acknowledgment of guilt, a profession of responsibility from a convicted heart which is a heart absolutely convinced of the reality and horror of sin. I believe that this is a revelatory act that comes only through the working of the Holy Spirit.'"[5]

That is what we see in Nehemiah's prayer. It is also observable in Daniel's intercessory prayer in Daniel Chapter 9 and Ezra's in Ezra Chapter 9. That is hard for us to embrace, in an increasingly individualistic western world where we tend to project our problems onto others.

Parker takes up this point when he writes,

> "The simple reason why Daniel and others own and offer to God a story for which they are not personally responsible is because they belong to that group. I cannot represent and confess the sins of the Japanese or American peoples because they are literally not my people. I can intercede for them, bless them and honor them and respect them all, but I cannot represent them.

However, when I understand the group stories of which I am a part, then I have a God-given mandate to represent my people before the throne of God... So then, because I am a member, I can carry my family story, my church story, my community and tribal story before the living God..."[6]

John Dawson of the International Reconciliation Coalition says:

"A repentant church, confessing the sins of the nation before God is the nation's only hope... The unredeemed cannot make atonement for the land... [They] cannot go up into the gap and present the blood of the Lamb... Our nation will be cursed, or blessed, according to the obedience or disobedience of the Church."[7]

The problem for me lies right here. What does one do when the Church in Ireland, and in the United States, is a part of the problem and cannot recognize it? At their governmental levels, there are massive historical and foundational, spiritual strongholds alive and well in both of our nations. They are seen in many of our denominational differences, in our politics, how we vote and how we related to others. Within the Northern Irish context—how can a sectarian Protestant Church pray against a sectarian spirit or reach out with the love of Christ across the sectarian divide? The reality is, we can't! Not until we deal with the sectarian spirits within! To rise above it can have grave ramifications for many, not only at a personal level but also at governmental levels in our historic Churches. We can lose our own cultural friends over it! It could split congregations. Clergy may lose their pulpits!

A few more considerations
Following on from the section above, it would seem to be a good place to mention something, which a Native American friend, Mark Charles, has thrown into the mix, the word: "conciliation."

One online dictionary described it as, a word very closely related to reconciliation.

> "As nouns, the difference between conciliation and reconciliation is that conciliation is the action of bringing peace and harmony; the action of ending strife while reconciliation is the reestablishment of friendly relations."[8]

An Inuit, John Amagoalik, giving his Native perspective on the subject, wrote:

"According to Dictionary.com, conciliate is defined as:

- to overcome the distrust or hostility of; placate; win over
- to win or gain (goodwill, regard, or favor)
- to make compatible
- to become agreeable

Since Europeans arrived on our shores more than five hundred years ago, there has never really been a harmonious relationship between the new arrivals and the original inhabitants of North America. The history of this relationship is marked by crushing colonialism, attempted genocide, wars, massacres, theft of land and resources, broken treaties, broken promises, abuse of human rights, relocations, residential schools, and so on. Because there has been no harmonious relationship, we must start with conciliation. We must overcome distrust and hostility, make things compatible, and become agreeable. For this to happen, from the Inuit perspective, many things need to be considered."[9]

Back to Mark Charles. He comments on Facebook that,

> "Reconciliation assumes a pre-existing harmony in the relationship. Conciliation is simply defined as the 'mediation of a dispute'... racial conciliation acknowledges the broken history of race in our nation. A history that began with the Doctrine of Discovery

and continues through systematic racism in existence today."

He also gives what he calls a working definition of "Racial Conciliation and biblical Reconciliation:"

> "In obedience to God, racial conciliation is a commitment to building cross-cultural relationships of forgiveness, love, and hope. Biblical reconciliation is walking in beauty with one another and with God."

I have pondered long and hard over this. To the best of my knowledge the Bible does not use the word "conciliation." Nevertheless, both John Amagoalik and Mark Charles in using phrases like "there has been no harmonious relationship" and "Reconciliation assumes a pre-existing harmony in the relationship" are right in highlighting an important and all too often missing relational aspect in the process.

It is sad, that both have felt, this about reconciliation. For me, reconciliation is not just a theological concept. I was not in a relationship with God when He reconciled me to himself. But what God did to make that possible, was in a very one-sided relational way. He sent His Son to live among us. This was how He identified with our lot on earth!

That is what the section above entitled "Identification—embracing God's heart" is all about. Having been brought into a relationship with our Creator, reconciliation must be relational! How can one embark on a reconciliation process with anyone without first entering into an identification process with them! Their comments imply that this has all too often been missing! Surely, conciliation should be an integral part of the reconciliation process!

At a personal level, reconciliation clearly began for me when I recognized what my sin had done to separate me from God; that he had reconciled me to Himself through Christ—what we call salvation. Christ the perfect has reached out to us, the imperfect, and made it possible. There is also a second, ongoing dynamic regarding it—when I, as a Christian, have grieved God though committing a sin, reconciliation with Him has also been made possible through repentance.

Thirdly, because I now have this relationship with my Creator, through his Son, He asks me to reach out and help others to have this relationship with him also. This can be at an evangelistic level and in counseling/discipling others. That can be a challenge at times—taking the risk of going to a person privately, to see them being restored; or seeking to bring healing to a broken relationship. Yet, this is a universal principle, not necessarily requiring a relationship with God. Something of significance happens when anyone acknowledges a wrong and says sorry for it.

Repentance and restitution issues regarding historic corporate sins

This is where it can start getting a bit more complicated. It is an area that has given rise to much confusion and debate, especially at a national/inter-community level.

For me there are three major groups to consider, which may at times intertwine:

1. Church (local/national). What can it repent of/make restitution for, e.g., towards Native Elders/Tribes?
2. Government. In the USA—this may be at Local, State and Federal levels.
3. At a personal level, as mentioned above in Point 2.

So, who repents and makes reconciliation and restitution for what? Within the U.S. context, there may be some things that only a National Church can acknowledge as wrong or make restitution for, e.g., their historic endorsement of the Doctrine of Discovery; the setting up and running of some of the residential boarding schools; processes of acculturating Tribal people, turning them into white-Christians. While at State or the Federal Government levels, there may be issues surrounding broken treaties or forced land removal that needs to be owned and responded to.

Equally, there may be issues that both Church and State have been corporately complicit in endorsing and overseeing and will need to be collectively acknowledged and dealt with. In Ireland, the Protestant Unionist political leaders were so closely connected to the historic Protestant Churches and the lead they gave regarding the formulation and signing of the Ulster Covenant in 1912. The actions of one continually enhanced the actions of the other! The primary role that the Churches played in this is the remit of my book, "*Heal Not Lightly.*"

That was further complicated with Sinn Fein making a covenant in 1916; the island being partitioned in 1922 (26 of the 32 counties formed the Republic of Ireland, and the other six counties became Northern Ireland). That led to what is known as "the troubles" (approx. 1968-1998); to Sinn Fein/IRA committing themselves to a restored 32 county Ireland and the Unionist/Loyalist paramilitaries to maintain their union with Britain. Now, how do you get national healing out of that?

Let us not forget, that as members of a society, we invariably adsorb at some level the outcomes of its history and the wrong actions of its institutions which have been prejudicially developed against others. Here we need to take personal responsibility for our own attitudes or actions, whatever the institutions do or don't do about it. That is what I and many others have had to do in Ireland regarding the Ulster Covenant—we had to repent of it and its influence in our lives.

Again, referring to Chapter 2, we are in a spiritual battle. As followers of Christ, we should no longer be partnering with Satan against God. Instead, with historical and spiritual insight, we, the church, should be aligning ourselves with God's heart for our nations. We, the church, as John Dawson reminded us, have access to God's presence. We alone, can bring God's Kingdom reign to earth and change the spiritual climate in the nation, by our prayers changing things in the spiritual/heavenly realm. That, in turn, frees something up in people's hearts/minds/spirits which can enable them to make right decisions which they otherwise could not have made. The activities of the principalities and powers in the heavenly realms (Ephesians 6:12) regarding a specific issue, having been successfully quelled.

That is exactly what happened in that event in Drumcree (also in Chapter 2) when the Orangemen acted in a way that was counter to their nature and public expectation. It is what happens when I go to someone that I am in an adversarial relationship with, and say, "I am sorry." It has the possibility of bringing healing and restoration because the foothold Satan has had in our relationship has been removed through that action! It neutralizes the caustic dynamics that were in operation! Reconciliation between us has not been assured—it takes two—but room has been made for a reciprocal response!

That is the position I arrived at personally, in Ireland: When I felt a prompting of the Holy Spirit, whether it was spontaneous or pre-arranged, I knew I had to respond—this may have meant either going to a person privately or speaking it out in a public meeting. I believe that I could confess before them the wrongs "my people" had done, and then repent of them. I have often had to add, that I am not acting as a delegated spokesperson for my group, nor do I have the authority to initiate restitution on their behalf. This is me, seeking to act with integrity before God, genuinely trying to respond to what I believe was the prompting of his Spirit!

Who knows, this could be the very means whereby a person or people group can start a journey with God to bring healing to the whole, which may include visiting, in a right spirit, issues surrounding justice and restitution. We can never underestimate such an action! I believe this can equally apply to a group of people, representative of a section of society, who in feeling led by God to do likewise—reach out in repentance, seeking to be reconciled to the other.

Fort Wayne and the Miami Tribe
What is most powerful to see is local Church leaders reaching out in unity, mindful of correct protocol, in repentance and reconciliation to the local Tribal Elders and Council.

At the end of January 2010, I experienced one example of that, when I had the incredible privilege of being invited by Terry and Darlene Wildman to participate in a gathering in Fort Wayne, Indiana called "Restoring Ancient Gates." Much of what I now share with you has been gleaned from Terry's book, *"Sign Language—A Look at the Historic and Prophetic Landscape of America."* Back in 2005, Darlene had a strong sense that God was calling them to move from Arizona to Fort Wayne and that this move would not only reconnect them with former friendships but would also involve developing relationships with the regions Indians.

As I mentioned above, this involved hitting the research trail. They were to discover that it was a

> "... local hotspot for relations between the Native Americans and the newly formed United States. The first major battles took place there because George Washington wanted to establish a fort at the junction of the three rivers, called Kekionga by the Miami Indians. Little Turtle, War Chief of the Miami, said it was 'The glorious gate through which all the good words of our Chiefs had to pass from the North to the South and from the East to the West.' It was a strategically important portage between the three rivers and the Wabash that led to the west. The Miami and 10 other tribes fought and won the first battles but eventually lost to General Anthony Wayne who established a fort there that was named after him – Fort Wayne.
>
> In Greenville, Ohio in 1795 the Treaty of Greenville was signed by the 10 Tribes and the United States (*mine*—The signing of this Treaty was to open the Northwest Territory leading to the formation of the following States: Ohio, Indiana, Michigan, Wisconsin, Illinois, and part of Minnesota). Eventually, that Treaty and all the others were broken by the US and the Miami were placed on reservations. Then in the mid-1800s they were forcefully removed to Kansas and finally to Oklahoma. Those who remained lost all their tribal homelands and their federal status as an Indian tribe."[10]

Intercession was key! Soon after moving to Fort Wayne the Wildman's introduced themselves to City-Wide Intercessors there, to find that God had already been at work, showing this group that some form of reconciliation with the local Tribe was very much needed. They had also been asking God that He would send them some assistance with this.

Initial contacts were made with the Miami Chief, Brian Buchanan and over the next few years, those relationships with the Miami grew, leading in 2009 to the prayerful planning for the "Restoring Ancient Gates" event in Heartland Church, led by Pastor Ron Allen, another key person in this whole journey.

To quote Terry again,

> "'… we gathered to listen with open hearts to Native American leaders, and to the teaching of others who have paved the way in reconciliation.' Then, Chief Buchanan was 'invited along with the Miami Council to come and share what is happening with the tribe. There would be an honoring ceremony and an acknowledgment from pastors in the city, and an offering would be received towards the Miami language camp as a step of restitution… Then we began meeting Pastors and leaders in the city and region. Soon there were many… representing over 100 churches… agreeing to be involved.'"[11]

On Saturday evening, approximately 500 people were gathered in the Heartland Church – the sanctuary having been set up in a large circle, powwow style. The evening culminated in presenting Chief Buchanan and the Tribal Council with a special plaque, inscribed: "In Honor of the Miami People, the Original Gatekeepers of the 'Glorious Gate,'" followed by one of the Pastors reading an Acknowledgement (See Appendix II for the wording). That, in turn, was signed by many of the Christian leaders present and other witnesses.

Prior to going there, in my own research, I was to find that this confederation of 10 tribes had aligned themselves with the English in

Canada, who were still smarting from loses made during the Revolutionary War. It was also clear to me that the Scotch-Irish frontiersmen, who had aligned themselves with Washington during the war, were now part of this new US army under General Wayne's command – whose father was a native of Ulster. The English retreated and left the Native Indians to their fate. Both sides of my cultural/ethnic identity interacted negatively with them in that process. At one point in the evening's proceedings, I had the privilege to kneel before Chief Buchanan, acknowledging and repenting of the sins of my Scotch-Irish and English forefathers towards them.

It has been exciting to see how things were developing in Fort Wayne since then—a reminder that reconciliation is not just an event! When we are dealing with deep-rooted historic issues, it is something that has got to be worked at and walked out over an extended period. Here are a few of them, which Terry mentioned:

- Shortly after it, the Miami Council invited the pastors along with Terry and Darlene to their tribal council meeting at which they presented them with a framed Certificate of Appreciation, signed by the Council
- The Associated Churches Council of Fort Wayne extended an invitation to Chief Buchanan to meet with them and share his heart with them. During which, a further offering was taken and presented to the Chief
- The Tribes Powwow Committee invited the Christian leaders to attend their gathering the following summer as honored dignitaries
- The Church at Heartland, having acquired a large drum, asked Chief Buchanan and a Senior Council member to come and participate in the naming ceremony
- In October 2010, the Miami Council sent out an invitation to the Christian leaders and churches to take part in a grieving ceremony. That has taken place for over 170 years as a way of remembering the members of their Tribe who were relocated to Oklahoma. It was a very significant invite, as this was the first time in their history such an event had been extended to

outsiders—especially church outsiders! The "Restoring Ancient Gates" event had been the catalyst

- The following year, by mutual cooperation, the Churches and the Miami Council held a New Beginnings Powwow at the Heartland Church.

Something changed in the heavenly realms because of that gathering–both dignity and destiny for many who attended were, I believe, being restored.

The Heartland Church, where the events had been held, has continued to deepen their relationship with the Tribe and has appointed one of its members, Byron Funnel, as its link person. He has been able, through invitations to attend various events, to build up a relationship with Chief Buchanan and other tribal members. My prayer is that it will inspire others in many communities across the U. S. to proactively fulfill this sacred ministry of reconciliation!

-oooOooo-

If a personal or group act of repentance is made regarding State or National issues, I believe that the parameters of such a "repentance" need to be clearly established. As already mentioned, at a personal level there is a need to make it clear, that this is how I/we feel God has been leading me/us: this is my/our conviction and I/we are most certainly not representing or acting on behalf of a State, Denomination or group without having their delegated authority. Rather, as a member of both/either/neither of these, I believe that we can own and therefore acknowledge certain issues and say, "We got it wrong"; "We did things in God's name that we shouldn't have;" "This is not the Jesus we know." "For this, I am sorry and repent."

Again, relating to Ireland, I needed to acknowledge before God the wrongs of the Ulster Covenant, repenting of its influence over me personally. On several occasions, I had felt led to repent before others, regarding what the Ulster Covenant had done to them and their people. But that did not rule out what I believe the relevant Churches still need to do at their Governmental levels—repent of it before God and before man.

I have also heard and read of Christians standing up on platforms, undoubtedly sincerely, to repent of what White people have done to Native Americans or Protestants have done to Catholic. It has often been expected, that a Native or Catholic person appropriately responds. What is not appropriate is for that person to speak forgiveness on behalf of the whole tribe or nation! They can speak on their own behalf – that in itself can be healing! Otherwise it can then be considered as being over, settled! More than likely not! Some things have happened in Northern Ireland that has resulted in lengthy tribunals to try and ascertain the rights and wrongs. Saying sorry—did not finish it! Again, as I have mentioned, there may be justice and restitution issues to be resolved, which the repenting Christians have no right or authority to deal with! E.g., Treaties made and broken by the State. We can, nevertheless intercede before God regarding the issue(s) and lobby the relevant governmental bodies and seek to reach out and build positive relationships with the offended group.

Appropriate Christian repentance can nevertheless pave the way for civil authorities to act in ways that they could not have done before. Satan had them tied into their predecessors' previous wrongs; repentance can, however, lead to a change in the spiritual atmosphere, by freeing people from his influence and enable them to respond by choice, in a "God way."

Some protocol and honor considerations

I mentioned earlier that we need to be "mindful of correct protocol." That is something that can vary widely from culture to culture. I know if someone has been invited to a function at which Queen Elizabeth II is present, that there is a whole list of protocols to be observed such as dress code; how you approach and address her, etc., To not take the time to understand this and embrace it, is acting honorably towards her! I was soon to learn, on attending my first Reignbridge gathering in Ventura, that protocol is incredibly central to Native American culture. I just love the way they honor people through it! I had a similar experience in March'17, when we attended a Conference in Fort Yates, North Dakota, much of the first evening was given over to this – it was a central and unrushed opening event.

Here are some helpful insights by Liz Lévesque-Metis, from a Paper she wrote on Native American Reconciliation. I get the sense that she is sharing specifically within a Church/Native Tribe reconciliation and restitution issues context, not at a person-to-person level:

> "From what I understand of the Native viewpoint on reconciliation, it is the purview of duly elected chiefs and council members to exercise the negotiations necessary to obtain the reconciliation. In my opinion, these chiefs and elders are the only ones who can truly negotiate on behalf of Native America. These traditional people, because they have been chosen and elected by their Native communities, have the 'legal' right to speak on behalf of 'their people' because they have been elected as spokespersons..."

It appears to me that many Natives who stand on platforms and accept these apologies for 'our people' are acting without authority and are seriously overstepping their bounds. This bothers me when duly elected Native leaders are not even invited to the table, perhaps on the charge that they are not Christians... Since when does reconciliation in the biblical sense only mean a bridging of the gap between Christian brothers and sisters? Is it not the intention of Creator-God to reconcile 'all' peoples back to Himself?

It is time for the biblical model of reconciliation followed by concrete restitution to arise and be implemented. That means that the Majority Church is going to invite duly elected local Native chiefs and council members to the table whether they are Christians or not... It is going to be committed to listen to the Native heart, concern and wisdom."[12]

I get the sense, in talking to others and in reading, that many Native American Christians are tired of "repentance meetings" which they considered as being more geared towards salving the conscience of the specific white church. They know it should be done; they may be sincere, but time has not been taken to "listen to the Native heart, concern, and wisdom." (Perhaps this is, in part, what Mark Charles is connecting into when he speaks of 'conciliation'!) It has not been relational; possible follow through meetings have not been

290

considered.

I am reminded of a challenging Indian Proverb quoted at the beginning of the "Bury My Heart at Wounded Knee" film, "It is easy to be brave at a distance." What some have seen as "platform repentance" could have, with understanding, been the beginning of a developing and deeply meaningful ongoing relationship; proximity; listening; opening the door into a journey where issues, as they surface, can be faced together! It brings us back to the conciliation/reconciliation issue mentioned earlier.

—oooOooo—

From my experience, as mentioned above, healing could begin when I have stood up in a gathering where Irish Catholics were present, and I confessed the sin of my people towards them, current and generationally. When I have acknowledged that there are things we have done to them, often in the name of God, that had nothing to do with Him, some in such gatherings have said that they had never heard a Protestant say sorry for anything that was done against them. These have been sacred moments when tears have been shed in God's presence, and repentance, forgiveness, reconciliation, and healing has started to flow. It may seem small, justice and restitution issues may not have been resolved, but healing has begun, dignity is being restored, a new sense of destiny has been released. It has also been my experience in America, that many Native Americans have never heard a sincere "I'm sorry for..." either!

One person, open to God! John Dawson has this to say:

> "[T]he greatest wounds in history... have not happened through the acts of individual perpetrators; rather through institutions, systems, philosophies, cultures, religions, and governments of humankind. Because of this, we as individuals are tempted to absolve ourselves of all individual responsibility. However, unless **someone** chooses to identify themselves with the corporate entities, such as the nation of our citizenship, or the subculture of our

291

ancestors, the act of honest confession will never take place. This leaves us in a world of injury and offense in which no corporate sin is ever acknowledged, reconciliation never begins and old hatreds deepen."[13] (emphasis – *mine*)

As we move from this, into the next chapter, I am left with the awareness, that justice and/or restitution is not always possible, particularly regarding issues concerning land. That has historically been a huge issue in Ireland, though clearly not on the same scale, as it is in the United States.

Yet, I am equally aware, that for many Native Americans, getting their lands back is not the central issue—that may never be possible. For them, it can be, as I have just mentioned, the receiving of our sincere repentance; our acknowledgment of them being the first people of the land; honoring; respecting, choosing to walk with them and were possible make restitution. This is a higher way which leads to the restoration of dignity for all parties!

References:

1. Source: http://www.merriam-webster.com/dictionary/reconciliation
2. Source: http://www.oxforddictionaries.com/definition/english/reconciliation
3. Philip Yancey, *"Disappointment with God."* Published by Zondervan, 1988, Pg. 15.
4. Russ Parker, *"Healing Wounded History."* Darton, Long, and Todd, 2001, Pg. 100.
5. Jim W. Goll, *"Father Forgive Us."* Destiny Image, 1999, Pg. 42.
6. Parker. Pgs. 97-98.
7. John Dawson, *"What Christians Should Know About Reconciliation."* Sovereign World. Pgs. 12-15.
8. Source: https://www.quora.com/Whats-the-difference-between-conciliation-and-reconciliation-What-is-an-example
9. Source: http://speakingmytruth.ca/?page_id=266
10. Terry M. Wildman, *"Sign Language – A Look at the Historic*

and Prophetic Landscape of America." Greater Thunder
Publishing, Maricopa, 2001. Pgs.184-185.

11. Ibid. Pg. 187.

12. Liz Lévesque-Metis, *"Reconciliation: A Native View."* Talking
Circle Journal, Editors: Ray Lévesques and Tony Laidig, 2004.

13. Dawson. Pgs. 22-23.

Chapter 20

A Right Mess

Something stirred deep within me as the writing of this book progressed! I was meeting a growing number of Native Americans who were either worshipping or seeking to worship Creator, in a culturally-relevant, rather than a Euro-American way, with a few Native add-ons! I was sensing that this was a legitimate longing in their hearts. But I was also finding that this has not been without its controversy within both the Native and White Church communities! It was to take me on yet another trail of discovery.

I **don't** feel particularly adequate for such a task, but it has not left me. Nor do I believe I am called to present a "How to do it" chapter. However, I do sense there is something of real importance here that needs to be "flagged up" regarding what is considered by some, as a contentious issue.

I have also become more aware, that this a worldwide issue being addressed within modern **missions'** training. Down through the centuries of colonial history, we had not fully understood what was on God's heart regarding issues connected to mission: evangelism, church planting, expressions of worship and discipleship—we tragically got it seriously wrong. How we saw these issues was deeply influenced by our European Roman Catholic or Protestant worldviews. Sadly, as we say here in Belfast, Northern Ireland, "we made a right mess of it!"

With a stretch of the imagination, "a right mess," could be given a more positive meaning when used for instance, within the context of bringing together all the ingredients for a fruitcake; it may not look or tastes great until it is baked! That is truly in keeping with God's heart regarding the bringing together in witness and worship, diverse people groups, each with their unique cultures—this could, at times, also appear to look a bit messy, but it can be such a rich expression of His character. God has no problem with diversity. As we look around the world and at creation, He designed it to be this way. He loves it! Indeed, I soon discovered that the meaning of the word "syncretism" started in that vein.

—oooOooo—

The word "syncretism," along with others like "indigenous," "contextualization," and "enculturation" were appearing in conversations and in my reading. So, before going any further, let us look at a few definitions. There are some things of critical importance here, related to Native Americans—perhaps, the least evangelized people group in the U.S.—and their embracing of Creator's Son, Jesus.

Coming to terms
Syncretism:
This word is thought to have its origins in Crete during the period of ancient classical literature. Plutarch used it in his work "Fraternal Love," in which he described the temporary union ("*synistanto*" in Greek) of two ideologically different political parties standing against a common enemy that was trying to invade their country.

By the 17th century, the word had evolved to become a Greek concept "*synkerannymi*." Which means "to mix," "to meld" or "to harmonize" doctrines, philosophies.[1] During this period there was a group within the Church led by Claxitus (1656) known as the "syncretics," who tried to foster good relationships between those that held different doctrinal views.[2] Used in this sense, it was seen as something positive. However, in the early stages of the Reformation, the meaning took on a negative twist, with many of the different emerging groups such as Calvinists and Armenians taking extreme adversarial stances on various doctrines, making attempts at finding a unified way forward, difficult.

Such attempts were increasingly regarded as being incompatible and compromising, and the word "syncretism" developed into a word with more negative connotations. So far, Richard Twiss is the only writer that I have come across, who draws our attention to both the positive and negative aspects of it. One of the advantages or disadvantages of living in Ireland is that I don't always know when I have "stood on someone's toes!" Mentioning his name—and indeed, this subject—has at times had that effect! Grace! Do continue to read! Perhaps he was a pioneer!

In more recent times others have, within the context of Spanish Catholic colonization of South America, coined the word "Christopaganism" to describe the mixing of animism with Christianity. Twiss, in *"Reflections on the Widespread Concern About Syncretism in Native North American and Indigenous Ministry,"* writes that this is an area of primary concern, seeing it as a "theological issue centered around Christology and allegiance... [the] borrow[ing of] elements of another religion, without critically passing them through the screen of Christianity, with Christianity being watered down or destroyed in the process."[3]

That was explicitly warned against in the Old and New Testaments by God. In the Ten Commandments, Moses was given precise and clear instructions:

> *"You shall have no other gods before me. You shall not make for yourself an image in the form of anything in heaven above or in the waters beneath. You shall not bow down to them or worship them..."* (Deuteronomy. 5:7-9)

The Apostle Paul makes it very clear what he thinks about negative syncretism when it appears in the early church in Galatia:

> *"I am astonished that you are so quickly deserting the one who called you to live in the grace of Christ and are turning to a different gospel—which is really no gospel at all. Evidently some people are throwing you into confusion and are trying to pervert the gospel, of Christ. But even if we or an angel from heaven should preach a gospel other than the one we preached to you,*

let them be under God's curse! As we have already said before, so now I say again: if anyone is preaching to you a gospel other than what you accepted, let him be under God's curse. " (Galatians 1:6-9)

So, today, syncretism is a word that is loaded with explosive connotations in the minds of some Christians involved in ministry among tribal/indigenous people. Carl Starkloff[4] writes that no other word in the ecumenical vocabulary has aroused more fears and created more unnecessary controversy. Sadly, it has created deep wounds, suspicions, and divisions among Christians. Healing is needed!

Further contributions:

Richard Twiss:

> "Syncretism, i.e., negative syncretism… is essentially the rejection of the centrality of the biblical, historical Jesus Christ as savior, redeemer, reconciler, sacrifice, healer, intercessor, mediator, atoner, protector, etc., because it assumes other religious beliefs/practices are equally God-honoring and dynamic in accomplishing the purposes of God for mankind… Syncretism is sin in that it directs one's allegiance to other than Jesus Christ by reason of a person's participation in a new religious system—one created from the blend which dilutes or redirects faith to other than Christ."[5]

Alan Tippett:

> "… it is inevitable that many missionaries whose roots are in Scripture will be predisposed to resist anything in the churches planted which would lead to syncretism."[6] He also mentions that "Syncretism may be defined as the union of two opposite forces, beliefs, systems or tenets so that the united form is a new thing, neither one nor the other."[7]

W. A. Visser't Hooft:

"It is the intermingling and combination of diverse religions" or the "synthesis of beliefs which are radically divergent."[8]

Harold Turner:

"If what is drawn from local sources retains its original religious meaning, and is merely amalgamated with other Christian elements, we have a religious syncretism. This is a hybrid or mixture in which Christ through the Scriptures does not control all elements, and at best it is only partly Christian."[9]

These last three quotes are expressions, in keeping with Richard Twiss' understanding, regarding negative mixture. Jesus was extremely clear about this, when he succinctly states, *"I am the way the truth and the life. No one comes to the Father except through me."* (John 14:6)

Indigenous:
In the Webster's International Dictionary, the adjective "Indigenous" is said to have come from the Indo-European and Latin compound word in+de+gena, meaning "to beget," which signifies that which is "born from within" or "that which comes from."

From this, according to Karl Kasdorf, comes a more contemporary word, "indigeneity," meaning "a natural belongingness." Relating it to the Church, he goes on to say that it is "that [which] has been planted by a foreign mission but comes under native leadership and support without foreign domination. An indigenous Church is a Church born and maintained within a given culture by people of that culture without direct outside human influence or control."[10]

Melvin Hodges defines it, "as a result of missionary effort, a native church has been produced which shares the life of the country in which it is planted and finds within itself the ability to govern itself, support itself and produce itself."[11]

While Bolaji Idowu describes it as follows: "it means when the church is planted, for example in Nigerian soil, it 'is obligated to afford Nigerians the means of worshiping, as Nigerians, in a way that is compatible with their spiritual temperament... singing to the glory of God in their own way, of praying to God and hearing His word in an idiom which is clearly intelligible to them.'... 'It is not a church that is still in the 'incubator,' of her founder.'"[12] I ask myself, "Why is it in many African Church settings, that Western forms of worship and dress code (suits and ties) are standard?"

Contextualization and Inculturation:

There is yet another aspect of mixing that is worth looking at. Both Fanny Crosby and William Booth (founder of the Salvation Army) would probably have been seen as being syncretistic when they used the music of popular tunes for hymns. In a biography about Booth, Helen Hosier mentions that George Scott Railton, author, and songwriter, who became his lieutenant-general in 1873, concluded an article "About Singing" (1874) with this impassioned plea: "Oh, let us rescue this precious instrument from the clutches of the devil, and make it, as it may be made, a bright and lively power for good!"[13]

That brings us to the cutting edge of the syncretism issue!

In 1972, Dr. Paul Hiebert from Trinity Evangelical Divinity School was credited to have coined the word "contextualization" to describe the process of using the scriptures to critically examine the culture of the missionaries as well as the group being reached, for the purposes of evangelism and discipleship. By employing this "critical examination," it was hoped that the Gospel would be presented in the "cultural forms, languages, and ceremony of the people" in ways that still reflected the integrity of biblical Christianity rather than Western civilization or culture. The desired outcome was that Christianity would be "owned" by the people as theirs, not as a foreign import.[14] He also distinguishes between "critical" and "uncritical." The later, in rejecting the absolutes and uniqueness of the Scriptures leads to theological and cultural relativism—all cultures and belief systems being equal!

Richard Twiss writes,

> "Around the world missionaries have gradually come to value the importance of critical contextualization, an anthropologically informed, biblical approach to evangelism and discipleship. The consideration and incorporation of cultural forms and expressions have become central in the missionary process. These changes have not occurred in the vacuum of isolated geographical locales, but are global in scope, affecting all indigenous communities."[15]

A closely aligned word, "inculturation," is simply stating that the non-Western church needs to develop its own cultural identities through which the Christian message "becomes a principle that animates, directs and unifies the culture, transforming it and remaking it so as to bring about a 'new creation.'"[16]

Tippett articulates it like this:

> "the basic principles of anthropology, communication theory and incarnational theology tell us that the churches we plant (and by churches here I mean the Christian fellowship groups, however simple) in cultures other than our own must be relevantly part of those cultures."[17]

—oooOooo—

Jesus made it abundantly clear that we are "to go into all the world," to every nation (*ethnos*), to call them to become his followers. It also becomes clear that the early disciples went out to share this message within a very definite, narrow cultural context. For them, the Gentiles had to become Jewish to worship Jesus. Not that long into Church history, this produced such a tension that it needed to be addressed by a special Council in Jerusalem. This is a lesson that still needs to be learned repeatedly!

It is implied, within what we call the "great commission" that individuals and societies need to embrace the transforming presence of Christ; that all is not well with them; that much has been distorted by both Satan and man. Instead of worshipping our Creator God, many have worshiped Satan, masquerading as a multitude of deities within our cultures. To challenge the validity of these deities and the worship of them is not popular in today's liberal, all accepting, multicultural Western world. And the reality is, Native American cultures are as open to issues of idolatry and syncretism as much as the rest of Western Society. Both fall within the remit of the Church's call to evangelize and disciple them; with that comes, like it or not, a shift in worldview and inevitably a change in cultural outlook. Therein lies the challenge!

It was not that long ago that conversations around mission would have had a predominantly Western slant, with Europe and North America having the greatest share in missionary training and sending. That has seen a dramatic change in recent years. Back in 1975, Alan Tippet wrote,

> "We now stand at a formative period in the history of the expansion of Christianity. An old era of mission has passed, and we are suffering the birth pangs of a new one."[18]

While Philip Jenkins observes that,

> "The center of gravity in the Christian world has shifted inexorably southward, to Africa, Asia, and Latin America."[19]

In 2010, Mission Frontiers Magazine carried an article by Richard Twiss entitled, "Making Jesus Known in Knowable Ways" which conveyed similar sentiments:

"While the colonial missions' paradigm still exists, it is waning around the world as indigenous theologians, scholars, pastors, and missiologists begin interpreting Scriptures for their own local contexts, opposing the pressure to reject their cultural ways, and instead embrace their histories and cultures. No longer wondering if God was involved in their histories and asking 'if' God can be found in their cultural ways, they are assuming God was always involved and are discovering ways to worship within their culture[e]... The Creator of heaven and earth, 'the God-who-was-always-there,' continues to make Jesus known in new and dynamic ways as we resolve to work towards a post-colonial Christendom for future generations."[20]

The day of the European colonially inspired measuring stick appears to be fading!

As I read these quotes, another one from Dr. Billy Graham came to mind:

"The greatest moments of Native history lie ahead of us if a great spiritual renewal and awakening should take place. The Native American has been a sleeping giant. He is awakening. The original Americans could become the evangelists who will help win America for Christ!"[21]

Such a statement by Billy Graham may be a difficult one for many to embrace. What, God using another culture? Difficult as it may be, we need as UK & Euro-American churches to allow God to search our hearts and our histories regarding the negative legacy we have handed down to the Native Americans through our evangelization since colonial days and appropriately respond. From the time that we first set foot on American soil, we demeaned them and their cultures, seeing everything as pagan, something to be renounced. At the same time, we saw our cultural and spiritual beliefs and values as correct, superior—something they had to embrace. Period!

Whichever way God chooses to move, we are in a season when ministries—White and Native—need to stand as equals, seeking "first the Kingdom of God" together. That is a scriptural given! The challenge is to not only deal with our own 'stuff' but also to give the many different cultures in our midst the right to work on what are and are not redeemable expressions of worship in theirs. Granted, this may require us sitting down and listening to each other in a mutually honoring and respectful way. In doing this, we might find that we are removing the logs from each other's eyes! The 'spec' in our brothers' eye may, indeed, be a reflection of the 'log' in our own! (Matthew 7:3-5)

That is especially so for many mainstream traditional Churches. In places like the U.S., and the UK, that have tended to see Indigenous people as the "mission field"; or who reach out to the Indigenous Churches with a "How can we help you?" Rather than a "How can we help each other?" mentality. Perhaps, it is the mainstream churches that are need of the Indigenous church to help them! I have greatly appreciated and have been enriched by hearing Native leaders explain 'why' they worship in different ways than I do. Their journey into contextualization!

I also need to remind myself that our historic Western expressions of Christianity are not without their expressions of syncretism! Some of these have been with us for so long that we do not even recognize them as such! E.g., Easter is thought to be named after the ancient Anglo-Saxon/Germanic fertility goddess Eastre or Eostra, which included customs involving eggs and rabbits. Add to that the influences of the Enlightenment and secular humanism.

Cross-cultural communication
This leads me on to another (yet connected) challenge, which arises out of the need to communicate the Scriptures across cultures. Tippett writes:

> "We are continually (and quite rightly) warned of the danger of planting foreign western Christianity on what we have for so long called 'the mission field'...

on the one hand we try to preserve a pure faith and an essential gospel, and on the other we seek to give it 'an indigenous garment'... The moment we translate a portion of Scripture into a language which has hitherto built its vocabulary only for a [non-Christian] worldview and belief, we are confronted with the problem not only of translation but of reception. Yet unless the written word of God can be incarnated in the linguistic flesh of the receptor people, the saving experience is not likely to be transmitted... The basic problem, therefore, would seem to be how to communicate the essential supracultural core of the gospel to new believers in other cultures without having it contaminated by the non-Christian forms with which it must be communicated and shared."[22]

This was most certainly not something my ancestors thought about as they confronted the Native Americans, pushed them off their lands and tried to bring them to a white European Protestant God - with a copy of the King James Bible, in hand! It is something Terry Wildman (Rain Ministries), has thought a lot about, as he worked on a recently published harmonized translation of the four Gospels for Native Americans—*"When The Great Spirit Walked Among Us."*[23] He has more recently been working with a team of 15 Bible translators representing many tribes, denominations, and churches within First Nations communities, along with OneBook Publishers, to produce the First Nations Version (FNV) of the New Testament.[24]

Richard Twiss has this to say about the term "supracultural:"

"... as Christians, we do not represent only one 'Christian' culture in terms of ethnicity or nations or origins. The things we have in common as followers of the Jesus Way are 'supracultural.' [Which] basically means for Christians that the Truth of the scripture is above, over, or outside of all human cultures, and stands as absolute critique and judgment of them all."[25]

304

We will pick this up again in the next chapter, as we look further at the debate within Native American Christian circles.

References:

1. Leonardo Boff, *"Church, Charism and Power."* New York, Crossroad Publishing Company. 1986. Pg. 178.
2. Hendrik Kraemer, *"Religion and Christian Faith."* Philadelphia, Westminster Press, 1956. Pg. 393.
3. Source: http://richardtwiss.blogspot.co.uk/2005/01/syncretism-work-in-progress-by-richard.html
4. Carl Starkloff, *"A Theology of the In-Between: The Value of Syncretic Process."* Milwaukee, WI, Marquette University Press. 2002. Pg. 10.
5. Richard Twiss, *"Reflections on the Widespread Concern About Syncretism in Native American and Indigenous Ministry."* Based on a Research Paper for a Doctor of Missiology Program, Asbury Theological Seminary. 2004, Pg. 1.
6. Ibid. Pg. 1.
7. Ibid. Pgs. 17-18.
8. W. A. Visser't Hooft, *"No Other Name."* Westminster Press, Philadelphia. 1963. Pg. 14.
9. Harold Turner, *"Syncretism."* in Stephen Neill, Gerald H Anderson and John Goodwin, eds., Concise Dictionary of Christian World Mission, London, Lutterworth. 1971. Pg. 580.
10. Hans Kasdorf, *"Indigenous Church Principles: A Survey of Origin and Development."* in Reading in Dynamic Indigeneity, edited by Charles H. Kraft and Tom N. Wisley. California: William Carey Library.1979. Pgs. 71-86.
11. Melvin Hodges, *"The Indigenous Church."* Springfield, MI. Gospel Publishing House. 1953.
12. Bolaji Idowu, *"Towards an Indigenous Church."* London: Oxford. 1965. Pgs. 11 & 14.
13. Helen K. Hosier, *"William and Catherine Booth: Founders of the Salvation Army."*
14. Richard Twiss, As 8 above. Footnote 3.
15. Ibid.
16. Fr Pedro Arrupe SJ, cited by Shorter. *"Theology of Inculturation."* Chapman. 1988. Pg. 11 in John Roxborogh.

"Syncretism and Identity." Christian Thought and History Seminar, Dept. of Theology and Religion, University of Otago, 2012.

17. Alan Tippett, *"Christopaganism or Indigenous Christianity."* Re-Published in Global Missiology. 2006. Pg. 1.

18. Alan Tippett, *"Christopaganism or Indigenous Christianity."* William Carey Press, South Pasadena, CA. 1975. Pg. 16.

19. Philip Jenkin, *"The Next Christendom: The Coming of Global Christianity."* New York, NY. Oxford University Press. 2002. Pgs. 1-2.

20. Richard Twiss, *"Making Jesus Known in Knowable Ways."* Mission Frontiers Magazine. Sept-Oct 2010. Pg. 6.

21. Billy Graham quote. http://www.consumingfire.com/native.php

22. Alan Tippett, Pg. 1.

23. Terry Wildman, *"When The Great Spirit Walked Among Us."* Great Thunder Publishing, Maricopa, Arizona, 2014.

24. Source: http://www.jumpintotheword.com/2016/03/01/first-nations-version/

25. Richard Twiss, *"Christ, Culture & The Kingdom-Seminar Study Guide."* Pg. 21.

Chapter 21

Native Worship: Healing the Divide

History has left its scars – the Native divide!

In my journeys in and out of the United States I have observed among Native American Christians, two distinct groups:

- There are those who have been evangelized, according to an older colonial Christian model (perhaps over two or three generations), who were taught that everything of their Native culture was wrong; of the devil and therefore had to be renounced and walked away from

- The other group has either partially found, or is in the process of searching for, an indigenous expression of Christianity. I say 'partially' in the sense of them being on a journey of discovery. They know Creator's Son, Jesus and are seeking for indigenous ways of worshiping him.

It is out of this that questions arose for me–if God made man in His image; made all the many ethnic identities in the world; if He put eternity in our hearts, then surely room must be made to worship Him in an ethnically relevant way? If we, because of sin entering the world, do not have everything in our culture perfectly aligned with God, have we not made room, consciously or otherwise, for the worship of Satan in a myriad of ways—occultism, shamanism, sacrifices, wrong covenants, etc.? How, then do we redeem our cultures so that God can be at the center and rightfully worshipped? In so doing, will we not become more complete—along with our Cherokee, Sioux, Apache brothers and sisters in Christ? More like what our Creator intended us to be? Surely this is at the very core of us having our dignity restored!

Growing up as a child in an Evangelical Church in Belfast, women going to church on Sunday in trousers or men not wearing a suit and tie, was unthinkable; so too was the use of drums and guitars—these were the Devils' instruments, ways of "the world!" If we can now dress more casually and use these instruments in our worship today, then surely such restrictions at that time were culturally determined, not sin? Can Native Americans not redeem the drum? Surely the drum is not the problem—it is who we worship with the drum that matters! If that is the case, what else can be redeemed?

This is when issues of syncretism and contextualization can become contentious. What are the criteria for such a discernment process? Should such a process be in the hands of the dominant invading culture or in the hands of the Christian Indians? Even in that a problem arises when the two groups of Christian Natives mentioned above, can be at variance with each other. History has left its scars!

—oooOooo—

In several places in the previous chapter, I quoted the late Richard Twiss. He was a Lakota Sioux (Rosebud Reservation, South Dakota), who headed up Wiconi International until what many felt was his untimely death in 2013. In its purpose statement, we read: "We seek to live and walk among all people in a good way, as we follow the ways of Jesus—affirming, respecting and embracing the God-given cultural realities of Native American and Indigenous people, not rejecting or demonizing these sacred cultural ways."[1] He would be perceived by some, as I have alluded to earlier, as a controversial figure, as he challenged the positions taken by some of the longer established Evangelical Native ministries regarding syncretism, on the basis that they were tainted by western colonial perspectives. He mentioned two of these ministries in an article entitled *"Reflections on the Widespread Concern About Syncretism in Native North American and Indigenous Ministry."*[2] (i) The Evangelical Native Leaders and (ii) The Native American District of the Christian & Missionary Alliance Denomination.

Twiss wrote, recognizing that a "shift toward a global Christianity has become normative Christian mission, in our commitment to present a biblically faithful, culturally meaningful message of faith and hope in Jesus Christ in a cross-cultural setting, we will always walk a fine line between syncretism and critical contextualization." That "there will always be a dynamic tension in contextualizing the gospel." Within that tension, he also recognized that there are twin fears, something that David Hesselgrave and Edward Rommen also articulate:

> "a fear of irrelevance if contextualization is not attempted, and the fear of compromise and syncretism if it is taken too far... Since, by definition, contextualization appropriates indigenous linguistic and cultural forms, it always risks cultural and religious syncretism. The only viable choice in the face of these two dangers is a contextualization that is true to both indigenous culture and the authority of Scripture."[3]

Regarding the "shift" that Twiss mentions, Philip Jenkins has this to say:

> "this shift is one of the transforming moments in the history of religion worldwide... over the past five centuries or so, the story of Christianity has been inextricably bound up with that of Europe and European-derived civilizations overseas, above all in North America... radical writers have seen Christianity as an ideological arm of Western imperialism."[4]

In his paper, Twiss recognizes that not everyone would embrace what he felt he could contextualize, but he has helped to bring the debate out into the open. I will look briefly at the two opposing positions I mentioned above, along with some of his comments. Hopefully, it will give some insight into the nature of the debate that has been going on out there:

The Evangelical Native Leaders (several dozen leaders under the banner of Chief Inc., Ministries) published a paper against syncretism, *"A Biblical Position by Native Leaders on Native Spirituality."* They defined it as the subtle attempt to integrate biblical truth and faith in Christ with non-biblical religious beliefs, practices, and forms—which produces "another gospel."[5]

"In their thesis, they affirm their belief that salvation is in the finished work of Christ and that nothing can be added to this that can improve right relationship with God. The central concern of the paper is summarized in its conclusion, [that] believers should not, therefore, use or attach any spiritual value to items regarded as sacred such as tobacco, cedar smoke, sweet grass, peyote,... masks, drums, dances, etc.; to places regarded as sacred... sweat lodges, or other traditional religious places of worship, etc.; or to spirit beings... or nature spirits, etc."[6]

Twiss continues,

"Syncretism for this group of First Nations leaders is primarily concerned with preserving 'orthodoxy' or theological integrity. Their concern has led them to assume an adversarial posture toward appropriating cultural forms and practices while presuming the 'correctness' of their conclusions; to the point of issuing a prohibition against using various items or places for Christian use. This conclusion would represent how Rosalind Shaw and Charles Stewart view syncretism as a contentious term, often taken to imply 'inauthenticity' or 'contamination,' the infiltration of a supposedly 'pure' tradition by symbols and meaning seen as belonging to other incompatible traditions.[7] In addition, the papers prohibition reflects a western interpretive bias that indigenous leaders have been forced to use in exegeting their own cultures in light of scriptures. This bias is a normative view for most North American evangelicals and systemically problematic, even oppressive, in Native mission endeavors today, particularly within denominational structures.

In tribal communities, religion is the core of the culture and permeates all of life, and there is no artificial separation of sacred and secular beliefs. In contrast, missionaries brought to tribal peoples a distinct 'dualism' or 'split-view' that separated the natural and supernatural realities from each other. It created spiritual and natural compartments that categorized native culture expression as 'spiritual' and thus pagan, demonic and evil, things needing elimination."[8]

While acknowledging how difficult it is to draw a sharp line between religious and non-religious practices, Paul Hiebert[9] says that missionaries tended to feel that most customs because they did have religious connotations, had to be rejected indiscriminately. Several generations on, this view has now been understood by many as a "Native evangelical perspective," when it is most likely the lingering effect of paternalism and fear of syncretism. The paper does not qualify meanings or uses of the items listed, nor apply commonly accepted missiological principles in their findings.

The conclusions of the CHIEF document seem to reflect the influence of the previous seventy-five years' missionary pattern, as Hiebert has noted, of indiscriminate and generalized rejection.[10]

The second positional paper on syncretism that he critiques is titled *"The Boundary Line,"* produced by **The Native American District of the Christian & Missionary Alliance Denomination**, under the leadership in 2000 of the acting Superintendent, Rev. Craig Smith. He makes similar comments regarding their determination on what can or cannot be used in Christian worship: "The paper's concern of syncretism rests on their premise that sacred objects used by animists are never neutral, (or sanctifiable), but dedicated to the demons." This, they believe, is the biblical position as it "forbids the use of, or the redeeming of the artifacts and practices of animism and admonishes the Christian to destroy them and forever distance themselves from the evil they represent."

Twiss holds that they do

"not critically exegete the culture in light of biblical principles of missiology and a theology of mission. [They do] not identify and acknowledge the difference

311

between 'forms or objects' used in 'so-called' spirit, from actual spirit worship. This is an issue of the heart—giving homage, praise, and worship to a spirit or idol. The Bible does not indict drums and guitars, or feathers and rattles, or dances and clapping, as expressions of worship, but utterly condemns giving worship to any god but Himself."[11]

He continues:

"There were many perverse practices involved in Satanic ritual and idol worship, which the Bible condemns; human sacrifice, torture, and mutilation, prostitution, fornication, drunkenness, sorcery, and divination, to name a few. The children of Israel, as the Boundary Lines paper notes, were told to tear down the 'high places' of Baal worship and to destroy the works of idolatry. When Moses came down from Mt. Sinai to find the people worshipping a golden calf, He did not command them to kill all the cows and destroy all the gold. He was angry not with beef and metal, but with idolatry—misplaced faith and allegiance. Later in King Solomon's Temple, gold was used profusely; all kinds of carvings of animals were erected, painted, and made statues of. All the instruments and dances (excepting those obviously perverse) were later used in the temple in worship to Jehovah."[12]

While praying about this, I was drawn again to the following passage of Old Testament scripture where God makes a covenant with Abram:

"I am the Lord, who brought you out of Ur of the Chaldeans to give you this land to take possession of it." But Abram said, "O Sovereign Lord, how can I know that I will gain possession of it?" So, the Lord said to him, "Bring me a heifer, a goat and a ram, each three years old, along with a dove and a young pigeon."

312

Abram brought all these to him, cut them in two and arranged the halves opposite each other; the birds, however, he did not cut in half. Then birds of prey came down on the carcasses, but Abram drove them away.

As the sun was setting, Abram fell into a deep sleep, and a thick and dreadful darkness came over him... When the sun had set and darkness had fallen, a smoking firepot with a blazing torch appeared and passed between the pieces. On that day the Lord made a covenant with Abram and said, "To your descendants I give this land, from the Wadi of Egypt to the great river, the Euphrates..." (Genesis 15:7-18)

I was drawn to the words *"Abram brought all these to him, cut them in two and arranged the halves opposite each other; the birds, however, he did not cut in half."* and noticed that there is no apparent instruction from God regarding what he should do with the animals. On looking up several reference books, the reason why became clear. What Moses did was normal practice in those days when tribal peoples in the region, such as the Chaldeans, entered covenants with each other. Abram did what he knew! Also, the tribal peoples in those days, in entering something as solemn as a covenant, called upon their deities during the process. Was God being negatively syncretistic? Surely not! God took what was the practice and redeemed it, put his stamp on it!

-oooOooo-

The views coming from the Native American leaders I mentioned above have generally been held by Native Christians who were discipled by a Western Evangelical Missions model, which believed that nothing within the Native culture was redeemable—the Indian had to be bred out of them! This would be the understanding of Mathias Zahniser in his analysis of The Boundary Line paper:

"The problem is that those who have judged and labeled as syncretistic, certain Native rituals, have all

313

done so from the perspective of the western outsider. Though the authors of the paper are indeed respected tribal cultural insiders, the analytical or hermeneutical schema they use to arrive at their conclusions seems to strongly reflect the cultural bias and prejudices introduced by early missionaries or western outsider."[13]

Counter to these two positions, Twiss writes that,

"William Shenk[14] takes a redemptive approach to cultural forms and items stating not all the expressions of culture and identity are to be abolished, but instead, are to be brought into captivity to the purposes of Jesus Christ. The gospel must come through in indigenous rhythm and speak its message to the heart. For the man from the forest, the worship must have the capacity to vibrate with the beat of the drum. Tippett states the arts and crafts of the group must be employed to absorb the energy, skills and dedication of the artists and craftsmen of the group, that their manual and mental competencies may be expressive of spirituality and help the group to worship the Lord in what, to their eyes and ears, may be described as 'the beauty of holiness,' even though discordant or grotesque to the westerner."[15]

—oooOooo—

This is a debate that will undoubtedly continue. You can now see what I mean when I use the word "contentious!" As John Roxborough writes,

"For many, syncretism is still a religious danger to be avoided rather than a natural process of cultural interchange whose outcomes can only be evaluated by attention to meaning, context, and the voices of interpretive communities."[16]

Herein lies my question: When we look at the list given by the above papers: sweat lodges, longhouses, tobacco, tipis, stick; smoke from cedar, sage, sweetgrass, peyote, other mediatory incense or sacred objects, fetish masks, drums, rattles, whistles, carvings, medicine pouches, dream catchers, totem poles, what criteria does one use to determine what can or cannot be "redeemed," "sanctified" from within a culture, to be used in our worship of God?

Some appear, to me as an uninformed Christian Western Irishman, quite clearly suspect! But on what basis do I/we make the decision that something can be accepted or rejected; is it negative syncretism or can it be contextualized? Outsiders may give input, but surely it is the insiders that have to sit down together and decide! The end reality is, Christians from all traditions, with all their differences, are all members of the one body of Christ—the ecclesia. Walking in the unity of the Spirit has to be steadily worked at, especially when there is such a dynamic clash of worldviews that have produced deep wounds over the centuries. That's a lot of "strongholds" to break down! Even Paul realized this when he instructs us, to *"strive to maintain the unity"* which we have in Christ. "Strive"—that's a very strong, action word!

This is certainly the reality we face here in Ireland. Can the historic Churches, both Catholic and Protestant, lay aside their centuries of sectarian baggage for the sake of evangelizing the next generation? Why should our Evangelical traditions continue to expect Catholics with Irish Nationalist politics, to become Northern Irish Protestants? Likewise, what is God asking of the white American Church, so profoundly shaped by European colonial history, as it responds to Native American Christians who are seeking to contextualize their faith in Christ?

One of the problems in Ireland regarding an issue like the Ulster Covenant, and especially in some of the historic denominational churches, is that the leaders tend to be either: locked into their own denominational and cultural histories; while others are invariably looking over their shoulder, aware that there are many critics out there who pay them their salaries. There are yet others, genuinely wanting to see change and to enter into meaningful dialogue but find it hard to "stick their heads above the parapet," for fear of the consequences.

315

Working at the "coal face" can understandably, be a very lonely and at times dangerous experience. We are desperately in need of anointed Apostolic, Prophetic leadership today!

Twiss, while referencing Carl Starkloff, observes:

> "While anthropologists, missiologists, and church historians have been able to objectively examine syncretism with relatively detached 'objectivity,' leaders of local churches have generally reacted with fear and opposition. Even though, in most cases, they have never seriously studied its meaning; it is simply taken to be synonymous with heresy. This is true among many Native pastors and leaders who have not had the opportunity to engage with others in honest dialogue outside their denominational or organizational structures. Frequently critical contextualization is mistaken for syncretism."[17]

—oooOooo—

By way of a reminder, I take you back to Chapter 2, where we looked at what makes up "Legal Footholds." I shared there some words from Paul:

> *"For though we live in this world, we do not wage war as the world does. The weapons we fight with are not the weapons of this world. On the contrary, they have divine power to demolish strongholds. We demolish arguments and every pretension that sets itself up against the knowledge of God, and we take every thought captive to make it obedient to Christ."* (2 Corinthians 10:3-5)

The word "stronghold" in the Greek means "to have or hold." In the New American Standard Bible, it is translated as "a fortress," i.e., a fort, a castle or a prison—a place in which something can be strongly held. Relating this to Satan, it implies that he has found a place within a person or group of people: a strong cultural belief system;

prejudices; sinful habits or addictions, which he can use to hold onto them tightly. Relating it to God, if we embrace what the Scriptures teach about marriage, then this has a positive outworking for society—marriage is a "stronghold" for God.

There is another word here that has relevance to what I am sharing—the word "arguments." Just as a reminder, it means the total of the accumulated wisdom and information learned over time. It becomes what we believe: our mindset, our worldview. These include philosophies, religions, racism, intellectualism, materialism, roots of rejection—anything that causes us to think, act or react in a specific way. This can have positive and negative connotations. So, if you take the position that all syncretism is negative, then you don't even have to visit this "argument." That will most probably mean that good syncretism (contextualization) is not on the table to be looked at either!

I ask myself, where do these "arguments" and "strongholds" come from? Like most people growing up in Northern Ireland, we have been strongly influenced by our tribal histories and myths regarding the other. What I learned in our segregated educational system of Irish history is hardly recognizable as the same history by the other culture. The same can be said of my ancestors coming to America from the British Isles and the Native Tribes they conquered. We came with a Christian worldview shaped by the Protestant Reformation, with the "add-ons" of the Doctrine of Discovery and the influences of the Age of Enlightenment. All of these shaped how they saw the world in and outside of Europe. They in turn, politically and in their evangelization transferred something of those "arguments" and "strongholds" on, to the Native Americans. Praying Villages and Boarding Schools, were such vehicles, designed for such a purpose, to breed the Indian out of them and instill a Western worldview.

The sad reality is, that we all have these "strongholds" to varying degrees, because of our upbringing, culture, history, etc., which often makes us very resistant to being changed even in the face of irrefutable information to the contrary. As we say here in Northern Ireland, "You get sectarianism in your mother's milk!" At the same time, we saw the need to emphasize doctrinal issues such as the fall; man's

317

consequential separation from God, etc., Wilbert Shenk reckoned that these were "applied disproportionately with regards to cultures outside the West. Because the measuring rod was determined by Western sensibilities, it was the non-Western cultures that were stigmatized. This approach encouraged a dismissive attitude towards their traditional cultures and religion." He saw that the *modus operandi* of mission, influenced by the Enlightenment, was "an essentially Western initiative."[18]

—oooOooo—

In closing...

In all my reading connected with this book, a few points stand out. Protestant and evangelical culture were dominant before and after the Revolution in America; Native Americans had nothing to contribute—they were the heathen; nothing within their culture was redeemable; all had to be destroyed. Starting with a "clean slate," they began the building program with Western civilization and our specific understanding of the Christian gospel, as the main currency. Negative syncretism was deeply embedded, without them even realizing it!

This, in turn, has produced an expression of Christianity, especially among 3rd/4th generation Christian Indians today, which often renders them incapable of embracing what current First Nations theologians are seeking to do today around the world—to biblically and missiologically challenge and correct, what in Richard Twiss's perspective is a "legalistic and narrow view of syncretism."

In the words of Randy Woodley,

> "We must realize that, to many people groups, the term Christian is not the good news we intend it to mean (both in Ireland and the United States – *mine*). Rather, it is the bad news of colonialism, oppression and even genocide. It is bad news, because many of those who named themselves after Christ, have acted in very un-Christlike ways, and the cultural baggage that comes with the name *Christian* is sometimes unnecessary,

318

and at other times actually opposed to Christ and His purposes."

What he says next profoundly resonates within me:

"If we take Him seriously, Christ calls us to examine everything in our culture, whether we consider it good or bad, and to turn it upside-down to see if it is aligned with His new Kingdom culture of righteousness... When we become Christ's followers, all cultures are suspect, especially our own, and we must re-examine them in the light of God's Word."[19]

Herein is my plea:

We are all part of the one body, the "body of Christ." Each follower of Christ is in a way, an organic cell that belongs to it while taking on different denominational or national characteristics. Every cell in the human body will carry the same DNA, and yet cells can be grouped together to form very different organs, each with their unique function and role to play for the benefit of the whole.

What I long for, is to see the Native parts of the Body of Christ in America increasingly find their place(s) in the Body—indigenous expressions included—for the purposes of not only having their dignity restored and for the evangelizing of their own people, but more significantly, so that they can more fully worship their Creator as He intended them to. This is healing! If a part of the Body is missing or is not functioning properly, then the "whole" does not function as it should! That has become my position because of my journey in reconciliation in the divided culture and Church in Ireland and out of my awareness of the wounds my tribe inflicted on the Native Americans because of our colonial exploits. I yearn to see those wounds healed!

References:
1. Source: www.wiconi.com
2. Richard Twiss. As 8 above.

3. David Hesselgrave and Edward Rommen, *"Contextualisation – Meanings, Methods, and Models."* Grand Rapids, MI, Baker. 1989. Pg. 55.
4. Philip Jenkins, *"Dream Catchers: How Mainstream America Discovered Native Spirituality."* New York, NY, Oxford University Press. 2004.
5. Twiss. As 8 above. Also Footnote 5.
6. Ibid.
7. Charles Shaw and Rosalind Stewart, *"Syncretism/Anti-Syncretism: The Politics of Religious Synthesis."* London and New York, Rutledge. 1994. Pg. 1. C. R. Stewart has studied with more than 50 professional instructors, trainers, and coaches. He traveled around the world, exploring diverse cultures and international business, and launched his own company at the age of 20. Rosalind Shaw is an associate professor of sociocultural anthropology at Tufts University.
8. Twiss. As 8 above.
9. Paul Hiebert, *"Anthropological Insights for Missionaries."* Grand Rapids MI, Baker Academic. 1985. Pg. 184.
10. Ibid.
11. Twiss. As 8 above.
12. Ibid.
13. Mathias Zahniser, *"Ritual Process and Christian Discipleship: Contextualizing a Buddhist Rite of Passage."* In Missiology: An International Review, January 1991. Darrell Whitehead, ed. Scottsdale, PA, American Society of Missiology, Pg. 16.
14. William Shenk, *"Recasting Theology of Mission: Impulses from the Non-Western World."* In International Bulletin of Missionary Research, July 2001. Denville, NJ. Overseas Missionary Study Center. Pg. 100.
15. Tippett. As 23 above. Pg. 28.
16. John Roxborogh, *"Syncretism: VI. Church History."*
17. Twiss. As 8 above, quoting Carl Starkloff. *"A Theology of the In-Between: The Value of Syncretic Process."* Milwaukee, WI, Marquette University Press. 2002. Pg. 12.
18. Wilbert Shenk. Pgs. 98-102.
19. Randy Woodley, *"Living in Color – embracing God's passion for diversity."* Chosen Books, Grand Rapids, MI, 2001. Pg. 5.

Chapter 22

Give It to Me

In this chapter, I want to share with you three things. The first, was for me, an unusual encounter with God; made all the more so, because He had never communicated with me in that way before. The others come out of a series of two Repentance and Forgiveness events: one in 2010 that culminated in a Summit in Ottawa, Canada and the other one in 2016 was a National Day of Prayer for the First Nations, called "All Tribes DC."

The first of these happened approximately twelve years ago when I was in the United States to attend a residential in Whidbey Island, Seattle. I had been staying in the area for a few days before it, to get over jet-lag. During my second night there, I woke up with a series of words coming into my mind. Somehow, I knew that it was a God moment! I equally knew that while it was spoken directly to me, it was not about me but was connected to Native Americans. I will share it as it came, along with some of my thoughts (in brackets) as I prayed and meditated on it. It started with these words repeatedly coming to me and continued, on and off, for nearly one hour:

> "A human 'right' is not the same as a Kingdom of God 'right.'"

(It was an 'out of personal context' sentence for me, and as more words kept coming, I eventually had to get up and write them down.)

Here is the rest of what I could only describe as a progressive "download from God":

> "Give it to me! Give it to me! My wisdom is not the wisdom of this world. That does not make less of your pain, your wound. It is not a denial of it—but give it to me!"

Verses from the New Testament then came into my mind from the Apostle Paul's second letter to the Church in Corinth, one of which was:

> *"[W]henever anyone turns to the Lord, the veil is taken away. Now the Lord is the Spirit, and where the Spirit of the Lord is, there is freedom. And we, who with unveiled faces all reflect* [some translations - *behold*] *the Lord's glory, are being transformed into his likeness..."* (2 Corinthians 3:16-18)

(The word "veil" was specifically highlighted, followed by the sense of a raped woman, seeking justice and retribution as a means of dealing with the past/drawing a line under the violation. She was in a sense owned by that person/that violation—a veil stood in the way of "glory"/transformation. The question also arises, "Do you want to be free?" See more below.)

> "Give it to me! With an unveiled face behold My glory."

> "As people and nations, you have been raped, just as England repeatedly did to Ireland. They [the Irish] have thought that their freedom was found in the 'Celtic Tiger' (see Reflections below for more info.) and not in Me. That has resulted in a culture, a society, paining and losing its way. Return to Him—give it to Him."

> "You may or may not get 'justice' as you see it. It does not matter (in the sense, that it does not become the driving force in your life)! For what I want for you is the Kingdom of God—my righteousness, peace, and joy. In that is your dignity restored. That is what I am after!"

> "There is a wisdom that comes, is given from:
> — The Chief of chiefs - the Father
> — The Elder of elders - Jesus

— The Spirit above all spirits - Holy Spirit."

"Your destiny, your full destiny was denied a long time ago—long before the white man came here. It was denied to all your tribes when an angel in heaven rebelled against me, and I cast him to earth, where he led mankind in rebellion. Something was profoundly lost and denied there. Back then, without the wisdom that comes from God, your elders even led you in ways that denied your destiny which I had planned for you."

"Your destiny as nations will never fully be restored here on earth. But what I want to give you is dignity, as people, as nations—DIGNITY IN ME!"

"Many came into your land also with their destinies denied—some of their own will, others through force of circumstance, and some were brought here against their own will."

—oooOooo—

A few reflections

- The overall sense I get from this is one of incredible hope for the Native American peoples of North America. There is the sense that God has been there among them all along, amid their pain, wounds, and imperfections, before and since the white man came to their shores.

- In Chapter 2, "Legal Footholds," I wrote that the word "veil" (Gk. *kalupsis*) means "to hide, cover up, wrap around," just as a bark veils the inside of a tree. Historical/social/psychological negative experiences and traumas such as genocide, land removal, broken treaties, removal to boarding schools have produced these veils over many Native American hearts, minds, and spirits. That is cultural rape!

Such a traumatizing experience can manifest itself in anger, depression, suicide, alcohol and drug addiction, high unemployment, diabetes, etc. It keeps people from seeing the true image of their Creator. That is the stuff that gives Satan the foothold into a culture and lives, that he is after. He does not want Native Americans to experience the full revelation of their Creator; healing through His Son.

- Contrast this with the image of an "unveiled face," where we can behold and contemplate God's glory, His face. Remember, that the word "revelation" is *apokalupsis: apo* means, "off or away"— quite literally an unveiling or uncovering. We are made for Him; everything is in place to enable us to live the "unveiled" life!

- The image of the raped girl is a very powerful one. Owned by an unknown "other" who inflicted a wound at the very core of her identity, daily felt, with no justice in sight, no day in Court, no hopeful means of being able to move on. For some, as I experienced first-hand, it is tangibly felt in places like the Pine Ridge Reservation.

There was a sense that God was in no way minimizing her trauma. He was asking her to hand it over to Him. To begin a journey into wholeness. It was a change of ownership. Both the violator and the violated had a strong ownership/hold on the current circumstances. She was now being asked to make a choice. An opportunity was at hand to draw a line under the whole traumatic experience, by giving it to her Creator God. He was offering a future and a hope! This is not, what I have heard some Euro-Americans say: "It's time they got over it and moved on." That attitude pains me. What God is asking here is not easy, but I know that grace is available, from Him.

- Today, there is also for some, a subtler "veil" in place. It grieves me that many 2nd & 3rd generation Native American Christians, no longer surrounded by their people or immersed in their culture, believe a lie, sold as truth, that nothing in their culture was redeemable. Today, when confronted with other Christian Indians, who sit in circles to dance their prayers and beat the drum, they cannot identify with it, embrace it, enter in – it is seen to be "of the devil," "not of God."

The real "truth" of who God created them to be has been hidden from them because of this demeaning and dishonoring past. Today there are a growing number of Native Christians who are seeking to worship God in an indigenous way and redeem their culture. (See Chapters 20 and 21.)

- The heart cry of Creator is, "Give it to me! I want to restore you!" The wisdom of this world has time upon time failed them. For differing reasons, government at Federal, State or Tribal levels have never been able to fully provide what is required because of wrong decisions that have been made. There is One who is there for them, the Trinity that is God: The Chief above all chiefs, the Elder above all elders the Spirit above all spirits.

The liberating truth for all of us is that He is the one who can remove our veils! He can, in the intimacy of His presence, transform us. There we can begin the journey of finding our true identity. Full justice may never come to the raped girl, but He can help her to make a new start, embrace a new identity, in the giving of it to Him.

- "A human 'right' is not the same as a Kingdom of God 'right.'" The Christian Scriptures speak of two kingdoms: God's and Satan's (or "the god if this age"). They conflict with each other.

> "*And even if our gospel is veiled, it is veiled to those who are perishing. The god of this age has blinded the minds of unbelievers, so that they cannot see the light of the gospel of the glory of Christ, who is the image of God.*" (2 Corinthians 4:3-4)

There are two rulers—God and Satan. And there are two totally opposite sets of values.

John Dawson in his book, "Taking Your Cities for God." writes:

"The only authority Satan has is a stolen human authority. He initially gains this authority when, at some point in history, human beings believe his lie, receive his accusation and are seduced into an allegiance to his plan... Whole countries are kept in darkness by satanic lies that have become cornerstones of a particular culture.

The whole of the Bible from Genesis to Revelation... speaks of a battle that has been going on since Satan was thrown out of God's presence—a battle against God waged by Satan. He is anti-God, anti-God's plan for the world and anti-God's people. He wants to distort the redemptive plans of God for us. He wants to keep people from not only having a right relationship with God but also from being His instruments and channels of healing and grace to those around them who may not yet know him. It is a battle that is instigated in the heavenlies and worked out on the earth among people, authority figures, and governmental structures."[1]

- The prevailing western world systems would say: hold on to your hurts; get even; it's pay-back time. Our histories and memories become the personal and corporate narratives that we can subconsciously live out of—good and bad! That which is "bad" is not God's way, His wisdom says, "Give it to me, I bore it already on the Cross. I have another way of dealing with it."

- It is easy for us to forget, as Catholics and Protestants; Indians or White or indeed Indian Tribe to Indian Tribe, that we can get caught up with how the "other side" has historically wounded us, forgetting how we may have wounded them or ourselves by our individual and corporate negative responses! How victimhood can blind us!

- The reference to Ireland and the "Celtic Tiger." At the time of

326

receiving these words, Ireland, as a member of the European Union was receiving a lot of financial investment from it. With this cash injection, their sense of National pride increased. For the first time, before and since its birth as a nation in 1922, it stood confidentially as an equal among its fellow European States. It was no longer under the shadow of its closest neighbor, the UK. With this came the throwing off, of many other restrictions from its past and the rapid secularization of Irish society. The controlling presence of the Roman Catholic Church hierarchy also crumbled. What has been embraced instead by many, has sadly, not been any more freeing for them!

—oooOooo—

National Forgiven Summit

The second one, which I followed closely on Facebook, is such a powerful example of giving our hurts, pains, and wounds over to God. It is choosing the "higher way," to live according to Gods' principles and His kingdom.

It is related to an event in Canada in 2010 (June 11-13) called the National Forgiven Summit. It was the culmination of a five-month "Journey of Freedom" across the nation, led by Chief Kenny Blacksmith (Cree Nation of Quebec). The Tour, focusing on the Residential Boarding Schools issue (see Chapter 17), "visited 20 cities and towns across Canada… promoting forgiveness as a means to let go of the past and move forward together, with hope."[2] It was directly connected to a Canadian Government apology, regarding Residential Schools, made in 2008 by the Prime Minister, Stephen Harper.

Here is part of a Report written by Chick Taylor of Indian Life Ministries[3]. It reminds me so much of similar, albeit smaller, events in Ireland which I had the privilege to be a part of. It truly is a powerful response to Gods' "Give it to me!"

> "Forgiveness, worship, dance, friendship, healing, tears, joy, freedom, unity, protocol, and celebration are all words that describe the National Forgiven Summit

of the First Peoples of Canada... This was a time that First Nations, Inuit and Métis people, came together from across Canada to give a formal response to their government, that had given an official apology... 'We forgive you' for the wrongs and abuses in the Residential Schools. Over 5,000 attended the weekend events.

Chief Kenny Blacksmith carried the vision and spearheaded this successful gathering. Blacksmith, a residential school survivor... said that 'at that moment, the onus was placed on our people as individuals to respond.'

There were several members of the government present, including Indian Affairs Minister Chuck Strahl, along with several tribal chiefs. First Nations from across the country gathered together and presented their government with the signed Charter of Forgiveness. Young adults also signed the Charter, representing the generation that followed those who were victims of the Residential School abuse.

'The only way to come into our full healing as the First Peoples of Canada is to forgive,' Blacksmith said in a statement. 'Forgiveness is not political; it cannot be bought or sold; it cannot be legislated. It is an individual choice that can break the generational cycle of victimization and accusation.'

... Dancers, musicians, singers all came together to lead in worshipping Creator God and to thank Him for the ability to forgive and be restored and set free, to be who He has created us all to be... To witness such an event as this was a privilege from above. Listening to those who were survivors of the residential schools, intentionally willing to forgive their government, was a testimony to the grace of Creator God, and willingness of the people to heal their lives and their land and walk in reconciliation. It was said more than once that this was just the beginning and for the people to move forward and keep moving forward in the love and freedom of Creator God. In witnessing protocol, it can be said that no one can out give First Nations people. Beautiful gifts from the heart were given to individuals in honor of who they were or what they have done.

After the formalities were over, a mighty celebration took place with different bands and dance groups joining in as one huge unified group of people on stage. There were no barriers, no distinctions. But rather, God's wonderful people enjoying and honoring each other and Him. It was a true picture of what heaven will be like—all nations, tribes, and tongues coming together to worship their Creator. When we choose to forgive and choose to honor, this is the heart of Creator God.'"

A similar gathering in the USA

And the third one was a similar gathering on October 12ᵗʰ, 2016 in Washington DC. Called "All Tribes DC," it was a National Day of Prayer for the First Nations. There have, since then, been other such gatherings, the most recent one in November 2018.

This day, organized by the Rev. Negiel Bigpond (a full-blood Euchee Indian), saw a representation of Native Americans from several hundred tribes gathering together with white Americans to prayer for the Nation. Along with other Native leaders, he formed a Tribal Council to oversee what was "the first of a kind" gathering. What was so remarkable about it was the fact that they reached out in forgiveness, without expecting anything in return, especially when, as Negiel Bigpond says, "unforgiveness and bitterness towards the United States have hurt native people."

One of the speakers at the event, Kevin D. Freeman (a Cherokee and author) wrote,

"This historic gathering at the Washington Monument will represent all the Native Peoples of America coming together to pray for our nation. This humbling effort of repentance has the power to heal our culture as forgiveness replaces demanding. It has the power to restore our economy as the blessings of God can be restored to America. And it has the power to defend our land as God's hand of protection returns to our nation... by offering forgiveness to the United States for centuries of atrocities and broken promises, unified Native American people can begin a healing process that will affect not only them but the entire nation."[4]

Below is part of a prayer which they collectively spoke out:

"We the people, the host people of this great nation and the original lovers of this land, stand united with one heart and mind to bring the power of forgiveness to bear. As the host people of Turtle Island... we forgive every atrocity and broken covenant ever designed to destroy us as a race of people. We break every curse and renounce every lie, purposed to decimate us as human beings. We forgive the government, the church, and the educational system for the use of residential schools that attempted to destroy our culture and silence our voice as people by stealing our language.

We stand in the gap for those who are unable or unwilling to forgive, and call upon the master of life to forgive us for harboring unforgiveness, resentment, hatred, bitterness, and rage; We repent of every curse spoken over America by our ancestors, and we release the power of forgiveness to bring healing and the peace of Creator God to this land... not returning evil for the evil perpetrated against us, but on the contrary, we choose to release a blessing, knowing that the father of us all has called us as his children to bless and not curse, that we may inherit a blessing."[5]

As we can see from the words *"We stand in the gap,"* this was an act of identificational repentance. The few on behalf of the many. Humbly done and led by the Holy Spirit this can have a very powerful effect. I believe it can radically change things in the heavenly realms; it sets people free from the principalities and powers that have been unleashed over a nation because of broken covenants, genocide, hurts, wounds, etc.

Such actions are a massive demonstration of what it means to "Give it to Me."

Perhaps, at both gatherings in Canada and Washington D.C., there was a missing element – representatives of my people, my tribe, humbly repenting of what we did through the introduction of the Doctrine of Discovery, land removal, genocide, etc., among the Native peoples of America! It is certainly something my people need to both own and respond out of!

References:
1. John Dawson, *"Taking Your Cities for God."* Pg. 53.
2. Rebekah Sears.
    http://www.cpj.ca/search/node/we%20are%20sorry
3. Chick Taylor, Indian Life Ministries,
    http://www.indianlife.org/about-us/what-about-here/212-summit-calls-for-repentance
4. Source:
    http://affluentinvestor.com/2016/10/native-american-prayer-rally-offer-forgiveness-america/
5. Source: http://www.tulsaworld.com/news/religion/oklahoma-minister-organizes-native-american-prayer-rally-in-dc/article_81c2f60f-545c-5411-9b4e-7f674288f064.html?mode=print

Chapter 23

It's Time to Rebuild

Throughout our time living in Rostrevor, we met daily as a residential community for prayer and worship from across the Catholic/Protestant divides. We also had regular prayer times over many years with others, not only from the local community but also from across Ireland and from around the world. Throughout that time, God frequently brought me back to the Old Testament book of Nehemiah, to teach us about developing strategies of prayer and action for the community. It continues to be one of my favorite books in the Bible.

At the beginning of the first chapter, we find Nehemiah exiled in Babylon with many of his fellow Jews, because of their long-term persistent disobedience of God. It opens with some of his old friends from Jerusalem visiting him. As was the case when we lived in the Netherlands and friends visited us, we were not long in asking, "How are things back in **Belfast**?" So, he enquired about Jerusalem. For Nehemiah, it was not good news,

> *"Those who survived the exile and are back in the province are in great trouble and disgrace. The wall of Jerusalem is broken down, and its gates have been burned with fire."* (Nehemiah 1:3)

His response was both instant and revealing,

> *"When I heard these things, I sat down and wept. For some days, I mourned and fasted and prayed before the God of heaven."* (Nehemiah 1:4)

He was away from home, away from the ongoing problems and difficulties there; things were going well for him, he was working in the palace as a wine taster to the King! It is, however, my understanding from this passage that Nehemiah never forgot home or what was happening to his people there. The depth of his instant response to the sad news portrays that. It also throws out a challenging question, "How do you feel about your community. Your town. Your Reservation?" In most cases in the western world, our cities may not have broken walls and burned gates, but if we look at the spiritual, moral and social decay in them, there are undoubtedly spiritual parallels!

For the 500 plus Native American Nations, I believe there have been many "broken wall" scenarios that could be readily recalled by them and are in immediate need of being rebuilt. I think of the many treaties and covenants made, only to be broken by my people throughout the colonial expansion era and since then by the United States Government as the ever-increasing westward expansion took place. If we make a treaty with someone and then break it, it is not only broken towards the other party; it is also broken before God.

Thankfully, it does not stop there, for we find Nehemiah carrying, what can only be described as a "spiritual burden." He had caught something of God's heart, and God had found someone that He could use to become a vital part of the solution. Despite their disobedience and exile, God was in the business of healing and restoring His people. I believe this applies to every nation (*ethnos* - though most nations today are made up of multiple ethnic groups. Each with their God-given uniqueness, to be woven into a rich ethnic tapestry). They are, after all, God's idea, He brought them into being, and the scriptures tell us that He put eternity into the very core of their existence. (Ecclesiastes 3:11) He has a plan for us, which Satan and sin have thwarted. Still, God is undeniably for us! Surely, this applies to the United Kingdom, Ireland and the United States of America today!

Chapter 1 begins in the month Chislev, and the next chapter finds us in the month of Nisan. That was a period of 9/10 months, during which God had been speaking into Nehemiah's heart, and it showed, as we see when the King enquires why he is sad in spirit. (Nehemiah 2:2) His sadness was due to the burden he carried for Jerusalem, and its people and the opportunity was now there to share this with the King.

When the king asks, *"What is it you want?"* he **didn't** have to say, *"Can I go away and pray about it and let you know next week?"* During those months of intercession, God had shown him exactly what he was being called to do and what he needed for the rebuilding of the walls of Jerusalem! So, he takes a deep breath and sends up a telegram prayer, *"I prayed to the God of heaven..."* and then makes this request, *"If it pleases the king and if your servant has found favor in his sight, let him send me to the city in Judah where my fathers are buried so that I can rebuild it."* (Nehemiah 2:3-5)

It should not surprise us, therefore, that we read: *"The gracious hand of the Lord was on me, the King granted me my requests"* (v.8).

Back home

When Nehemiah returned to Jerusalem, we read that he went out with a few friends by night to see the state of the walls and the gates for himself. Only then did he approach the Officials and Spiritual Leaders and envision them,

> *"You see the trouble we are in: Jerusalem lies in ruins, and its gates have been burned with fire. Come, let us rebuild the wall of Jerusalem, and we will no longer be in disgrace.' I also told them about the gracious hand of my God upon me and what the king had said to me. They replied, 'Let us start rebuilding.' So, they began this good work."* (Nehemiah 2:17-18)

We too may need to do our "prayer walking"—go on a research trail of our own communities and their history—if we are going to effectively bring about reconciliation and restoration within them. In a sense, this book has been very much about this. My journey of research into the Puritan and Scotch-Irish roots has been an essential part of it, unearthing not only our woundedness but also the wounds we inflicted on the Native Irish and the Native Americans. But it has led to more than that; it has also meant that God wanted me to embrace something of His heart regarding these groups.

334

Clearing the rubble

As Nehemiah assessed the state of the walls, it will have occurred to him, that there was an incredible amount of rubble; all of which would have to be cleared out of the way and sifted through. Some of it was undoubtedly beyond use, but there would also have been a lot that could have been taken, cleaned up, and reused in the repair work. Is that not a parable in the making: What can God take out of the broken walls, the stones, and mortar of our lives, our histories, cultures, churches, and reuse in the rebuilding process? That is in part what Chapters 20 and 21 are all about, as we looked at issues surrounding syncretism and contextualization.

Next to

As we move into Nehemiah Chapter 3, we see that it is one of those chapters that could readily be passed over, with its list of people's names and the sections of the wall they were repairing. Without looking too closely at all those details, let us nevertheless reflect on something important—the big picture in this chapter!

There were when you take the time to count them, 41 different sections mentioned here. I can vividly remember God giving me a strong mental image regarding this—a bird's eye view, like an eagle hovering over the rebuilding of the city of Jerusalem. I could see all the groups working away, yet as I dropped height and drew closer, I could see that each of the sections had straight edges. My immediate thought was, "They are not building one wall; they are building 41 walls!" That was quite a shock to me, as I was instantly made aware of the implications; what God was saying to me about our local communities.

In each of the villages and towns near us, there were many different denominational expressions of the Church. Some of them, to varying degrees, recognized and worked with each other but sadly there were many who didn't. The divisions were more than the historic Irish Catholic/Protestant Church divide, in many instances, many of the Protestant Churches couldn't work with each other either. It came down to how many boxes did each church need to tick: doctrinal issues, dress codes, worship styles, governmental types, which translation of the Bible was used, etc., before they could work with and for each other and their communities. These are all historical developmental issues—doctrinal and cultural—within our church history, which have so often caused much division, even unto death. All of these led to building the straight edges of our protection mechanisms.

Clearly the wounds of history have to be bi-laterally recognized and understood before such cooperation is possible and a Kingdom of God vision is embraced by the whole body of Christ in a Community—Catholic/Protestant, Black, White, Native, Hispanic, etc., what my' Navajo friend Mark Charles calls "developing a common memory." That may start, as was often the case in Northern Ireland, with members of the dominant Protestant community reaching out in repentance and reconciliation towards the other. Reconcilers become, in a sense, the interconnectors, helping the wall sections to become one.

Building the Kingdom of God together is not without its problems; it takes humility and a desire to see "the other" as well as ourselves, from God's perspective. There could well be, as there was in the building of Jerusalem's wall, opposition from within and without. Despite that, we read, *"So we rebuilt the wall till all of it reached half its height, for the people worked with all their heart."* (Nehemiah 4:6). THEY WERE ALL BUILDING ONLY ONE WALL!

Level ground

The good news is—the ground at the foot of the cross is level! If I meet Him there as my Savior and you meet Him there, as yours, then we are brothers and sisters in Christ, we both have the same Father, the Creator of all, we are members of the one family. Period!

We may all "do" church differently; we may all be on different journeys to Christian maturity; we will never have all of our theology sorted out; we will certainly not attain perfection this side of heaven, but we are called by God to journey together and become tools in His hands at "growing each other" and in helping others to find Him.

Each country in the world will have its own mix regarding this. In the USA, it will include White, Native, Black, etc. The point I am making is that at all levels from local to State to National we are all called by Christ to be builders of His "body," the Church, in our communities and Nation. Like the rebuilding of Jerusalem's walls, there should not be any defined divisions—just one wall! Jesus prayed that *"we may be one so that the world may know."* The converse of that implies that disunity may lead people to reject Christ—which is sadly a shocking reality!

How we build each section may be different; each culture should reflect something of its unique difference. Some had to build gates, others the walls and yet others both walls and gates. Just a thought regarding the gates – who are the gatekeepers today? Surely the Native American people need to be highly represented here? We also read how some sections were being built very close to where they lived—that will certainly ensure a good build if your protection depends on it! Let's not fall out over methodology! There will be some things we can learn from the guys next door! And there may be times when we require each other's expertise. Unity with diversity is a compelling expression of the Kingdom of God.

In keeping with the building theme, Paul writes to the Church in Ephesus:

> *"You are no longer foreigners and strangers, but fellow-citizens with God's people and also members of God's household... with Christ himself as the chief cornerstone. In him, the whole building is joined together and rises to become a holy temple in the Lord. And in him, you too are being built together to become a dwelling in which God lives by his Spirit."* (Ephesians 2:19-22)

In Nehemiah chapter 4 we read:

> *"... the man who sounded the trumpet stayed with me... The work is very extensive and spread out, and we are widely separated from each other along the*

*wall. Wherever you hear the sound of the trumpet, join
us there. Our God will fight for us."* (vs. 18-19)!

Each section will undoubtedly have its leaders, its overseers, but there
may be times when we need to come together and stand with each
other. If one part of the church in a community is attacked, then the
whole church is under attack because we are one. That could equally
apply to a pressing need that a church may have. Unity is bigger than
cooperation. We can cooperate over an event, but this is not
necessarily unity. It is, however, an expression of it!

I realize however that certain issues can make this unity/building work
difficult. For instance, within the Irish context, when you consider that
the terms "protestant" and "catholic" are as much cultural and political
and that the Greek word for church is *"ecclesia"* meaning "the called-
out ones" (not a building or a regular church attendee), then everyone
affiliated with *ecclesia* may not necessarily have a genuine Christian
commitment. Also, one can often see in churches that family dynasties
and individuals, with or without any real living faith, can be in
positions of influence, authority and control in them. Added to that,
many people in the denominational Protestant Churches I grew up
with, are bound by the dominant cultural strongholds attached to the
Orange Order, Free Masonry and the covenant of 1912 that leaves
them locked into deep sectarian attitudes. All of these make for
difficulties when we seek to walk in unity, as they have become key
elements in the building of our straight sectarian edges! Nevertheless,
one can start, even with a few Spirit-led leaders and prayerful folk
who agree with God's diagnosis and His heart for our communities
and begin to lay a new foundation. We should never underestimate
what a small group like this can achieve under God's guidance.
Nehemiah started out, one man—with God!

Jesus calls us to *"seek first the kingdom and His righteousness..."* If
we divisively seek first a denominational or an ethnic/cultural identity,
that is idolatry; it has nothing to do with having a kingdom heart and
vision. There is nothing wrong with denominations, but there is
everything wrong with denominationalism. There is nothing wrong
with having different cultural expressions, but there is everything
wrong with a heart or mindset of cultural exclusivism or nationalism,

especially when it is imposed on another people group. Instead, we can be greatly enriched as the different national and denominational expressions work together. We are together to build only one wall, one Kingdom, and we are being empowered and inspired by one Holy Spirit to do it. There is only one body of Christ in your community!

How we need to continually realign ourselves with the mind of Christ. He is our plumb line! Even in the prayer that Jesus gave to his disciples, we see it when he taught us to pray:

> *"**Our** Father in heaven, hallowed be your name, your kingdom come, your will be done on earth as it is in heaven..."* (Matthew 6:9)

He is **"Our** Father." We are part of his family, in community with everyone who knows him. We pray, many of us every day, "your kingdom come... on earth AS IT IS in heaven." Surely, seeking to live in unity as members of His body is central to that! Connect that with Jesus's other key prayer in John 17, and we see clearly the importance in His thinking, regarding this issue:

> *"My prayer is not for them alone. I pray also for those who will believe in me through their message, that all of them may be one. Father, just as you are in me and I am in you. May they also be in us so that the world may believe that you have sent me. I have given them the glory that you gave me, that they may be one as we are one: I in them and you in me. May they be brought to complete unity to let the world know that you sent me and have loved them even as you have loved me."* (vs. 20-23)

Paul succinctly puts it in Ephesians 2:14-18, regarding Jewish and Gentile reconciliation—surely this reflects the **Father's** heart in heaven as to what He still wants to see made manifest on earth, in and through us:

> *"For he himself is our peace, who has made the two one and has destroyed the barrier, the dividing wall of*

hostility, by abolishing in his flesh the law with its commandments and regulations. His purpose was to create in himself one new humanity out of the two, thus making peace, and in this one body to reconcile both of them to God through the cross, by which he put to death their hostility. He came and preached peace to you who were far away and peace to those who were near. For through him we both have access to the Father by the one Spirit."

Should Native American/Euro-American unity in Christ be any different?

In the writing of this chapter, I became very conscious (as I mentioned earlier) of another important issue related to mission. Here in Ireland, many Catholics and Protestants have become disenchanted with the sectarian nature of their churches. If they did not give up on their faith, what were the alternative means for meeting? Many people started to explore what it meant to be Irish and Christian—full stop! For a "Catholic" to become a "Protestant" was not a considered option!

I have found that many Native American Christians are on a similar quest. Why should they have to worship God with a Euro-American expression of faith—historical baggage included! What does an Indigenous expression look like? These are questions modern missiology has been grappling with all around the world. It led me, as I have mentioned above, on yet another research trail and to the writing of Chapter 20, "A right mess!" Reading it has undoubtedly been a challenge to many, as it has been to me, particularly if you are from a European, Euro-American or 2nd and 3rd generation Native American evangelical mindsets!

There is a building work going on! I have had the joy of being in gatherings of Native American followers of Christ who are reaching out to their own tribal members, introducing them to a Native American Jesus. They are finding him, they are being set free from hopelessness, despair, the 'spirits' of depression, suicide, alcoholism...

—oooOooo—

Questions

So, what has all of this to do with Dignity Restored? EVERYTHING1

For me personally, it nevertheless throws up a lot of other questions. How does God want me to continue to walk this out? He has made it clear that I am not to proactively develop any personal ministry through this. It is not about me! My forefathers came to America uninvited by the First Nations people to what became the original 13 States, whereas I am to come in the opposite spirit, by invitation! Among those in the U.S. that I am already walking with on this journey, there are those that I have received an endorsement from. That encourages me to believe that what I profoundly carry in my spirit, is of God.

Nevertheless, I ask myself, is it enough for me to come, walk among both Native and Euro-Americans, to listen, learn, research, write and when I feel it appropriate, to repent of the sins of my forefathers and then go back home again?

How does God want us to walk this out? I wholeheartedly believe that there is something that God wants me, along with present-day English, Scots, and Scotch-Irish to do, as part of the healing of America's wounds, that we have not yet fully experienced. I frequently ask myself what should our response be regarding the Doctrine of Discovery? That is an issue that is hardly on the radar, even within the Reconciliation Movement in the UK!

In the United States of America, you may have your independence from Britain, but what a negative legacy we left you! One that in so many instances you have continued to build on! That fills me with a profound sadness. We gave Satan many footholds into the formation of the nation, as well as giving him multiple footholds into the Native American peoples, through our attitudes towards them: superiority, genocides, broken treaties, land removals, boarding schools, reservations... the list goes on!

341

A U.S. Church response?

A number of U.S. Churches have set up committees to look into the Doctrine of Discovery. As far as I know all but one of them have been seeking for the Pope to repudiate the Doctrine – the Episcopal Church. Back in 2009, they passed a Resolution which asked Queen Elizabeth II to "disavow, and repudiate publicly, the claimed validity of the Christian Doctrine of Discovery." (See Appendix III for the full wording.)

From what you have been reading in this book it is my belief that the other Denominations have been looking in the wrong direction. Let me explain: While acknowledging that the Papacy developed the dynamics behind the Doctrine of Discovery, it did not introduce it into the foundations of what became the United States of America. The DOD was introduced by a strongly anti-Catholic Protestant British Crown, Government, and Church before the War of Independence.

Where the Roman Catholic Church may still have some accountability today is in the Southern States, such as New Mexico, Southern California and Arizona, where the Spanish Empire introduced the DOD prior to them becoming States within the USA.

—oooOooo—

Where do we start?

The core sentiments of 2 Corinthians 6:11 (bold – *mine*) seems like an appropriate scripture for me to begin with:

> *"**We have** spoken freely to you Corinthians and **opened wide our hearts to you**. We are not withholding our affection from you, but you are withholding yours from us. As a fair exchange—I speak as to my children—**open wide your hearts also**."*

I have shared my heart with you!

It is clichéd, but Paul is right: "the issue of the heart is at the heart of the issue!"

Is there a role that God wants you to play in your community? If you are not Native American, on which tribes' traditional land are you living on? What do you know about them? Have you reached out to them? In the United States, the Native American Christian communities are meant to be an essential element in any wall built in your communities. They have to be included! They are after all the first people of the land, it's gatekeepers!

Do you have God's heart for your community? That's where it started for Nehemiah! Do you have a Kingdom of God vision, especially as it relates to building the walls of the Church, not a straight-edged section of it?

Dr. Randy Woodley, shared 4 very helpful and practical suggestions for such a process, in an article entitled, *"A Theological Declaration on Christian Faith and White Supremacy."*[1] and was précised in a blog by Cherice Bock· called *"Decolonizing Thanksgiving."*[2]

1. **"Listen**: create and/or attend conferences (national, local, regional) or have conversations with people, listening actively, attentively, and vulnerably to those of different experiences of Christianity than your own.

2. **Lament**: we all have much to be grateful for, but pain and hardship are not equally shared. True lament requires really seeing the suffering of the others and being near enough to them to truly lament together as parts of the family of God.

3. **Repent** (turn around): recognizing we have lived by an interpretation of Christianity that does not reflect the heart of Christ, apologizing, and beginning to live out our faith with humility and courage, to be radicle disciples.

4. **Re-imagine**: opening up to visions for a future expression of Christianity that truly leads to reconciliation between people groups, God, and creation. This includes a new understanding of Whiteness, a way for those of us of European descent to feel dignity and belovedness in ways that don't have to be based on

343

power-over, but instead living out love and care for and alongside all those in the community of creation."

My prayer...

One thing I do know is that I have been called by God to carry something of His heart in mine, in intercession for the United States of America. The Apostle John writes, *"He who believes in me...* *'From his innermost being will flow rivers of living water.'"* Now, this *he said about the Spirit..."* (John 7:38, NASB). "Innermost being" or as other translations put it, "the heart," is a translation from the Greek *koilia,* which literally means 'the womb.' It is the place of birthing! When the Spirit of our Creator God plants something of His heart in ours, we become an integral part of birthing, bringing into reality, that very thing. This, I am convinced, is the experience of Nehemiah which I shared with you at the beginning of this chapter. That was the starting point for his journey, his God assignment! What started as something very invisible within him, soon became manifest, nation-changing!

As I finish this chapter and therefore, this book, it is my prayer that having read it, you will commence or continue further along the road of Gods' journey in reconciliation, for you. A journey into the heart of Creator, a Spirit journey, to be an extension of His healing presence wherever He places you and in whatever He puts in your heart.

Thank you for sharing in a little piece of mine!

References:

1. Dr. Randy Woodley, *"A Theological Declaration on Christian Faith and White Supremacy."*
   Complete text:
   https://thedeclaration.net/read and
   https://thedeclaration.net/action
2. Cherice Bock, *"Decolonizing Thanksgiving"*
   www.watersheddiscipleship.org

Appendix I

Key Elements of The Doctrine of Discovery

Below, in brief, are what Professor Robert J Miller considered to be the ten key components that constitute the Doctrine of Discovery. I have adapted them from his book: "Native America, Discovered and Conquered: Thomas Jefferson, Lewis & Clark, and Manifest Destiny." Pgs. 3-4.

First discovery. When a European country discovered a land that no other European country had previously found, they could claim both sovereignty and property rights to them over the native peoples. That was however only considered as an incomplete title.

Actual occupancy and current possession. For a title to become an actual occupancy, the discovering European country had to show evidence of both its possession and occupation, i.e., building settlements or a fort that is occupied, within what was considered a reasonable time of claiming the title.

European title or preemption. The first discovering country had the primary right to buy the claimed land from the Indigenous people. That prevented or preempted other European governments or person from buying the land from its native owners. That is something the United States still lays claim to regarding Indian lands. (25 U.S.C. section 177 (2006))

Indian title. After a land was first discovered, the Euro-American legal systems held that the Indigenous peoples no longer had full property rights/ownership to them. From then on, the natives only kept the rights to both occupy and use the lands. If a Native tribe never consented to sell their land to the country that held the preemptive power over them, those rights to occupancy and use could last forever.

Limited sovereignty and commercial rights. Following first discovery some aspects of the Indigenous Nations own sovereignty; trade rights and diplomatic relations were curtailed. They could, from then on, only deal with the Government of the country that first discovered them.

Contiguity. This had several elements:

- When two different European countries claimed land close to each other, Contiguity enabled each of them to hold rights to land to the halfway point between each other.

- It also held that when a river mouth was discovered, the discovering country could lay claim to the entire river basin— even if it was over a thousand square miles of territory.

Terra nullius. It is land that is null, void, empty. If it was not occupied, possessed or used in a way predetermined by European legal and property regulations, it was "empty" and therefore available for discovery. This meant that if Indigenous Peoples were using the land but not according to either Euro-American laws or cultural ways, it could be deemed "vacant" and therefore available for Discovery. The Indigenous Tribes had more of a sense of stewarding the land rather than owning it.

Christianity. This had a very significant place in the Doctrine of Discover, as all non-Christians were considered as inferior and unable to hold the same rights as Christians to either land, sovereignty or self-determination.

Civilization. Another very important aspect regarding Discovery. We were seen as superior, and our Christian role was, therefore, to paternally evangelize, civilize and educate the Native.

Conquest. "Just" and "necessary" wars against an Indian tribe was a sufficient means of laying claim to their lands.

Appendix II

Restoring Ancient Gated Conference, Fort Wayne, January 2010 – The Wording of The Acknowledgment

This is the Acknowledgement that was signed by pastors and ministry leaders, following the presentation of a plaque to the Miami Council, 30th January 2010. It had inscribed on it: "In Honor of the Miami People, the Original Gatekeepers of the 'Glorious Gate.'"

The acknowledgment

We as pastors and spiritual leaders, representing several churches in Fort Wayne and the surrounding region, do corporately acknowledge our sins in relation to the Miami people. We not only acknowledge the unjust acts against your peoples by our ancestors but also our failure to act on your behalf, to publicly acknowledge or attempt to rectify those wrongs, in the generations that followed. In all of this, we have corporately failed to represent a good witness to our faith in Jesus Christ.

We acknowledge the historical sins of our ancestors—

- In the unjust acquisition of your ancestral homelands and the breaking of treaties and covenants;
- In the forceful removal of your ancestors from the homeland and to bring division and devastation to the many families represented;
- In the dehumanizing of the Miami peoples and the cultural genocide that followed;
- In the abuse of families and children by the removal of children to boarding schools that degraded their way of life and language.

Today we recognize and honor the authority and rights of the Miami peoples as the original gamekeepers and caretakers of this land. Even though we may differ in the beliefs and practices of our spiritual ways, we commit to respecting the Miami as a spiritual people who desire to honor the Creator of the world, who have a rich and beautiful cultural heritage, and a unique and important role in the healing of this land and the future well-being of this city and region.

We realize that words will not make up for the wrongs done. So, in the spirit of humility, we now extend our hands in friendship to the Miami peoples in hope that we might begin a process that will allow us to walk forward to a better future for all peoples.

Source: *"Sign Language. A Look at the Historic and Prophetic Landscape of America."* **Terry Wildman**, Great Thunder Publishing, Maricopa, 2011. Pgs. 189, 190.

Appendix III

Episcopal Church Repudiates Doctrine of Discovery Urges US Adoption of The UN Declaration

The resolution was passed unanimously by the Episcopal House of Bishops, and by an overwhelming majority of the House of Delegates during the church's 76th General Convention July 8-17, 2009 in Anaheim, California.

Episcopal Church-DOD FINAL VERSION-Concurred

Resolution: D035
Title: Repudiate the Doctrine of Discovery
Topic: Reconciliation
Committee: 09-National and International Concerns
House of Initial Action: Deputies
Proposer: Dr. John Chaffee

Resolved, the House of Bishops concurring, that the 76th General Convention repudiates and renounces the Doctrine of Discovery as fundamentally opposed to the Gospel of Jesus Christ and our understanding of the inherent rights that individuals and peoples have received from God, and that this declaration be proclaimed among our churches and shared with the United Nations and all the nations and peoples located within The Episcopal Church's boundaries. This doctrine, which originated with Henry VII in 1496, held that Christian sovereigns and their representative explorers could assert dominion and title over non-Christian lands with the full blessing and sanction of the Church. It continues to be invoked, in only slightly modified form, in court cases and in the many destructive policies of governments and other institutions of the modern nation-state that lead to the colonizing dispossession of the lands of indigenous peoples and the disruption of their way of life; and be it further

Resolved, that The Episcopal Church review its policies and programs with a view to exposing the historical reality and impact of the Doctrine of Discovery and eliminating its presence in its contemporary policies, program, and structures and, further, that this body directs the appropriate representatives of the House of Bishops and House of Deputies, to inform all relevant governmental bodies in The United States of its action and suggest similar and equivalent review of historical and contemporary policies that contribute to the continuing colonization of Indigenous Peoples and, further, to write to Queen Elizabeth II, the Supreme Governor of the Church of England, requesting that her Majesty disavow, and repudiate publicly, the claimed validity of the Christian Doctrine of Discovery; and be it further

Resolved, that each diocese within the Episcopal Church be encouraged to reflect upon its own history, in light of these actions and encourage all Episcopalians to seek a greater understanding of the Indigenous Peoples within the geopolitical boundaries claimed by the United States and other nation states located within the Episcopal Church's boundaries, and to support those peoples in their ongoing efforts for their inherent sovereignty and fundamental human rights as peoples to be respected; and be it further

Resolved, that the 76th General Convention direct the Office of Government Relations to advocate for the U.S. government's endorsement of the "United Nations Declaration on the Rights of Indigenous Peoples," which the United States has refused to endorse (only the U.S., Canada, New Zealand, and Australia have failed to sign on).

Source: http://doctrineofdiscovery.org/episcopalrepud.htm

Lightning Source UK Ltd.
Milton Keynes UK
UKHW022046070419
340626UK00004B/69/P